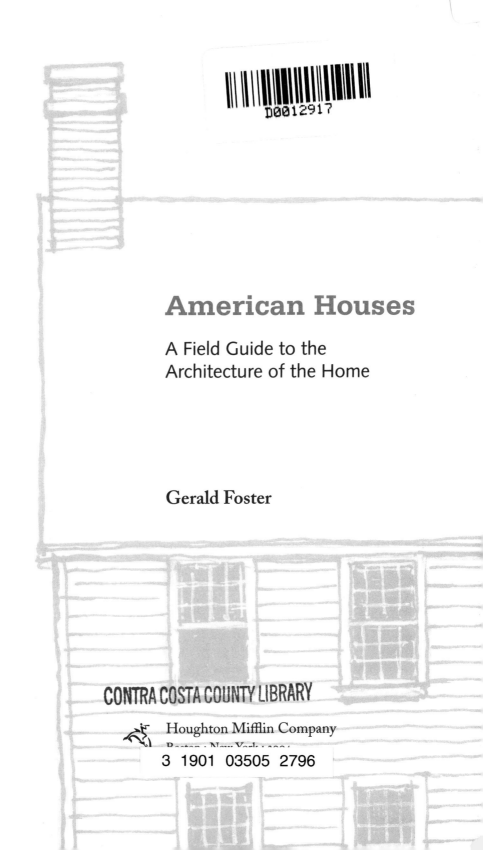

American Houses

A Field Guide to the Architecture of the Home

Gerald Foster

Houghton Mifflin Company
Boston · New York · 2004

For information about permission to reproduce selections from
this book, write to Permissions, Houghton Mifflin Company,
215 Park Avenue South, New York, New York 10003.

Visit our Web site: www.houghtonmifflinbooks.com.

Library of Congress Cataloging-in-Publication Data

Foster, Gerald L.
American houses : a field guide to the architecture of the home
/ Gerald Foster.

p.   cm.
Includes bibliographical references and index.
ISBN 0-618-38799-4
1. Architecture, Domestic—United States.   I. Title.
NA7205.F67 2004
728'.37'0973—dc22   2003056705

Book design by Gerald Foster and Erin Wells

Printed in the United States of America

MP 10 9 8 7 6 5 4 3 2 1

American Houses

Also by Gerald Foster

A Field Guide to Airplanes
A Field Guide to Trains

Gratefully dedicated to my son Mark Foster

Acknowledgments

Many people helped with both inspiration and information as I worked on this book.

At the Library of Congress, many thanks to Kia Campbell of the marvelous Historic American Buildings Survey (HABS) collection of architectural photographs, which were so necessary to my work. With friendly enthusiasm, she helped me select and order the prints I needed.

At the anthropology department of the University of Massachusetts, Professors John Cole and Robert Paynter were always ready with good suggestions and a willingness to discuss my ideas. Marjorie Abel's writing program was especially valuable.

Many sources helped to motivate me at difficult times — meetings of the Vernacular Architectural Forum, for example, and the research department at the Colonial Williamsburg Foundation, particularly Carl Lounsbury, Mark Wenger, Edward Chappell, and Willie Graham. Their expertise goes well beyond Virginia. And there are the writings of many scholarly enthusiasts to whom I owe a considerable debt: Abbott Lowell Cummings, Dell Upton, Henry Glassie, John Michael Vlach, Chris Wilson, and many others. I am truly thankful for the many historical societies and their hard work in recording and maintaining our architectural history. Books of this type would be impossible without their help, and they deserve our generous support. My local resource, the Lincoln Public Library, was very helpful in tracking down research materials far from home.

Special thanks to Harry Foster, my very patient editor at Houghton Mifflin, who unwaveringly supported this project through its lengthy gestation. Beth Kluckhohn helped to coordinate the various pieces of this endeavor, Luise Erdmann's editing helped make it readable, and Peg Anderson's attention to detail brought it all together.

The book's designer, Erin Wells, determinedly and very successfully pulled together its myriad visual aspects into a harmonious whole.

Finally, without the continuous encouragement and enthusiasm of my son Mark, this book would still be just an idea. He was there at the beginning, and his assistance has been crucial to me all the way. Whatever success this book may find will owe much to his efforts and his unflagging confidence that I could actually pull it off.

Contents

An Introduction to American Houses

The single-family home has traditionally assumed an unusual importance in the United States, compared with other Western societies. Buying a home is an American rite of passage, and the house has been a symbol of independence and security, as well as social and economic status, since the Europeans settled here in the 1600s. A house not only provides shelter; it informs neighbors and passersby of its inhabitants' wealth, taste, and degree of conformity to community values. This was as true in the early Colonial era as it is today.

In the planning and building of a house, no matter how simple, aesthetic decisions are made: the placement of windows, the selection of materials, the building's orientation on its site. Should the front door be centered on the exterior wall, or should its location be determined by interior convenience? Should the corners be turned with corner boards or quoins? Should the windows be tall and narrow or shorter and wider?

Earlier in our history, these questions were answered by building traditions evolved from ethnic and cultural preferences, adapted to local conditions and available materials. These traditions create an expectation of what "looks right," and eventually a distinct, recognizable architectural style may be established.

But what makes a building "look right"? The first American settlers built houses that resembled as much as possible the ones they had known at home. Most of these regional styles, however, were subsumed by the English Georgian influence that eventually dominated the settled Colonial landscape, even affecting areas in the lower Mississippi, for example. In the 19th century, Classical scholars and architects found what "looked right" to them in the architecture of Greece and Rome. Reducing the proportions of temples and their elements to sets of universal design principles, they essentially created styles from archaeological discoveries. Specific formulas were published for building according to the Classical orders, and architectural plan books proliferated, instructing architects and contractors how to apply Classical forms to their projects. Schools of architecture sprang up to interpret and codify these design principles further and train architects in the Classical language.

In reaction to the rigid formality of the Classical orders, an opposing design philosophy arose that found visual satisfaction in a building's harmonious relationship to the landscape. Houses modeled after Italian villas, and the later Shingle Style, reflect this more relaxed and flexible "picturesque" aesthetic. The tension between the Classical and picturesque characterized the development of architectural styles throughout the 1800s, with late Classical revivals vying with the Arts and Crafts Movement at the close of the century.

The Industrial Revolution led to dramatic changes in construction techniques and architectural styles in the 20th century, but in building homes, the primary impact of industrial change was on the quantity of houses built and the standardization of elements, not design. While houses inspired by the Bauhaus or Frank Lloyd Wright received attention out of all proportion to their numbers from architects and critics, most new American homes were increasingly built according to published plans with exteriors loosely based on historical styles, particularly Colonial Revival. In the past, only a relatively few houses (usually the more expensive) were designed by professional architects, but these homes often established the styles that added flavor to American architecture. Now, though more and more expansive and expensive houses are being built, architects are less and less involved, and owners and buyers ask for little in the way of originality or innovation in design. Million-dollar homes are built from standard plans designed for a generic site, with a Colonial shell—pick your colony—enveloping an attempt at a modern open floor plan. The exterior and interior, the form and the function, no longer relate.

We have no truly distinctive American residential style at present, but fortunately we have streets lined with houses displaying the architectural styles of the past. This book is a guide to their visual characteristics, cultural origins, and history. Our first styles arose from

An Introduction to American Houses

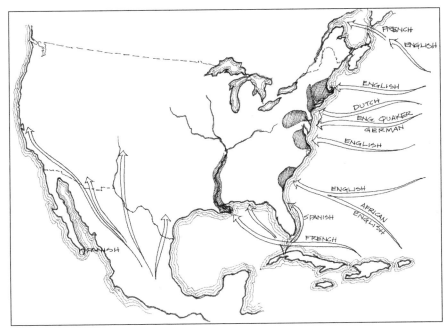

The Colonial hearths

the 17th-century core settlement areas, or "hearths," which are described in the chapters on Colonial architectural traditions.

Throughout the book, the discussion of each style begins with a list of its "field marks," the visual characteristics that identify it and distinguish it from other styles. First is Form: the roof shape, height, proportions, mass, and overall shape of a house. Next is Stylistic Detail: siding, doors, windows, moldings, and other features that are often the result of specific aesthetic decisions made by the owner or builder. Third is Construction: how the houses were built and what materials were commonly used.

Following this list is a fuller discussion of the history, geography, social and cultural influences, and other important and interesting aspects of each style.

Photographs show specific examples of the different styles, but the primary visual tools in this guide are illustrations that emphasize the key field marks described and eliminate the individual quirks that can obscure a house's origins.

A distinguishing feature of this book compared with other guides to American architecture is the inclusion of floor plans as well as exterior views. Where reliable information was available, I have indicated the uses of individual rooms. Architecture is much more than street façades, and understanding how a house was designed to be lived in adds greatly to the appreciation of any style.

Identifying the style of a house is inherently less precise than identifying the species of a bird or the model of an airplane. Houses may have elements of more than one style and are likely to have been re-sided, remodeled, and expanded, obscuring their original character. Still, a careful examination of a house and its original floor plan can usually lead to a fairly precise identification.

This book puts strong emphasis on the Colonial period and the 19th century, because many of the residential styles that have arisen since then are recycled from these earlier forms or are short-lived curios with little widespread influence. Indeed, the book reflects the fact that no vigorous American style has emerged in the last fifty years, in contrast to the vitality of domestic architectural design in the 19th and early 20th centuries. Real estate agents continue to define styles as "Colonial," (window glass divided into small panes), "contemporary" (more glass), or "Dutch" Colonial—anything with a gambrel roof. As up-to-date as our world is in many respects, our houses for the most part attempt to reflect an earlier time, and there is a great sameness in domestic design today. It is my hope that this book will help spur a wider awareness of our architectural heritage and a renewed interest not only in the preservation of distinctive styles but in a more critical appraisal of American home design generally.

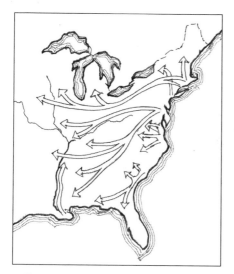

Diffusion paths from the original
Colonial hearths

Part One
Colonial Traditions

The New England Hearth

Some 21,000 English settlers immigrated to New England between 1629 and 1640, and in only a few generations their descendants would spread over much of the eastern seaboard north of Delaware and move west across New York, northern Pennsylvania, and the Northwest Territories (the area north of the Ohio River that in time became Ohio, Indiana, Illinois, Wisconsin, Michigan, and northeastern Minnesota). They swept through the Hudson Valley's Dutch culture and the remnants of French influence while relentlessly pushing uprooted indigenous societies ahead of them. Compared to the other original European settlements, the New England Hearth, or core settlement area, had the greatest influence on American architecture and culture.

It is important to remember that the early-17th-century English immigrants were largely middle-class yeomen farmers, traders, and artisans who were escaping not poverty as much as religious and political persecution, disease, and the economic distress that followed England's wars with France and Spain. Dozens of British ships brought skilled carpenters, joiners, and masons to build the characteristic villages of New England. In their new landscape, they found an almost endless supply of timber and clay but little lime for mixing mortar. They found very cold winters and short growing seasons. They found plenty of space but had to contend with the indigenous peoples who were (not surprisingly) unwilling to abandon it. The factors that shaped English architecture on the New England shore were the available natural materials, a harsh climate, and security.

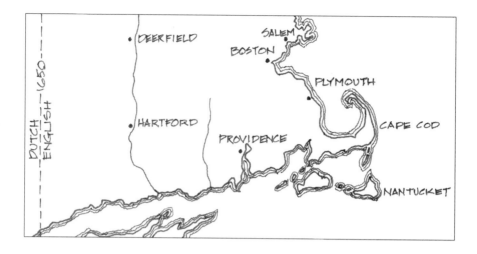

The Massachusetts Bay settlers came largely from the more densely populated counties of southeast England, where wood construction was common. Their vernacular rural house form was generally well suited to New England, and English cottages sprang up as quickly as land could be cleared. The first one- and two-room homes led to simple two-story houses, Garrisons, Saltboxes, and finally, in the 18th century, to the New England Large House, built from Maine west into New York State. Other adaptations, such as the Cape Cod Cottage and the Rhode Island Stone-Ender, were developed nearby. The construction of these sturdy buildings indicates, and records confirm, the use of fine tools brought from England.

Typical of each of these house types was the heavy timber frame, the massive masonry chimney, and a low exposed-timber ceiling. Four corner posts supported perimeter beams while a central "summer beam,"

running from chimney to end wall, further supported the attic or second-floor joists that spanned the house from front to rear.

Posts and beams were hewn from logs and connected with oak pins driven through chiseled mortise-and-tenon joints. Walls were built of somewhat lighter studs "let into" the sills and beams, then filled with sticks

The New England Hearth

and caked mud (wattle-and-daub). To protect the mud walls from the weather, the exterior was covered with sawn planks or clapboards and shingles split from logs. Until the establishment of sawmills, planks were laboriously cut from logs with two-man pit saws. In another method of wall construction, not common in England, heavy vertical planks were face-nailed to the sill and beam in place of studs. This technique was commonly used in the Cape Cod Cottage.

Roofs were framed with common rafters stabilized by purlins, then thatched or, later, boarded and shingled. Chimneys were often built of sticks and mud rather than brick, given the lack of lime for mixing mortar. Windows were covered with cloth and oiled paper until the arrival of affordable glass panes from England, when diamond-paned casements became commonplace. Hand-wrought nails were used except for the oak pegs in the structural frame. Nails were expensive, and stories are told of settlers, tired of the poor and rocky New England soil, burning their houses to recover the nails before moving west.

Amenities such as flooring, interior paneling, and masonry fireplaces depended on the owners' resources. Decorative detail was sparse, typically carved "drops" and brackets under garrison overhangs ("jetties"). Occasionally, exposed corner-post heads and beam ends were tooled as well.

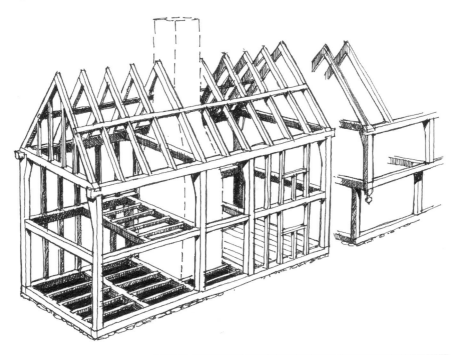

The New England Hearth

House styles were not uniform throughout New England. The rigid religious societies established by the Puritans and Pilgrims produced the Massachusetts Bay Colony's own refugees, who fled or were expelled to Rhode Island or the Connecticut River valley. They were joined by more liberal immigrants from other parts of England and established different housing patterns, which can be attributed to variations in available building materials and personal taste. The Rhode Island Stone-Ender and the 17th-century houses along the Connecticut River, while similar to those in the Massachusetts Bay Colony, are more relaxed and varied in form.

New Englanders took their building traditions with them as they moved west in search of better land, but well before they reached Ohio they were overtaken by the rush toward the more formal symmetry we now call the Georgian style. For the first time, a broader architectural expression began to erode regional traditions of house design. With improved travel conditions, communications, and the emergence of "professional" architects and designers in the later 18th century, the Georgian evolved into a national style.

A hundred years later, after the Revolutionary War, prominent American architects touring New England in search of their architectural heritage rediscovered the honest dignity of Colonial architecture. They created the Colonial Revival still with us today, as thousands upon thousands of "builders' Colonials" strive for some connection, however obscure, with the 18th-century New England Large House or Georgian mansion. The charm, the efficiency, and the validity of the original concepts are gone, however, with perhaps only the symmetry and clapboards remaining. Meanwhile, the current pace of new development promises many more three-car-garage "Colonials" in our future.

NEW ENGLAND SALTBOX

Peak House, *Medfield, Mass., late 17th c. (restoration)*

The One- and Two-Room English Cottage (1620–1800)

FORM: Simple 1½-story, gable-end structure with a large chimney at one end of the 1-room cottage, a central chimney in the 2-room form. Steeply pitched roof.

STYLISTIC DETAIL: None. Later versions had diamond-paned windows. Interior beams often chamfered.

CONSTRUCTION: A timber frame with thatched roof and wood siding. Later examples had shingle or board roofs. Early chimneys were mud and stick, later replaced by brick masonry. Wood sills rested on low, stone foundations.

Arriving on the New England shore, the 17th-century English settlers immediately erected Native American huts and wigwams or dug into the earth for temporary shelter. For more permanent housing, they drew on their own experience and built simple cottages based on familiar English homes. These houses were constructed by skilled carpenters using the fine tools they had brought from England.

In Massachusetts, particularly, house types common to England's southeastern counties were reproduced: rectangular, one-room, single-story huts with steeply pitched thatched roofs, typically 16–22 feet deep and 22–28 feet long. A fireplace and chimney occupied most of one end. The only outside door opened directly into a small entry "porch" beside the fireplace. Here was also a steep, ladder-like staircase leading to a sizable loft. An interior door generally separated the porch from the main hall, creating a further buffer between the public and private space.

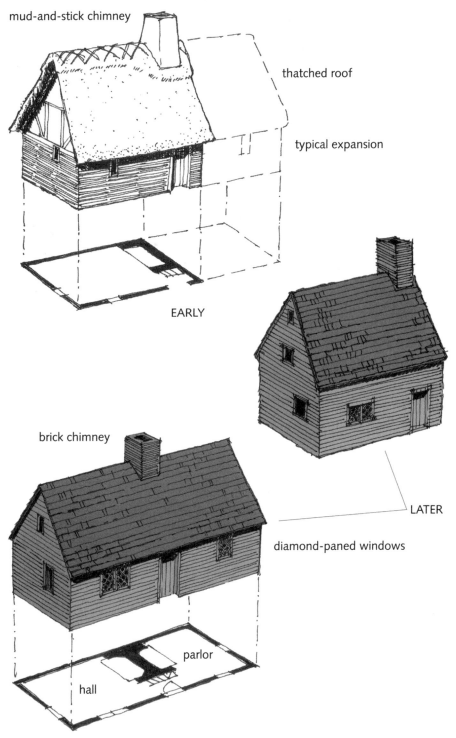

mud-and-stick chimney

thatched roof

typical expansion

EARLY

brick chimney

LATER

diamond-paned windows

parlor

hall

These cottages were often expanded longitudinally by adding another room beyond the fireplace, thus creating a near-symmetrical central chimney plan. This basic arrangement remained characteristic of New England house architecture until the multiple chimneys of the 18th-century Georgian style. Some cottages were built initially with two-room, hall-and-parlor floor plans, each fireplace venting into the central chimney. The hall, accessed from outside, remained the reception, entertaining, and cooking space, and the parlor was used for sleeping and less public family functions. The earliest surviving frame house, the Fairbanks House (c. 1637) in Dedham, Massachusetts, was originally a two-room cottage before many later additions.

As in the English cottages of the time, the structure of the one or two-room cottage in New England consisted of heavy timber corner posts supporting beams or plates and the exterior clad in clapboards or planks. The early houses had dirt floors and mud-and-stick chimneys, largely due to the lack of lime for mixing mortar. Improvements like framed wood floors and brick fireplaces emerged as immigrants settled in and discovered new resources. (In Rhode Island, where lime deposits were more plentiful, builders developed what have come to be known as stone-ender cottages.) It is important to note that these simple cottages were not replaced as a type by the advent of larger houses; they con-tinued to be built in great numbers throughout the Colonial period in New England.

New England houses can be contrasted with the Virginia hall and hall-and-parlor dwellings in the Chesapeake Bay Hearth, where the fireplaces were at the ends of the house, often outside the end wall.

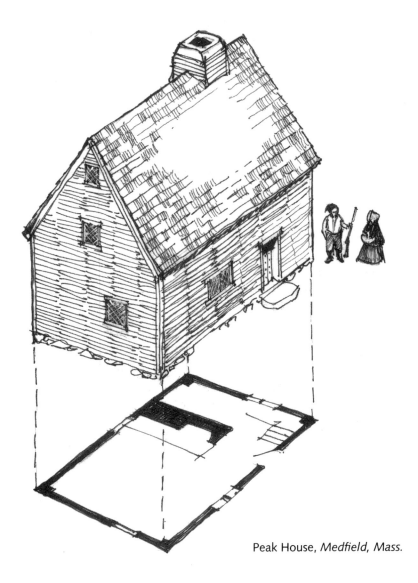

Peak House, *Medfield, Mass.*

Parson Capen House, *Topsfield, Mass., 1683*

Two-Story Houses: Saltbox and Garrison (1620–1700)

FORM: Typically a 2½-story gable-end structure, 1 room deep, under a steeply pitched roof. The Saltbox has a full-length shed extension at the rear. Massive chimney. Low foundations.

STYLISTIC DETAIL: Generally none except for Garrison homes, which often have carved pendants and brackets, usually at the front corners and at either side of the entry but occasionally at the gable-end corners as well. Plain expanses of clapboard wall are broken by small windows. The brick chimney may show a cornice, paneling, or fluting and a prominent drip edge. Diamond-paned casement windows are typical and often paired.

CONSTRUCTION: Heavy timber-framed structure with a shingle or clapboard roof and siding. Low stone foundation.

These house styles came directly from medieval England as two-story versions of the simple English cottage and became very common in the 17th century. One of the most important of them was the Saltbox, named for its similarity to that object and called a "catslide" in England. Developed in response to the need for more and distinct spaces for specific household activities, the Saltbox was either built initially in that form or was created by adding to an existing two-story house.

The Saltbox's full-length shed typically housed a kitchen flanked by a dairy or buttery, later called the pantry, and a small bedroom or

HALL-AND-PARLOR TWO-STORY HOUSE

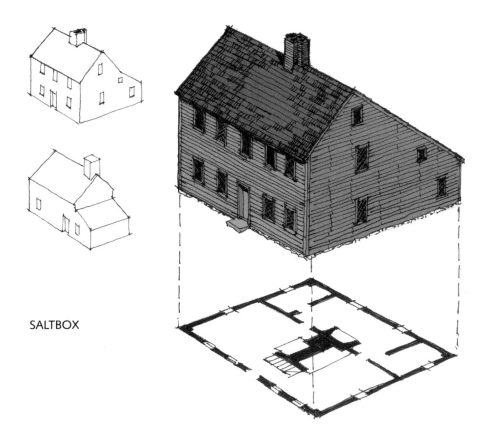

SALTBOX

chamber, perhaps for an elderly relative. A garret over these spaces provided storage or, later in the period, room for a slave or servant. In larger examples, a separate stair to the garret was installed. The shed roof was built as a smooth continuation of the upper roof or with a change in slope, causing a break in the roofline. A "broken" roofline suggests an addition, whereas new construction typically showed an unbroken pitch.

Beginning about 1660, some Saltboxes and two-story houses were built with jetties (the second-story overhangs we now call Garrison façades) on the long, entrance side of the house. The name Garrison reflects the overhang's resemblance to the jetties on a frontier fortress, or garrison. While the forts' wider projections shielded the defenders, allowing them to fire down on an enemy, the smaller jetty of the Garrison house had more peaceful roots. Elizabethan houses often had second-story extensions over the street that served several functions. They increased the amount of living space on the second floor, sheltered the shops and pedestrians below from the elements, protected a fashionably plastered first-floor façade, and could be decorated with pendants and brackets. Some say that they could also simplify framing at the second level. In less crowded New England, the overhang may have been primarily decorative, breaking up the large expanse of exterior wall with a horizontal shadow line. Still, the entry was protected, and a few square feet were added easily to the second floor. The overhang was also occasionally seen along a gable end, sometimes at an eave line, indicating the attic floor. An interesting design element, the overhang created a brief vernacular style lasting only about thirty years but familiar to us because of the Salem witch trials and Nathaniel Hawthorne's *House of the Seven Gables*. Today it is a common feature on suburban houses.

Most 17th-century jetties were built by extending the second-story framing out over the first. Another technique simply used a larger girt, or perimeter beam, at the second-floor level set into full-height, two-story posts that were wider above the second level. This assembly protruded only a few inches over the floor below, but it was enough to create the desired horizontal break in the two-story façade, though it lacked space for pendants and brackets. This latter form persisted into the 19th century, especially in Connecticut, where it was applied to other house types, even occasionally to a Georgian façade.

Another feature of the Elizabethan house that was brought to New England was the façade gable. No doubt it was partly ornamental and perhaps a status symbol, but it could also be used to direct rainwater away

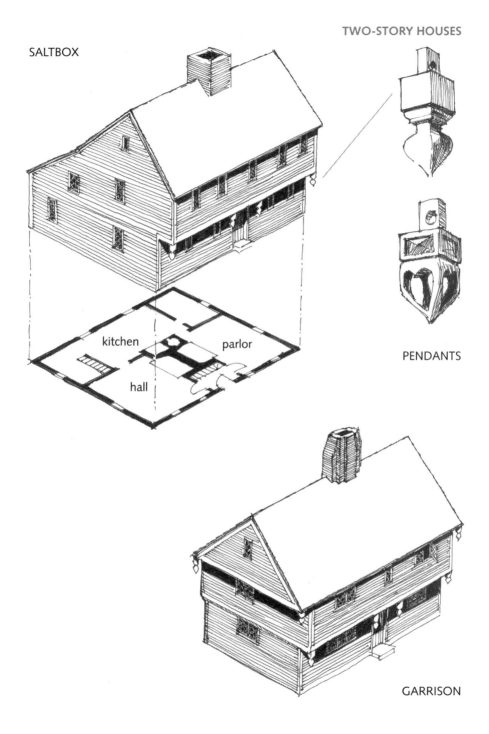

SALTBOX

TWO-STORY HOUSES

PENDANTS

kitchen

parlor

hall

GARRISON

from the entry while letting light into the living and storage spaces in the attic. It is thought to have originated in English towns where houses stood shoulder to shoulder, blocking gable-end locations for windows. In New England the façade gable flourished briefly and appeared most often on Garrison houses, but it fell from favor after about 1700. Façade gables were later frequently removed, as medieval architecture came to be seen as hopelessly out of date compared to the suddenly fashionable and strictly symmetrical Georgian style.

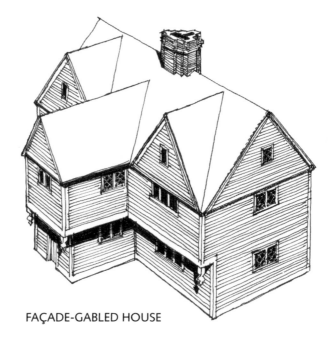

FAÇADE-GABLED HOUSE

METHODS OF
FRAMING JETTIES

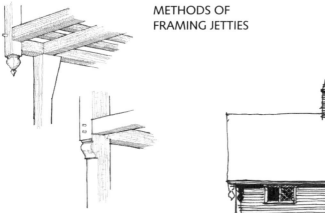

FAÇADE-GABLED HOUSES

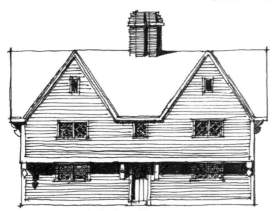

Rural English cottage, *16th c.*

New England Large House, *Scotland, Conn.*

The New England Large House (1690–1850)
New England Farmhouse

FORM: A 2½-story, 2-room-deep rectangular block, end-gabled. Large central chimney. Symmetrical 5-bay façade with 2-bay end walls typical. Roof slope not as steep as on other New England types. Attic dormers are often added. Gambrel roofs are not uncommon.

STYLISTIC DETAIL: Occasional Classical detailing at the front entry. Possible ornament at first-floor window heads, 12-over-12 symmetrically spaced sash windows. Window shutters are common.

CONSTRUCTION: A timber frame on a stone foundation. Clapboard siding and wood-shingled roof. Masonry chimney.

The evolution of the New England two-story house was a logical progression from the first two-story, one-room house through the Saltbox silhouette to the New England Large House, with a plan two rooms deep on both floors. This expansive design indicated the growing prosperity of a few citizens of the Colonies. Enclosing more volume for its footprint than the Saltbox, the New England Large House responded to the growing interest in entertaining, individual privacy, and separate spaces for different activities.

The Renaissance influence makes its first serious appearance in the Colonies with the Large House's symmetrical front façade, a feature typical of American residential design up to and beyond the Picturesque

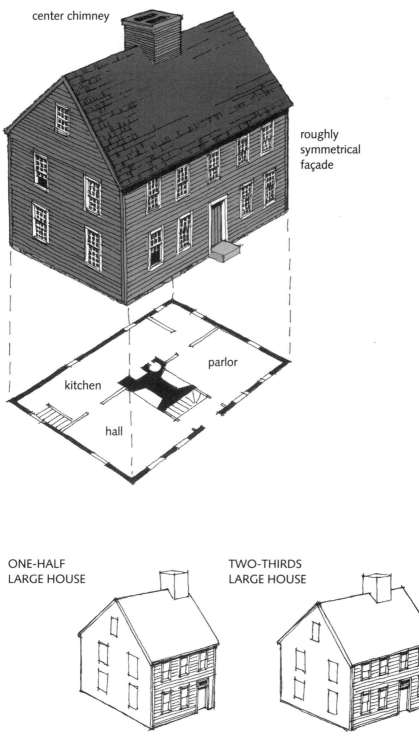

center chimney

roughly
symmetrical
façade

parlor

kitchen

hall

ONE-HALF
LARGE HOUSE

TWO-THIRDS
LARGE HOUSE

Movement of the 19th century. It often incorporated a Classically ornamented entry and symmetrically arranged sash windows of equal size. With its gentler roof pitch, lack of dormers, and higher ceilings, the Large House was a departure from the medieval character of its contemporaries.

Although it originated before King George's reign, the New England Large House is often mistakenly described as Georgian. There is a tendency to call any center-entry, symmetrically arranged façade Georgian, but in fact the New England Large House is more properly classified as a transition from late-medieval houses to the Georgian style. Its floor plan is quite different from the Georgian: it retains the central fireplaces with their massive chimney rather than a center passage, and thus it has an entirely different flow in terms of both ventilation and the separation of rooms by function. In a New England Large House the floor plan is virtually identical to that of a Saltbox, with the kitchen and other service functions at the rear.

Noting the central chimney paired with symmetrical gable ends is essential when identifying a New England Large House. As with the Cape Cod Cottage, the New England Large House was built in partial versions of three and four bays for those who didn't need or couldn't afford the space (and were not obsessed with symmetry). The style was built throughout New England and west, well into New York State. Today, modern oversize versions are standard models in housing developments, some even with fake central chimneys.

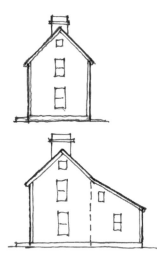

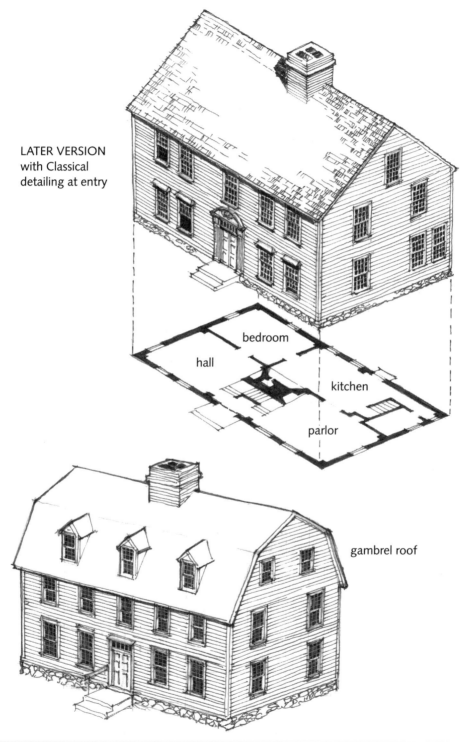

LATER VERSION
with Classical
detailing at entry

bedroom

hall

kitchen

parlor

gambrel roof

Jonathan Collins House, *Truro, Mass.*

The Cape Cod Cottage (1690–1800)

FORM: A compact, nearly square, 1½-story house, 2 rooms deep, with a steeply pitched gabled roof. Gambrel roofs are occasionally seen. A large central chimney and symmetrical 5-bay façade on the eave side. Minimal roof overhangs. Dormers on original examples are later additions.

STYLISTIC DETAIL: Little ornament except occasionally at the entry on later versions. Symmetrical façade. Multiple-pane sash windows, often with shutters.

CONSTRUCTION: A timber-frame structure vertically planked and sheathed with cedar shingles at the roof and walls or, less commonly, clapboards, sometimes on the front elevation only.

Resembling in form if not materials the stone fisherman's cottages of southwestern England, Cape Cod Cottages can be traced to the late 1600s in New England. Built along coastal waterways, they were shaped and oriented to withstand the prevailing winds and weather off the Atlantic. Compared to Saltboxes and Garrisons, the Cape Cod was reduced in scale, made of smaller, more easily handled parts and thus simpler to erect by smaller crews of builders. The vertically planked exterior walls created an extremely rigid structure, presenting a good surface for the characteristic cedar shingles. This sturdiness was also helpful in moving the houses, which was frequently necessary as sandy beaches shifted or a better location was found. They were floated as far as Nantucket as well as moved overland.

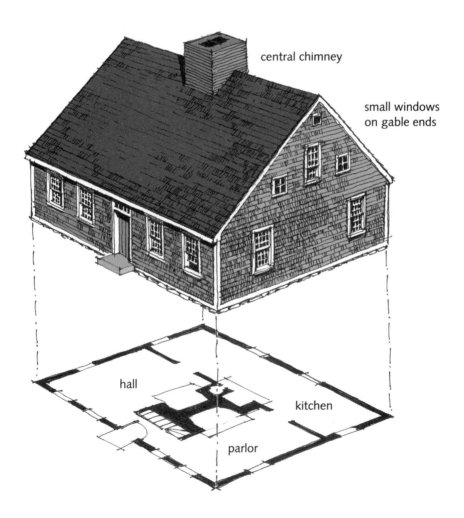

central chimney

small windows
on gable ends

hall

kitchen

parlor

With their relatively large windows, even original Capes look deceptively modern and, when compared with other early New England houses, are open and breezy, an advantage in combating the seasonal dampness of the Atlantic shore. The shingles turn from buff to gray to nearly black with exposure to the sun, salt air, and rain. The central entry may show Georgian or even Greek Revival detailing in later or updated examples. The symmetrically arranged sash windows were originally single-hung, with the often smaller bottom sash movable and the top fixed. Surviving original houses have usually been fitted with double-hung replacements.

The efficient first-floor plan resembles that of a Saltbox or New England Large House. The main rooms—the hall, parlor, and kitchen—surround a large central chimney with a fireplace in each space. Gable windows ventilate the sleeping chambers upstairs. Those not needing the space or not yet able to afford the complete house could build a half or three-quarter Cape, which could be expanded laterally at the owner's discretion, though many remained as built. At one time, a half Cape was called a house and a full Cape a double house.

The Cape Cod Cottage has had an enduring effect on residential design throughout the country and its history. Revived in the 20th century because of its simple construction and efficient use of space, Capes have been built in many versions, some duplicated block after block in large, post-World War II housing developments. Although generally lacking the central chimney, they are recognizable as Cape

Cod derivatives by the distinctive, simple roof shape and a usually symmetrical façade. The arrival of good wood stoves followed by central heating did away with the central chimney and thus the original floor plan.

The Cape Cod Cottage originally ranged along the North Atlantic coast from Long Island Sound to southern Maine. It was concentrated on Cape Cod and the nearby islands, eventually finding its way upriver into Connecticut, Rhode Island, and the rest of Massachusetts.

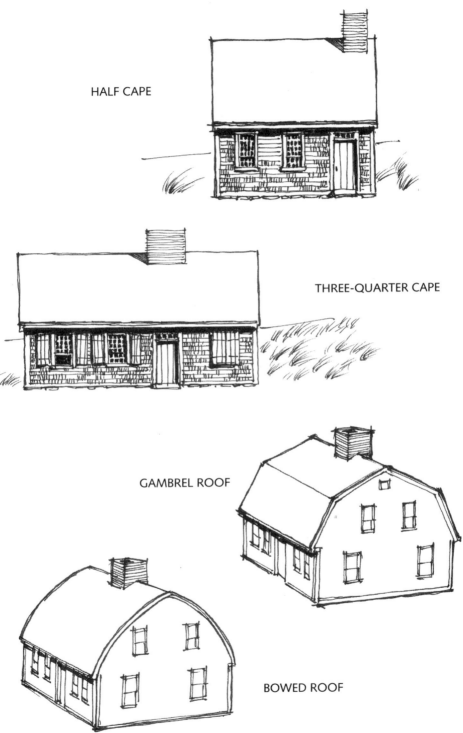

THE CAPE COD COTTAGE

HALF CAPE

THREE-QUARTER CAPE

GAMBREL ROOF

BOWED ROOF

Thomas Clemence House, *Johnston, R.I., c. 1679*

The Rhode Island Stone-Ender (1640–1700)

FORM: A small 1½- or 2-story gable-end house with a steep roof pitch, possibly with a cross gable. A massive stone chimney forms most or all of the north wall. The façade lacks symmetry.

STYLISTIC DETAIL: No applied ornament, but the stone chimney was commonly embellished with at least a heavy cornice if not multiple pilasters. Diamond-paned leaded glass was typical in small casement windows.

CONSTRUCTION: A timber frame with stone masonry fireplace and chimney. Thatched or wood-shingled roof. Clapboard or plank wall cladding.

Once common in and around Providence, Rhode Island, and south-eastern Massachusetts, the Rhode Island Stone-Ender had a different character than that of the Colonial houses of the Massachusetts Bay area and the Connecticut River valley. Although extremely rare today (the remaining examples having been greatly altered over the generations), they are important to include as a variation on the ubiquitous English Cottage.

With the lime needed to make mortar scarce in 17th-century Massachusetts, builders were forced to import it from England, making stone or brick masonry expensive. Early Massachusetts masons set their fireplace and chimney bricks in clay, using lime mortar only above the roof, where the chimney was exposed to the weather. However, lime did occur naturally around Narragansett Bay, in Rhode Island, and stone was

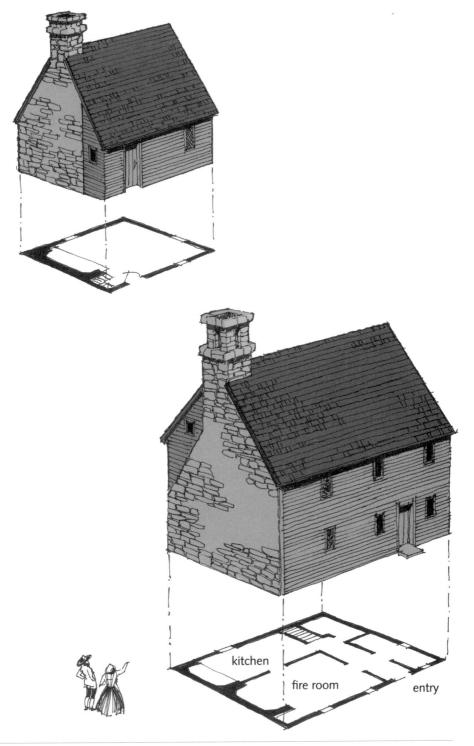

kitchen

fire room

entry

commonly used for very large fireplaces and chimneys. As a result, these houses had a different architectural character both inside and out.

The Stone-Ender seems to have begun as a typical one-room English cottage with sleeping space upstairs, but a massive stone fireplace made up nearly one entire end of the house. Subsequent additions deepened the house by adding a second room and an additional chimney under a Saltbox type of roof, with the new space becoming the kitchen. Only then was the house made longer, into a four-room or four-room-with-hall plan, the new rooms often used as bedchambers. As with all our earliest buildings, additions and attached sheds may obscure the original form of the house.

The steeply gabled roof reflects the medieval English tradition of thatching (steep thatched roofs let the water run off quickly), although planks or shingles soon replaced the thatch. Occasionally an equally steep Elizabethan façade gable was added to the front. The door and window arrangements are usually not symmetrical but reflect the interior layout. Most of the original diamond-shaped leaded-glass panes in small casement windows have long since disappeared, but they may be found in good restorations. Like other houses of the period, the Stone-Ender sits low on the ground, showing little of its stone foundation.

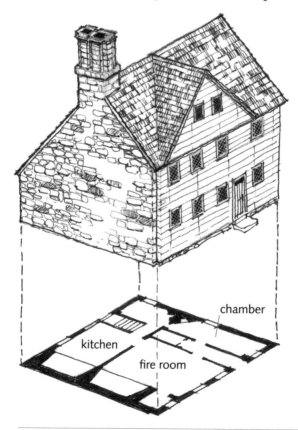

Eleazer Arnold House with façade gable, *1687*

chamber

kitchen

fire room

The New England Hearth

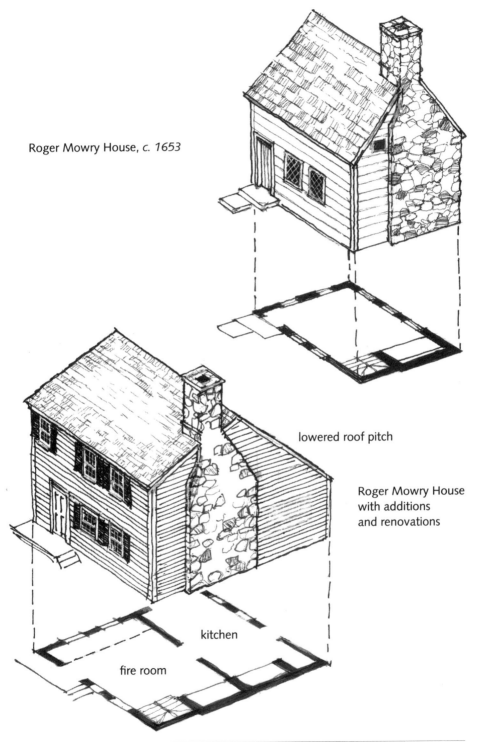

Roger Mowry House, *c. 1653*

lowered roof pitch

Roger Mowry House
with additions
and renovations

kitchen

fire room

Longfellow House, *Cambridge, Mass., c. 1759*

The New England Georgian (1700–80)

FORM: Typically an end-gabled, 2-story rectangular block on a raised basement; 2 rooms deep and anywhere from 3 to 7 bays wide, though 5 bays was the most common. The center-entry façade is strictly symmetrical. Roof types include the characteristic hipped roof as well as gable-end and gambrel. One or two chimneys toward each end, either at the end walls or within the house. Attic dormers common but may also be later additions.

STYLISTIC DETAIL: Ranges from relatively quiet décor, with attempts at Classical ornament around the entry, to elaborately ornamental houses with roof balustrades, full-height corner pilasters, and a projecting front gable at the entry. Paneled doors may have a rectangular transom light or, later and less commonly, a fanlight. Sash windows may be pedimented or hooded, typically at the first floor only. Glazing was generally 9-over-9 or 12-over-12 with thick muntins. Quoins were common, including wood panels rusticated and sanded to imitate stone. Decorative cornices with dentils were common.

CONSTRUCTION: Brick masonry or timber frame with clapboard siding is most typical, stone masonry less frequent.

What is now called the Georgian style consists of innumerable variations on a very simple English architectural theme: the symmetrical, two-story house with center-entry façade. This aesthetic, combined with the two-room-deep center-passage floor plan, was the basis for thousands upon

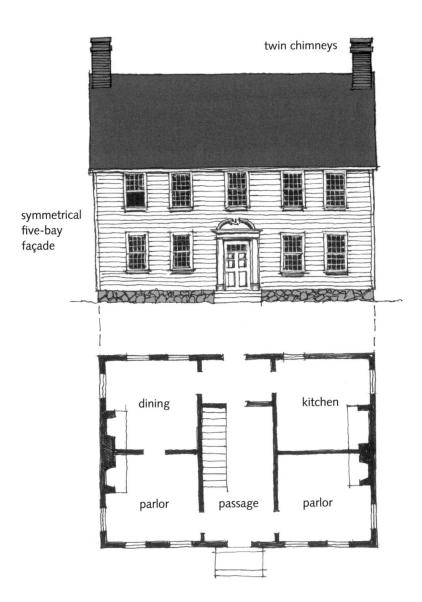

twin chimneys

symmetrical
five-bay
façade

dining

kitchen

parlor

passage

parlor

thousands of fashionable homes built on the eastern seaboard during the 18th century.

The free-standing detached urban house of middle-class society arose in England as a consequence of a burgeoning mercantile prosperity and emulated, on a slightly smaller scale, the aristocracy's large country manors. These homes had been designed by architects increasingly influenced by interpretations of Classical Roman architecture, particularly the published works of the great 16th-century Renaissance architect Andrea Palladio.

While early- to mid-17th-century architects applied Renaissance ornamentation to the many-towered or -pavilioned Elizabethan and Jacobean mansions, a few began to work with the Renaissance concepts literally from the ground up, resulting in some strikingly original large houses. Architects began to compose large, refined, rectangular blocks, Classically detailed. Irregular rooflines were flattened or hipped, and larger sash windows, although carefully aligned, were isolated from other design elements in the walls. Symmetry was paramount, with the emphasis on the horizontal. Inigo Jones is often considered an early leader of this movement; his Queen's House in Greenwich (1616–35) and Roger Pratt's Coleshill House (c. 1650) are extravagant but notable examples and had a wide influence.

This architectural "modernization" was interrupted during Cromwell's revolution, but after the restoration of the Crown, Sir Christopher Wren (1632–1723) continued the trend, adding to English estate houses the fashionable baroque touches that eventually migrated to the New World and embellished fashionable homes in Massachusetts and Virginia. It was during this time that stylish, well-made, middle-class detached townhouses, scaled-down versions of Coleshill, proliferated in English towns. They have come to be called Wren-type houses, although Wren himself had little to do with designing them. It is this style we now call Georgian, coinciding as it did with the rule of the four Georges, commencing in 1714, although it was brought to the American Colonies near the end of the 17th century.

Interestingly, neither Jones nor Wren rose from the master stonemasons' guilds, as did most architects of the time. Jones began his career devising backdrops for royal pageants and masques; Wren was scientifically and mathematically inclined, well known in those fields before taking up architecture. Significantly, both had visited Italy and had been strongly impressed with the designs of Andrea Palladio from a century earlier.

Coleshill House, *Berkshire, England, 1650*

MIDDLE-CLASS TOWNHOUSE
The Moot, *Downton, Wiltshire, c. 1700*

In the Colonies, the tight symmetry of the Georgian house implied order and dignity, while the refined level of finish, particularly inside, spoke of its owner's prosperity and social position. Mostly executed in wood in the Northeast, brick typically south of Baltimore, and occasionally in stone around Philadelphia, Georgian houses could be both lavish and modest. (See the entries for Georgian architecture in the Mid-Atlantic and Tidewater hearths.)

The defining feature of most 17th-century New England interiors was the low, exposed-timber ceiling, but the Georgian house had high ceilings of 10 or 11 feet and was smoothly plastered, painted, and occasionally decorated with molded or carved ornament. Elaborate mantelpieces, stairways, and arched openings were fashioned from instructions in pattern books imported from England or the imaginations of the builders themselves.

Outside, the front doorway in particular received close attention. Pilasters supported weighty pediments or entablature. Paneled doors were topped by transoms of small square panes or, less frequently and later in the period, round-topped transoms with graceful fan-shaped panes. Large sash windows of many small panes created a new texture in the elevation.

Georgian architecture can be confused with the Federal style (see page 222) that followed it, as well as with the much later Colonial or Georgian Revival (see page 284). The Federal style is relatively restrained, with more delicate ornament. The Colonial Revival of the late 19th century led to everything from deceptively close copies of Colonial Georgian houses to ordinary homes with only the vaguest hints of an 18th-century heritage.

It is important to note that the lengthy dominance of Georgian architecture in the Colonies involved much more than an architectural style: it represented the material aspect of an evolving, stratifying culture. Correct social behavior of all kinds was prescribed in books of etiquette that covered table settings, dining, attire, and "gentle" manners for "gentlemen." Like the architectural pattern books, these English manuals enabled those with wealth and an awareness of fashion to demonstrate their superiority over those less fortunate and unable to read, thus with a lower social standing. The orderly, predictable façades of the Georgian house reassured its owners that they belonged to polite society. Eventually, however, as with every fashion, the Georgian motif filtered down through social levels, reaching those who, unaware of its origins, knew only that it was somehow desirable.

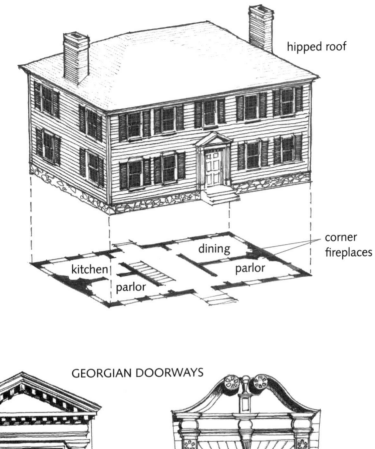

hipped roof

corner
fireplaces

dining

kitchen

parlor

parlor

GEORGIAN DOORWAYS

Col. Robert Means House,
Amherst, N.H., c. 1785

Williams House,
Old Deerfield, Mass., c. 1756

The Hudson River Valley Hearth

Dutch Colonial is not nearly as simple and narrow an architectural heritage as modern real estate advertisements may suggest, often applying the term to any gambrel-roofed suburban house with a two-piece "Dutch" door and possibly an overhanging eave. These houses bear no resemblance to the houses built by Dutch émigrés during the brief period of Dutch colonization in the mid-17th century.

The story of the Dutch in North America began in 1609, when Henry Hudson, sailing under the Netherlands' flag, explored the river later named for him while seeking the elusive Northwest Passage. By 1614 the first traders had begun to trickle in to New Netherlands, and in 1621 the Dutch West India Company was founded and given near feudal powers to administer the colony and attract permanent settlers. Favored proprietors were granted vast "patroonships," or plantations, covering dozens of square miles up and down the river. Few people were attracted, however, by the prospect of becoming little more than sharecroppers, and the area remained sparsely settled. Those who did arrive came from several areas of northern Europe in addition to Holland.

Unlike the other Europeans on the American continent—many of whom came to plunder or escape religious or political persecution and to convert, drive off, or exterminate the natives—the Dutch hoped to establish strategic trading posts for the acquisition of beaver pelts, a highly profitable commodity in Europe. However, they had difficulty maintaining good relations with the Native American tribes, who competed with one another to supply the Europeans. Eventually the Dutch succumbed to the standard Colonial pattern of domination

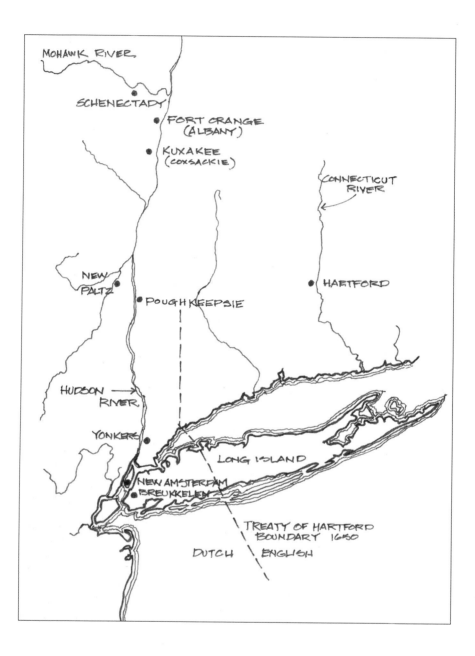

MOHAWK RIVER

SCHENECTADY

FORT ORANGE
(ALBANY)

KUXAKEE
(COXSACKIE)

CONNECTICUT
RIVER

NEW
PALTZ

POUGHKEEPSIE

HARTFORD

HUDSON
RIVER

YONKERS

LONG ISLAND

NEW AMSTERDAM
BREUKKELEN

TREATY OF HARTFORD
BOUNDARY 1650

DUTCH   ENGLISH

by force, first out of fear, then as a way of acquiring land for agriculture and speculation.

New Netherlands lasted only until 1664, when the English king Charles II sent his brother James, the duke of York, to occupy the Dutch claim, which stretched south from around Schenectady along the Hudson into New Jersey and western Long Island. Although many buildings were built before the British took over, none remain from the actual Dutch Colonial period.

The English offered the settlers more favorable terms, and emigrants came in considerable numbers from northern Europe, bringing with them a variety of housing traditions. The historic "Dutch" houses seen now along the Hudson were in fact built when the area was a British colony. Under a relatively relaxed British administration, the Dutch social traditions continued, particularly community organization and church customs, and Dutch houses continued to be built. Eventually, however, as would happen with the French settlements on the lower Mississippi and with the German farmers of Pennsylvania, the dominant English culture, exemplified by its Georgian symmetry, diminished the Dutch influence in the Hudson River valley as New Englanders moved west during the 18th century.

Branford House, *Wyckoff, N.J., 1745–75*

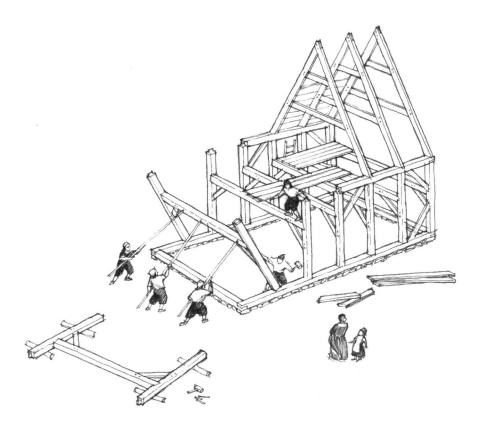

The Dutch housing traditions did not travel, and the surviving examples of authentic Dutch residential architecture remain in river towns along the Hudson and its tributaries in New York and northern New Jersey and in eastern Long Island. These houses can be grouped into four fairly distinct styles, roughly defined by their building materials, floor plans, and period of construction. The early manufacture of brick in New Amsterdam (New York) and Fort Orange (Albany) permitted the reproduction of typical Netherlands townhouses, with similar structures adapted for the nearby countryside. Old engravings as well as photographs of more recently lost buildings in New York and Albany show houses similar to those in 17th-century Amsterdam: parapet-gabled brick houses of two or more stories with steep roofs and many with stepped gables. Few were built in the Colonies after 1730, and the Adam Yates house in Schenectady is the only surviving Dutch townhouse from that time. New York City demolished its last Dutch townhouses as recently as the 1920s.

Along the Hudson between Albany and New York, stone was readily available and was used to construct simpler rural, side-entry, one-and-a-half-story dwellings. Many of them remain and are used today. At the time, stone was considered inferior to the more expensive brick.

The style we think of today as Dutch Colonial evolved in northern New Jersey and Long Island, areas settled largely by groups other than the Dutch and Flemish: Huguenots, English, and Scots-Irish, in particular. They soon developed the now familiar configuration of a gracefully proportioned gambrel roof and curved, extended eaves. The availability of wood on Long Island helped to distinguish its homes from those in New Jersey, where the red sandstone gave similar designs a somewhat different character.

What unites these variations as Dutch architecture is the anchor-bent frame, which is derived from Dutch and German barn construction in medieval northwestern Europe. Heavy timbers form a wide H-shaped bent with the crossbar at the attic floor, and the bents are spaced approximately 4 feet apart for the length of the house. The roof was then attached at the plate on the upright legs, not at the attic level, as in English one- or one-and-a-half-story houses. It is this structural system that gives most "Dutch" houses from Schenectady to New Jersey their distinctive, high-shouldered look. The resulting extra wall height allows for the smooth integration of the flared eaves that have become, along with the broad gambrel roof, the defining elements of our Dutch Colonial style. Not all Dutch houses were built this way, particularly later ones, but even when other framing techniques were used, the proportions of the anchor-bent framed house were retained.

Jan Bries House, *East Greenbush, N.Y., c. 1723*

The Brick Farmhouse (1650–1750)
Albany Brick Cottage

FORM: Typically a 1½-story house with steeply pitched parapet gables and roof. Gambrel roofs were occasionally seen. Continental dormers. Minimal eaves. Larger, 2½-story manor houses were rare.

STYLISTIC DETAIL: Smooth façades with flat or segmented arches over windows and doors. Decorative dagger-shaped anchor plates or beam anchors tie masonry walls to the timber frame. Originally fitted with casements, but vertical sliding sash windows installed after 1750. Brick was laid in a Dutch cross-bond coursing, with special "mouse-tooth" brick detailing along the parapets. Smooth, not "crow-stepped," gables.

CONSTRUCTION: Brick veneer over an anchor-bent timber frame on a stone foundation. Rare examples were built of stone. Later versions may have masonry bearing walls. Wood siding occasionally used. Roofing evolved from thatching to flat tiles to wood shingles.

A few drawings and old photographs show the streets of Fort Orange (Albany) and New Amsterdam (New York) lined with structures similar to the traditional urban houses of Holland. The Brick Farmhouse was similar to the Dutch townhouse but adapted for rural use, resembling the farmhouses in 17th-century landscape paintings by van Ruisdael and other Dutch artists. Unlike the urban house, the farmhouse had its entry in the long, or eave, side of the house rather than the gable end.

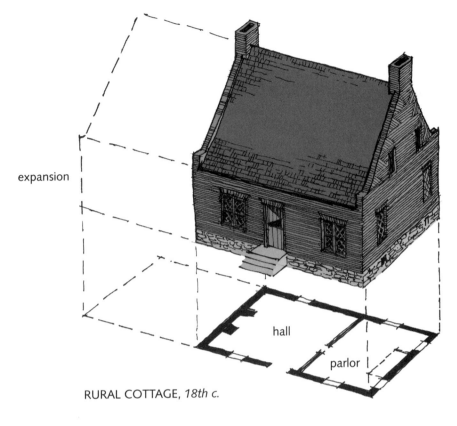

expansion

hall

parlor

RURAL COTTAGE, *18th c.*

URBAN TRADITION

dagger-shaped
anchor plates

Adam Yates House,
Schenectady, N.Y., mid-18th c.

The Hudson River Valley Hearth

43

Fortunately, a few examples have survived along the Hudson River. They were initially one- or two-room cottages, the one-room being about 12 by 12 feet, the two-room 12 by 18, with fireplaces at both ends. The steep roofs allowed for attic space even above the generous loft. Larger, two-and-a-half-story plantation versions were also built, such as the Crailo House in Rensselaer and the gambrel-roofed Herkimer House on the Mohawk.

In the northern part of the Dutch settlement, brick was the common building material, as it was in Holland. However, the basic load-bearing structure was the anchor-bent timber frame with brick cladding. Early brick houses (before 1700) used thin Dutch bricks in a Dutch cross-bond pattern. Smoothing the top surface of the exposed parapets resulted in an unusual brick detail called muisetanden, mouse-tooth coursing, a medieval detail found in Flanders as well as parts of England. Patterns of glazed brick decorated the gable ends, sometimes including names and dates. Slots said to be gun ports are found on several early houses, indicating the need for defense either from Indian attack or perhaps, on the larger houses, from angry tenants.

Several of these sturdy farmhouses can be seen in the area from Kingston north to Albany and along the Mohawk River: the Leendert Bronck House (1738) in Coxsackie, the Bries House (1723) in East Greenbush, and the Mabie House (c. 1706) in Rotterdam are worth searching out. Note that all were built well after the Dutch colony was taken over by the English.

John Mabie House, *Rotterdam, N.Y., original house 1670*

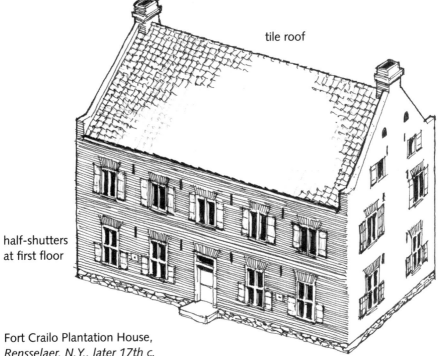

tile roof

half-shutters
at first floor

Fort Crailo Plantation House,
Rensselaer, N.Y., later 17th c.

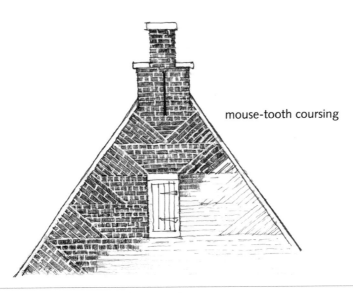

mouse-tooth coursing

Bevier-Elting House, *New Paltz, N.Y., c. 1698*

The Stone Farmhouse (1700–1800)

FORM: 1½-story house, sitting low to the ground, with two or more rooms arranged in a line. The moderately sloping gabled roof has minimal overhangs. Note the typically Dutch high eave line. English gambrel roofs are not unusual. Additional wings and sheds or lean-tos at the rear are common. Shed dormers may be later additions. End chimneys flush with the gable-end walls are typical. Multiple chimneys indicate later additions.

STYLISTIC DETAIL: Plain asymmetrical façades. A divided Dutch door under a cantilevered hood is typical. Doors may have a simple, rectangular, multiple-pane transom light. Shutters, when present, are plain and solid (not louvered). Chimneys are not elaborate. Windows are leaded casements opening outward during the 17th century, double-hung sash after 1700, usually 12-over-12.

CONSTRUCTION: Irregular fieldstone and, less commonly, coursed ashlar stone, usually covering the heavy, anchor-bent timber frames. Clapboards are typical at the gable ends, particularly above the upper-story windows or collar ties.

Along the Hudson between Albany and New York, stone was plentiful and became the primary building material, due largely to the expense of hauling the much-preferred brick from the urban centers where it was made. Accordingly, the houses were quite different in character from the medieval, steep-roofed brick farmhouses to the north and the later two-room-deep houses of southern New York and northern New Jersey.

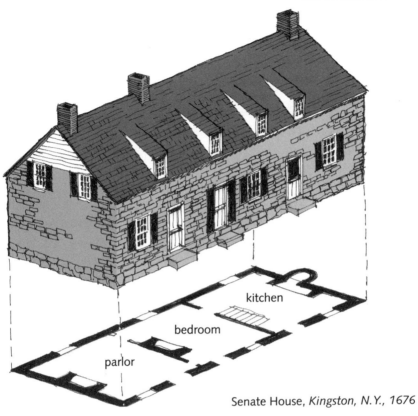

kitchen

bedroom

parlor

Senate House, *Kingston, N.Y., 1676*

TYPICAL RURAL FARMHOUSE FLOOR PLAN

gambrel roof
not original

Ariaantje Coeymans House,
Coeymans, N.Y., c. 1716–23

The Hudson River Valley Hearth

Often beginning as one-room cottages, Stone Farmhouses grew as new rooms were added at the ends, continuing the roofline. A chimney and a new front door were usually added for each room. Additions at the rear for kitchens and bedrooms frequently resulted in a Saltbox profile and a kitchen that was a few steps down from the main house. The extra garret space gained above could accommodate slaves.

Benjamin Ten Broeck House, *Kingston vicinity, N.Y., c. 1751, 1765*

In later-18th-century houses, the English concept of an unheated center passage appeared, probably adapted from the Georgian mansions being built in the area. The center passage led inevitably to the two-room-deep floor plans that found favor throughout the Colonies. Along the Hudson, the deeper plan was frequently covered with a gambrel roof, allowing longer transverse spans and greater second- or third-floor headroom. Two-thirds Georgian plans similar to those in the Middle Atlantic region were also built (see page 69). In the first quarter of the 19th century, as the New Englanders moved west and south, English residential architecture came to dominate the Hudson, ending two hundred years of Dutch construction.

kitchen
addition

Ten Eyck House, *Horley, N.Y., c. 1700*

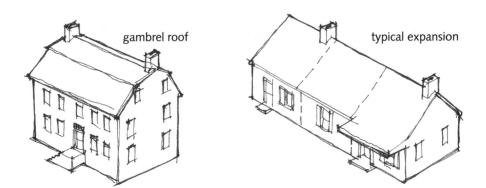

gambrel roof

typical expansion

Dewerk Peter Herring House, *Old Tappan, N.J., c. 1712*

The Lower Hudson River Farmhouse (1750–1835)
Dutch Colonial, Flemish Farmhouse, Flemish Colonial

FORM: 1½-story side-gabled house with extended eaves, typically flared at the
front or at both front and rear. Roof may be gabled or gambreled. Typical Dutch
high eave line. Additional wings at either or both ends are common. Minimal roof
overhangs at the gable ends. Shed dormers may be original; gabled dormers are
later additions.

STYLISTIC DETAIL: The signature flared eaves may extend from 2 to several feet
and are occasionally supported by posts, creating a full-length porch. Almost
symmetrical façade of 3 or 5 bays. Simple detailing. Large sash windows.

CONSTRUCTION: Generally of wood frame in southern New York and western
Long Island, of stone and wood in eastern New Jersey.

Flemish, French Huguenot, and Dutch immigrants, as well as French
Canadians and anonymous but inventive 18th-century local housewrights,
have been credited with the flared-eave, gambrel-roofed farmhouse. Its
origins remain unclear, although surely it is some combination of the
Low Country tradition and the settlers' ingenuity.

Often referred to as a "bell-cast" eave or a "Dutch kick," the
graceful, curved continuation of the roof slope gives these houses their
distinctive look whether the roof line is gabled or gambrel. The flare is
made possible by the traditional Dutch high-shouldered eave line, which

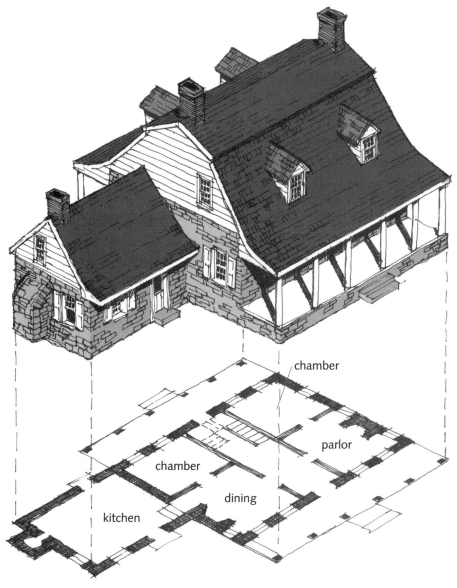

CENTER-PASSAGE FLOOR PLAN

descended from the early, anchor-bent timber construction technique, perhaps the house's only claim to a northern European ancestry.

Although the earliest examples retain the peaked gable roof, it is the gambrel that is typically associated with the so-called Dutch Colonial house. It is generally

Tabreskie-Christie House, *Dumont, N.J., 1810*

believed that the English introduced gambrel roofs to the eastern seaboard, particularly to eastern Long Island (next to the Dutch settlements), but in New York and New Jersey the upper pitch is much shorter and flatter, leaving a second long, gentle slope ending in the flare. It is as though the top slope was flattened to save the extra construction of finishing off the peak. Considerable second-floor space was created, as well as a useful attic.

Floor plans were invariably of the center-passage type, becoming more formally symmetrical as the Georgian influence was felt. Typically, there were two large rooms in front, with fireplaces, and two smaller rooms to the rear. Kitchens were often added at a gable end (or were occasionally built before the main house).

Today, it is common to find a builder's so-called Dutch Colonial among the ubiquitous Georgian Colonials that continue to clog our suburbs. From about 1890 through the 1930s, there was a revival of the Dutch style, with a few scrupulously accurate examples built. Most, however, were ordinary houses with a few Dutch features, and they bore little resemblance to genuine examples of 18th-century farmhouses other than an extended, sometimes even curved, eave line and a horizontally divided door. Dutch Colonials nevertheless remain a respected house type, especially in corners of the country that never saw the real thing. (It is not unusual for real estate offices to call any gambrel-roofed house with a large shed dormer a Dutch Colonial.)

Many of the handsome original houses still survive in northern New Jersey (typically of stone) and western Long Island (wood).

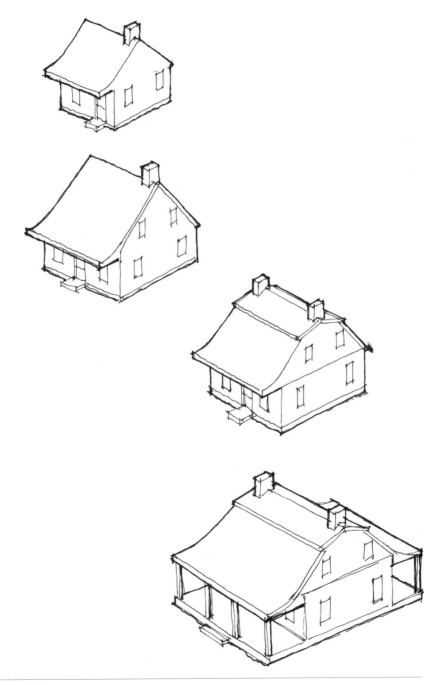

The Mid-Atlantic Hearth and the Upland South

The Mid-Atlantic (or Delaware River) Hearth has a more complex pattern of settlement than New England and Tidewater regions, which were more homogeneous. The greater variety of political and religious refugees settling on this mid-Atlantic landscape resulted in a blend of building customs as the different groups adapted their familiar European house types to a new environment. The climate was milder than New England's and less "tropical" and disease-prone than that of the southern colonies; its fertile, rolling countryside held ample resources of clay, lime, stone, and timber. More important, its native peoples were somewhat friendlier to European settlers than those to the north and south.

Geographically, the core of the Mid-Atlantic Hearth includes southern New Jersey, northern Delaware, southeastern Pennsylvania, and parts of northern and western Maryland. In time, the Delaware Valley culture extended itself by launching streams of settlers down the Appalachian Mountains and valleys into the upland South and along the Ohio River valley to the lower Midwest. The settlers took vernacular European building traditions with them through southeastern Pennsylvania and Maryland, eventually influencing house design in what is now every southern state, plus Texas, Oklahoma, and Missouri, as well as the midwestern states along the Ohio River. This is the migration that carried the storied pioneer log cabin and the ubiquitous "I" house (see page 72) to the interior, influencing the appearance of countless towns and rural landscapes.

Given the usual bias toward affluent English culture in American history books, the Philadelphia mansions of the Mid-Atlantic Hearth are generally overrepresented and the rural domestic architecture slighted, referred to simplistically as stone farmhouses or, worse, a "Pennsylvania Dutch" style. The considerable variation among rural mid-Atlantic house types can be baffling, but the history of the European settlement in the region organizes representative examples into a distinct pattern. As is usually the case, it is the floor plan that distinguishes these houses, not merely the façade or applied ornament. The vitality of these houses is often ignored by historians until the mid-18th century, when more symmetrical façades could be labeled Georgian.

The mid-Atlantic area saw the arrival of a few Swedish, Finnish, and Dutch settlers in the 1630s. However, New Sweden, as the original colony was known, faltered from lack of support and was taken over by the Dutch, who were settling along the Hudson River, in northern

New Jersey, and in western Long Island at the time. When the Dutch capitulated to the British in 1664, the mid-Atlantic was in line for official English colonization. The English Quaker William Penn was granted the land west of the Delaware River, south of New York, and north of Lord Baltimore's Maryland grant. Penn scouted Europe for Quakers and others affected by the uncertainties and religious upheavals of the 17th century. His own group of English Quakers was the first to arrive in significant number, in 1675. By 1715, 23,000 North Midland English and Irish, as well as some German and Dutch Friends, settled in the valley. They were soon followed by even greater numbers of Protestant Swiss, Germans, and Moravians from the upper Rhine River region as well as other areas. Both the Germans and English brought building traditions that shaped the Delaware Valley architecture quite differently from those of the settlements to the north and south.

In the 1720s, a surge of energetic and restless Scottish and Irish immigrants from the northern English borderlands and northern Ireland came ashore. Urged to move on by the staid and disapproving Quakers and German farmers, they pushed west through southern Pennsylvania and south through Maryland into the Shenandoah Valley, taking mid-Atlantic building traditions with them. Waves of Scotch-Irish continued until 1775, expanding the American frontier through the upland South and lower Midwest. With such a history of ethnic settlement, there is much more variety of house styles in early Delaware, New Jersey, and Pennsylvania than just the familiar Philadelphia Georgian homes of the Revolutionary period.

The essential materials of 18th-century mid-Atlantic residential architecture were logs, brick, and stone. The architectural vitality still apparent to anyone traveling through southern Pennsylvania was not derived from the nearby Chesapeake Bay Tidewater traditions, although there may occasionally be some resemblances. Mid-Atlantic architecture is also the story of English Quakers and German Pietists adapting their traditions to the conditions at hand.

These groups used a variety of floor plans during the Colonial period, but the primary building materials, solid and well handled, gave this area its outward character.

Taylor-Parke House, *Chester County, Pa., c. 1768*

The Quaker Plan House (1675–1800)
Penn Plan, Swedish Plan

FORM: Typically 2-story, nearly square block of 3 or 4 bays with a moderately pitched gable-end roof. Chimneys appear at one or (more typically) both ends. Wide porches are likely to have been added later.

STYLISTIC DETAIL: Plain except for attempts at Georgian façade symmetry. Dentils, broken cornices, and returned cornices are not unusual but may have been added later. Pent eaves (partial projecting roofs) are common across either the front entry façade or on all sides. A rectangular, 4-pane transom light is typical over the front door.

CONSTRUCTION: Stone or brick masonry bearing walls. Log and wood-frame versions were stuccoed or sheathed with weatherboards.

Three-room house plans played a significant role in late-17th- and early-18th-century architecture in the Delaware Valley, for Penn recommended a three-room plan as a "beginner's house" in advertising for his new colonists in 1684. When the Germans and Swiss of the upper Rhine Valley and the Quakers from the North Midlands of England immigrated to Penn's mid-Atlantic colony to escape religious persecution, they followed his advice. There has been much discussion about whether the German and English houses have a common origin. It seems likely that the Quakers and Germans each brought with them their own traditional three-room arrangement but, in adapting it to their

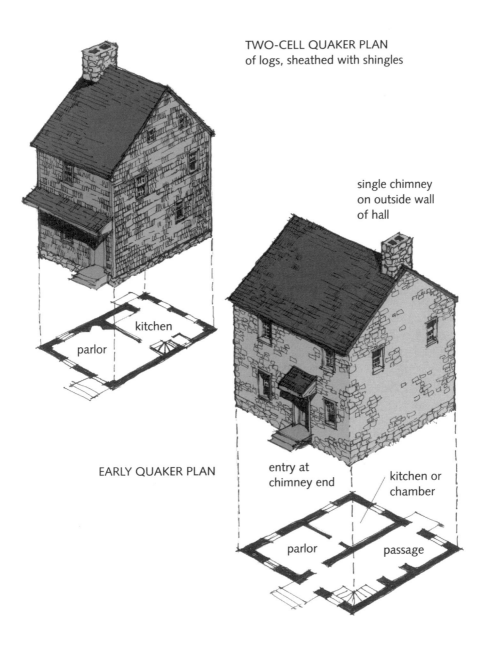

TWO-CELL QUAKER PLAN
of logs, sheathed with shingles

single chimney
on outside wall
of hall

kitchen

parlor

EARLY QUAKER PLAN

entry at
chimney end

kitchen or
chamber

parlor

passage

new conditions—a moderate climate and plenty of wood, clay, and, especially west of the Delaware River, stone—ended up with similar building styles.

The Quaker Plan—or Penn Plan, as it is sometimes called—is a squarish, two-story, side-passage design something like a two-thirds Georgian house (see page 69), though the passage, a hall in this case, is much wider, about the size of the other two rooms combined. (Some claim this plan was inspired by the houses already built in the valley by earlier Swedish settlers, hence Swedish Plan.) Such a house was originally built with a fireplace only at the hall's gable end, but later designs added another chimney at the opposite gable, serving two adjacent or two corner fireplaces back-to-back. Corner fireplaces are often attributed to Swedish influences, as it was common for the Swedish settlers in this area to use them in one- or two-room log houses. However, there is plenty of precedent for corner fireplaces in other English settlements. The kitchen was in the rear room behind the parlor, in the basement, or in an addition on the hall side. Occasionally it occupied a separate structure, probably indicating the owner's prosperity.

Quaker three-room plans can generally be identified by either the single chimney at the hall gable end or chimneys in both gables. The three-bay front elevation is typically not quite symmetrical, due to the off-center doorway required by the hall's width. The door may be in the first or third bay, depending on the handedness of the plan. In later four-bay versions, the door is in the second bay from the end and the façade appears virtually symmetrical. There is always a chimney in the door bay. There are examples of a narrow, two-room, double-cell Quaker plan, with no hall and just one room front and rear. It is sometimes considered a one-third Georgian house (see page 69).

Of the various Pennsylvania three-room plans, only the Quaker (or Penn) Plan seems to have traveled west in any number, becoming familiar in eastern Tennessee, for example. Three-room-plan houses were also reportedly built to the south, as Quakers migrated into Georgia and North Carolina. The English Quakers built other types of houses as well, but all were generally plain and unadorned, consistent with their disdain for ostentation. By the mid-18th century, with greater prosperity and a partial relaxing of attitudes, Quaker homes, particularly in Philadelphia, began to incorporate more stylish and decorative features.

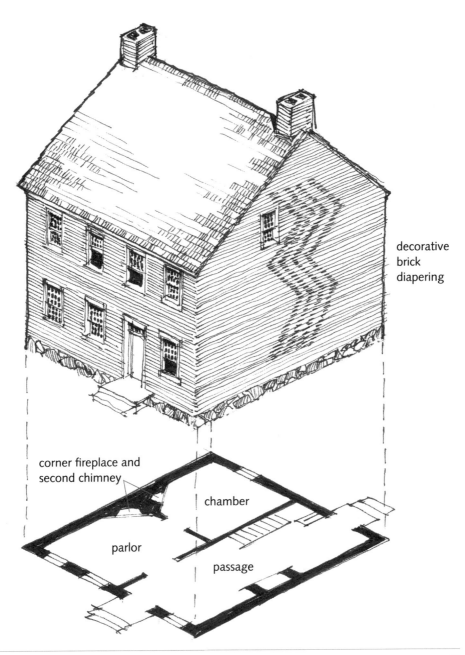

decorative
brick
diapering

corner fireplace and
second chimney

chamber

parlor

passage

Hans Herr House, *Lancaster County, Pa., c. 1719*

The Continental Plan House (1715–1800)
Pennsylvania Farmhouse, *Flurkuchenhaus*

FORM: A nearly square, 3-bay, 2-story house under a side-gabled roof, with a single chimney offset toward the entry bay. Later versions may have two end chimneys and a nearly symmetrical 4-bay façade.

STYLISTIC DETAIL: Simple exterior trim, although quoins are common, frequently of ashlar stone. Segmental arches at door and window openings are typical. Full-width pent eaves at the second-floor façade over the entry are common.

STRUCTURE: Stone or brick masonry bearing walls. Log and wood frame versions stuccoed or sheathed in weatherboards.

The mid-Atlantic Continental three-room house is reported to have a forebear in the two-room *Flurkuchenhaus* (hall-kitchen house) of the upper Rhine Valley that, in larger, squarer versions, could be divided into three- and even four-room plans.

It accompanied first- and second-generation German and Swiss immigrants from Pennsylvania into northern upland Virginia and as far as North Carolina. In the latter states, it was gradually replaced by the ubiquitous but satisfyingly symmetrical English "I" house after 1800, as ethnic Rhenish-German traditions were abandoned in favor of the Anglo-American material culture.

In Pennsylvania the German three-room floor plan appears similar to the English Quaker plan, but it has a long, relatively narrow

The Mid-Atlantic Hearth and the Upland South

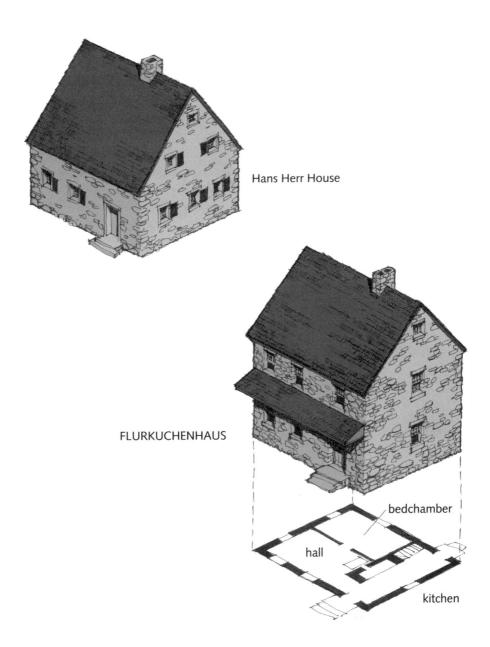

Hans Herr House

FLURKUCHENHAUS

bedchamber

hall

kitchen

kitchen running front to rear. The front door opens into the kitchen (*Küche*), which is likely to have a rear door as well. There is a very large cooking fireplace along the inside wall, with a tight stair in a corner beyond that leads to sleeping space upstairs. An opening in the rear wall of the fireplace serves a masonry stove in the adjoining room. The remaining space is divided into a heated parlor (*Stube*) in the front and a bedchamber (*Zimmer*) to the rear. With this design, the kitchen, and whoever occupies it, controls access to the interior, a different concept entirely from the English floor plans since the early hall-and-parlor house.

Storage cellars were common, and German houses were frequently sited on a hillside, allowing for outside access to the cellar at grade. These basements were often subdivided, with the inner space perhaps vaulted and the outer room finished as a workspace, even with a fireplace. A similar Swiss plan, the Swiss Bank House, has its gable end pushed into the hillside to provide a nearly constant temperature in the cellar, ideal for storing the products of home breweries and wineries, as well as milk and cheese. Its plan was similar to that of the *Flurkuchenhaus* but typically placed the kitchen at the lower level.

QUAKER PLAN

Reflecting the powerful English Georgian influence, builders adjusted and balanced the front elevation of the Germanic Continental Plan while moving fireplaces and chimneys to the gable ends; it retained a semblance of its unique layout inside. In many cases, the resulting nearly symmetrical four-bay façade (three windows and a door almost evenly spaced) still didn't quite satisfy. In response to the prevailing craze for symmetry, a second front entry to the parlor was added, replacing a window. Even then, perfectly equal bay spacing could be difficult to achieve due to the narrow kitchen. Gable ends also received 2-over-2 Georgian window arrangements at this time. Houses with this exterior reworking are often called Pennsylvania Farmhouses to distinguish them from the original three-room Continental Plan house.

CONTINENTAL PLAN

PENNSYLVANIA
FARMHOUSE

PENNSYLVANIA FARMHOUSE

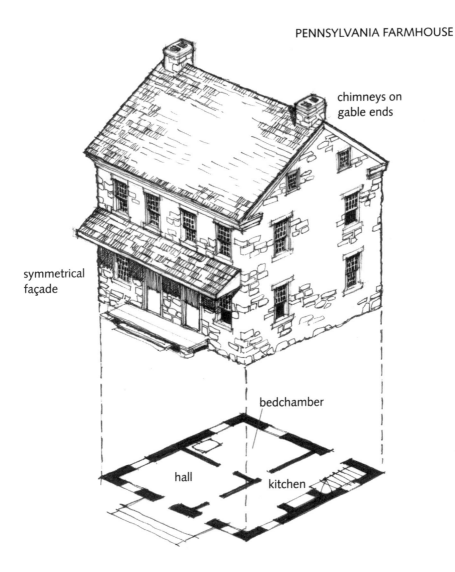

chimneys on
gable ends

symmetrical
façade

bedchamber

hall

kitchen

Warren Point, *Chester County, Pa., c. 1756*

The Mid-Atlantic Georgian (1750–1875)
Four-over-Four

FORM: A 2-story block under a gently sloping roof, gable ended or hipped, with chimneys at each gable end. Entry is centered on the long side under the front eave. A 5-bay symmetrical façade reflects the symmetrical floor plan. One-story versions are less common.

STYLISTIC DETAIL: Variable, but can be restricted to a mildly ornamented entry. Broken pediment is common. May have pent roofs over the first level on the front only or also at the gable ends. Cornices may be carried across the gable ends as pent eaves; 12-over-12 sash windows are typical. Projecting door hoods and rectangular transom lights are common, as are paneled shutters and doors. Wide front porches are likely to be later additions. Ornamental patterns (zigzag, diamond) in brick end walls are common, as are flat arches over windows in brick houses. Later, fashionable urban examples may show all the typical excesses, such as quoins, elaborate cornices, a projecting central pavilion, and ornamented chimneys.

CONSTRUCTION: Typically of stone: ashlar, random-coursed, or fieldstone. Also of brick, log, and wood frame covered with weatherboards or stuccoed. Brick is more common in southern New Jersey, stone in Pennsylvania. Wood frame examples may have brick nogging between studs.

The story of what Americans call Georgian began with the Italian Renaissance and Palladio's monumental symmetrical villas. Interpreted

evolving Georgian façade
on three-bay "I" house

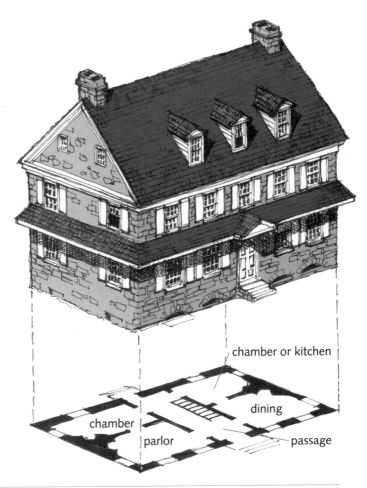

chamber or kitchen

dining

chamber

parlor

passage

by 17th-century English architects, the Georgian style arrived in the Colonies around 1700, becoming popular roughly at the time of the Colonial rule of George I, II, and III (1714–75); historians later named the period for those kings. However vague, the term Georgian is now so ingrained in American architectural conversation that it cannot be avoided, although it more aptly describes an era rather than a house style. The main ingredient of Georgian design is symmetry—as much as can be worked into both the elevations and floor plans.

After a few British aristocrats broke with the Tudor-Jacobean tradition of ponderous country homes and took up the simpler Palladian mode, the new style became fashionable for the increasingly prosperous and ambitious English mercantile middle class. Accordingly, the more formal configuration of a simple block with symmetrical elevations and relatively symmetrical floor plans eventually became popular throughout the British colonies. Pattern books and other class-conscious, tastemaker publications, as well as the arrival of colonists and artisans familiar with the new fashion, contributed to its widespread acceptance. As the Georgian style became universally popular in the Colonies as a sign of gentility, in the mid-Atlantic area it came to dominate the rural vernacular landscape as well as affluent estates.

Noticeable variants can be seen within the broad Georgian designation. Like the Cape Cod Cottage, the Georgian house was also built in partial versions, to be expanded later if so desired. A two-thirds, three-bay model is common to the mid-Atlantic region, retaining the passage (or hall) with stair and with two rooms on each floor. A smaller kitchen wing is commonly added to the gable end off the passage. The three-bay Georgian can be distinguished from the outwardly similar and shortened Quaker Plan House by its chimney—typically at the gable end farthest from the entry.

There is also a one-third Georgian type, two bays wide with just one room front and rear, similar to the "double-cell" Quaker Plan House (page 59). These narrow houses, whether called Georgian or Quaker, were well adapted to tight urban building sites but seem strange in rural settings. A great many of these houses were built as urban row houses, often paired, in mid-Atlantic cities and towns as well as in Baltimore, Washington, and Richmond.

The urban houses were larger and grander than the rural versions. The Georgian homes in Philadelphia, although mainly of stone or brick, resembled the wood mansions around Boston but offered more ornament in their quoins, pilasters, and pedimented center pavilions at the entries.

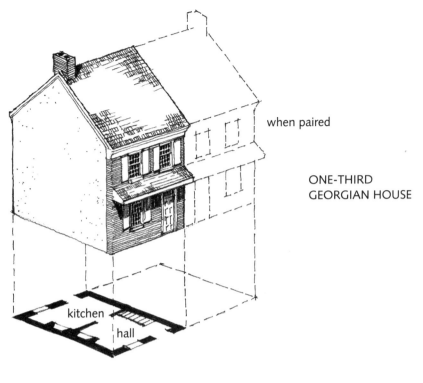

when paired

ONE-THIRD
GEORGIAN HOUSE

kitchen

hall

TWO-THIRDS
GEORGIAN HOUSE

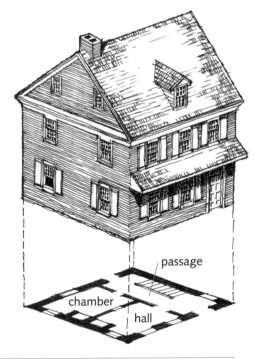

passage

chamber

hall

Although originally quite austere in their architectural taste, the Quakers, influenced by their new prosperity and the easing of Quaker doctrine, began to build houses as elaborate as those of their Yankee neighbors. These mansions were an expression of economic and social class rather than rural or urban siting, for many modest Georgians were built in mid-Atlantic cities, towns, and villages as well.

William Corbit House, *Odessa, Del., c. 1773*

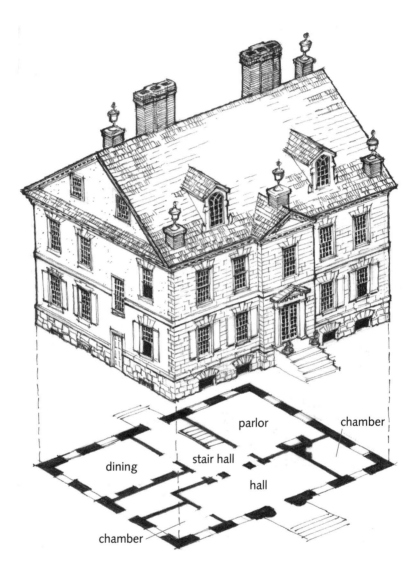

parlor

chamber

dining

stair hall

hall

chamber

Cliveden, *Germantown, Pa., 1763–64*

Weikert House, *Adams County, Pa.*

The Mid-Atlantic "I" House (1700–1915)

FORM: Always a full 2-story, 1-room-deep rectangular block of 3 or 5 bays. Length and height are at least twice the depth. Moderately pitched gabled roofs were typical, but gambrel roofs were not uncommon. Full-length pent eaves were common on the front elevation over the entry or on all sides. Wide porches are likely to have been added later.

STYLISTIC DETAIL: Early examples are plain with little aesthetic expression other than glazed brick patterning (diapering) at the blank gable ends and attempts at Georgian symmetry. Brick may be laid in English or Flemish bond. Stone masonry texture varies from rough fieldstone to ashlar. Symmetrical 5-bay façade and 2-bay gable ends typical after the mid-18th century. Dentils, broken cornices, and returned cornices not unusual. Rectangular transom lights common. The 19th-century examples may be trimmed with Greek or Gothic ornament.

CONSTRUCTION: Stone or brick masonry. Also log and wood frame, either stuccoed or sheathed with weatherboards.

Well known in England, the "I" house became a common sight in the English communities of the mid-Atlantic colonies in the 18th century. It was also familiar from the Chesapeake Bay Tidewater region south into North Carolina and north into New England, although it is not often called an "I" house there. This term, which arose only recently, may refer to its relatively tall, thin profile as seen from the end or to the long, narrow floor plan—or, it is also suggested, to the three states where

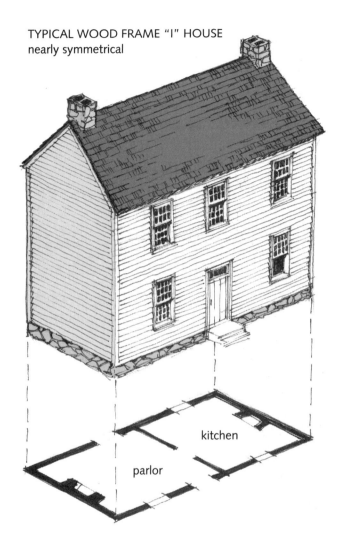

TYPICAL WOOD FRAME "I" HOUSE
nearly symmetrical

kitchen

parlor

"I" houses proliferated: Indiana, Illinois, and Iowa. In the mid-Atlantic region, it almost completely replaced the Quaker and Continental plans in the 19th century as the most popular type of farmhouse. With its short spans it was simple to build, and it provided good ventilation in hot, sticky climates. It could also be adapted to the fashionable, symmetrical Georgian façade, allowing a relatively modest farmhouse to present a full Georgian face to the public. This style became strongly associated with rural prosperity.

Floor plans ranged over time from the simple hall-and-parlor to the center-passage, and by the mid-18th century they were tidied up to balance the front elevation. Kitchens and other spaces often occupied wings to the rear. As with the Mid-Atlantic Georgian house and the Cape Cod Cottage in New England, partial "I" houses were built. These were usually three-bay, two-thirds houses consisting of one room (sometimes called a 1-over-1) or one room and a hall on each floor. On the two-thirds house, a one-story kitchen was often attached to the entry gable end.

Very early on, there were a few linear three-room houses that might be considered "I" houses. They repeated a common vernacular English style, with a hall, parlor, and kitchen arranged in a row, and were seen, if infrequently, in all the English colonies, though more typically in the 17th-century mid-Atlantic and Tidewater areas. Houses known as Swedish Gambrels in southern New Jersey can also be called "I" houses with gambrel roofs.

Robert Ashton House, *New Castle, Del., c. 1700*

The "I" house went on to become the standard dwelling, with many variations, of successful farmers in the South and West. It was the dominant vernacular house type for generations throughout the Piedmont, upland South, and Midwest, even into the 20th-century Ozarks, where a few have Greek or Gothic ornament, centered cross gables, and two-story porticoes.

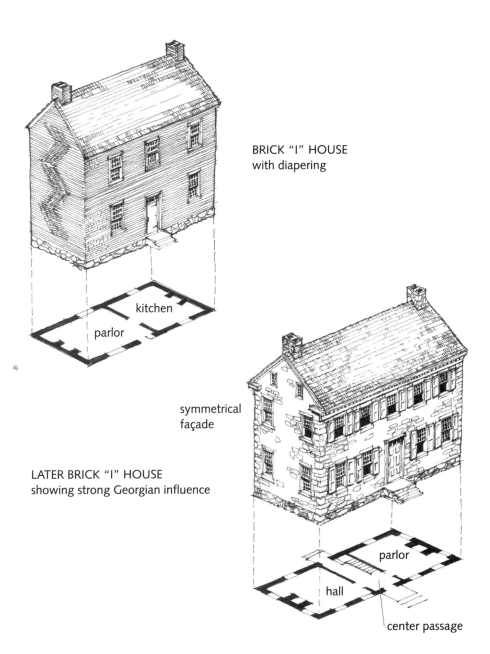

BRICK "I" HOUSE
with diapering

kitchen

parlor

symmetrical
façade

LATER BRICK "I" HOUSE
showing strong Georgian influence

parlor

hall

center passage

Wertz-Lashee House, *York County, Pa., c. 1765*

Log Building Traditions (1640–1850)

A symbol of the American frontier, the log cabin first appeared in
the Mid-Atlantic Hearth in 1638 with the arrival of a few Swedish
adventurers who hoped to acquire furs from the native population.
Bringing with them traditional Scandinavian log construction
techniques, they fashioned small dwellings from the plentiful timber of
the new territory. None of their cabins remains today, but they certainly
set an example for later arrivals. Cabins built in the Swedish style were
noted for round-log construction and corner fireplaces.

The Germans, arriving in large numbers in the early 18th century,
brought their own log building traditions. They are often credited with
the log cabin's explosive proliferation on the constantly expanding
frontier, a process driven by the need for quick, temporary construction
and the readily available timber. The first houses used the round-log
method with much necessary mud chinking. Soon, however, square-
hewn timbers made for a tighter (and tidier) result. Well-crafted corner
notches gave a more finished appearance as well as a drier house.
Several styles of notching were used, with the square notch and the
half dovetail becoming more common for houses and the saddle notch
for less important outbuildings. Many Pennsylvania Quakers and
German farmers built sizable homes of logs, often covering them with
weatherboards or even brick, making them hard to identify as
log structures.

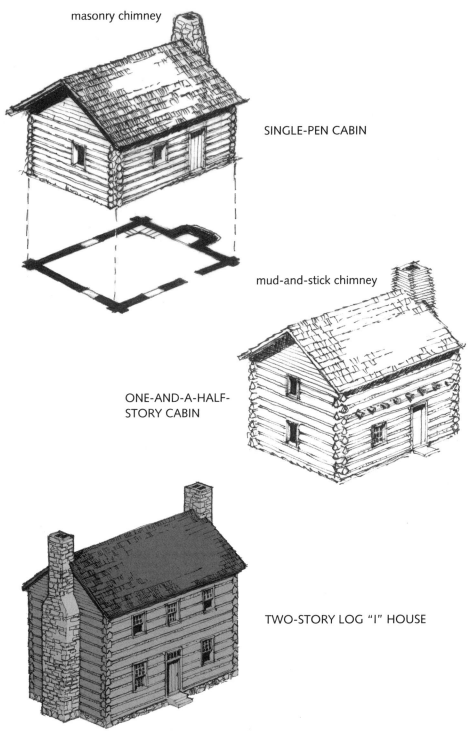

masonry chimney

SINGLE-PEN CABIN

mud-and-stick chimney

ONE-AND-A-HALF-
STORY CABIN

TWO-STORY LOG "I" HOUSE

The flood of immigrants that later passed through Pennsylvania (mostly Scots-Irish and English from the northern borderlands) took the tradition with them as they moved through the upland South and Midwest, building log cabins as they went. Most were low, crudely built structures, dark, with dirt floors, one room, one door, and a fireplace.

However, in Pennsylvania and beyond, the one-room cabin, or Single-Pen type, was not the only common style. With room sizes limited by the length of logs to about 20 feet—beyond that the natural taper of the tree trunk would leave too wide a gap between logs—the best way to add space was to attach another cabin to the original or to build one close to it and connect them. Two-room Double-Pen, Saddle Bag, and Dog-Trot cabins were built continuously throughout the upland South and, eventually, west beyond the Mississippi River.

Untold variations on the log cabin were used as slave quarters, ranch and farm buildings, and miners' and trappers' shelters from the Deep South all the way to California. In the 19th century, Norwegian and Finnish settlers brought Scandinavian log construction to rural areas of the northern Midwest.

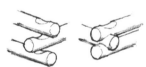

SADDLE NOTCH,
S.E. Pa. upland South

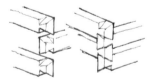

HEWN V-NOTCH,
S.E. Pa. German

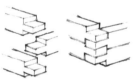

SQUARE NOTCH,
northern Midwest

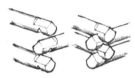

ROUND V-NOTCH,
upland South, Midwest

DOVETAIL,
S.E. Pa. German

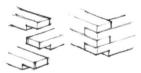

HALF-SQUARE NOTCH

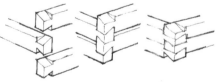

DIAMOND NOTCH, N.C.   HALF DOVETAIL, upland South

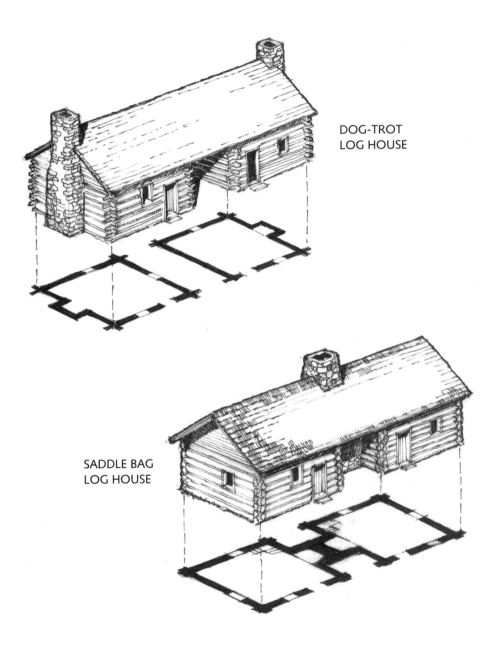

DOG-TROT
LOG HOUSE

SADDLE BAG
LOG HOUSE

The Chesapeake Bay Tidewater Hearth

The Tidewater region, the lowland area of Maryland and Virginia dominated by the expanse of the Chesapeake Bay, clearly defined the English settlements and their architecture. More than 150 rivers flow into its 200-mile width along 2,000 miles of shoreline. Both the low, rolling hills of the western shore and the flatlands to the east lend themselves to agriculture, while the bay itself is a rich source of fish and waterfowl. Summers are hot and humid and the winters short and cool, with little snow.

The English first entered the region at their ill-fated settlement on Roanoke Island in 1585, then, more successfully, at Jamestown in 1607. It was a difficult environment. The humid lowlands were rife with disease-carrying mosquitoes. Typhoid, dysentery, and yellow fever took their toll, as well as malaria, brought first from England and later in a more deadly strain from Africa. The early colonists, though surrounded by rich natural resources, knew little of hunting and planting. While other English colonies were founded by religious refugees and those who expected to settle permanently, the Virginia colony was seen as a commercial venture from the beginning. The English went to Virginia to get rich, hoping first to find gold but settling for the basic cash crop tobacco, which unfortunately grew best in the disease-ridden low country. The commercial nature of the colony, the expectation of a quick return to England, and the scattered, independent tobacco plantations did little to build a sense of community. While some colonists did make their fortune, their self-interest combined with the environment made

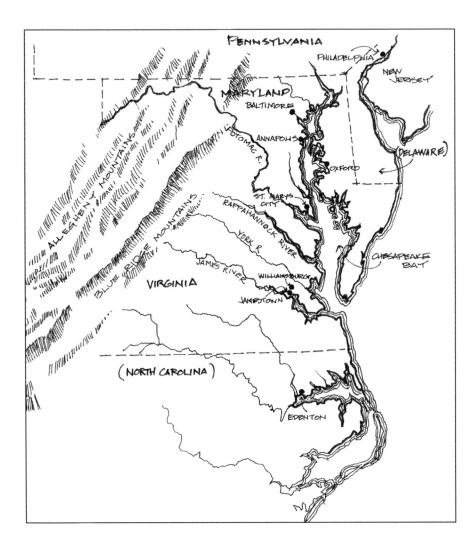

early Virginia a deadly place for the English, and many more died than went home wealthy.

Not until the 1640s did the colony stabilize under the authoritarian leadership of Sir William Berkeley, appointed governor by King Charles I in 1641. Berkeley recruited the English elite whose descendants would control Virginia politics from the 17th century to the Civil War and beyond. In this agricultural society, it was land that provided wealth and status, land distributed by the royal governor and his council. Thus a planter elite emerged in the 1640s and 1650s with its wealth based on large, distant plantations. At the same time immigration increased, although most of the newcomers were indentured servants, unskilled and illiterate, from the rural south and west of England; men outnumbered women by four to one.

Most of the planters were also from the south and west of England. They tended to be the younger sons of aristocratic families who had supported the king in England's Civil War of 1642–48 and who were forced to leave England with Cromwell's victory.

A society of almost feudal stratification developed under Berkeley. The planters, about 10 percent of the population, owned most of the land. These tracts were eventually worked by groups of African slaves and English indentured servants, both auctioned off when their ships reached shore. Plantations became villages unto themselves, maintaining their own carpentry and blacksmith shops as well as other necessities. During the early days, the relationships between master and servant were relatively informal, masters, servants, and guests often sleeping and eating in the same one-room cottages typical of early settlements. Small market towns dotted the landscape, but there were no cities to compare with those developing in the North, and the Tidewater region remained essentially rural and agrarian. There were few roads, as the landscape was constantly interrupted by creeks and rivers, so the waterways provided the main routes of transportation and communication. Ideally, each plantation had direct access to the water, where ships could load and unload from a planter's own wharf. There were no major port cities.

Maryland was colonized in 1634 by the brothers Leonard Calvert and Cecil Calvert, Lord Baltimore. They had received a royal charter and hoped to create a haven for Roman Catholics that would also be tolerant of other Christian religions. They set up a manorial system of managers and tenant farmers (mostly indentured servants) to produce rental income. Better prepared than the early Virginians, the colonists in Maryland immediately began farming tobacco and were soon shipping it in volume back to England. Initially the farms were small, but with the arrival of slave labor came larger plantations, although generally not on the same scale as those in Virginia.

Although power, both economic and political, remained in the hands of only a few families, the 18th century saw a number of significant changes. The tobacco crop eventually exhausted the soil around the Chesapeake, forcing small farmers to abandon their land. Plantation owners, however, with huge landholdings, could afford to rotate their crops. They absorbed the smaller farms, further increasing the gap between rich and poor.

African slaves largely replaced English indentured servants in the 18th century, and the relations between master and servant became much more rigid. This new order was reflected in the architecture. Plantations, which began as informal arrangements of a simple house with servants' quarters and other outbuildings, became much more elaborate. The prospering southern Colonial planters were for the first time able to attempt fashionable English architectural styles on a relatively grand scale. Following the ideas of the Italian Renaissance architect Andrea Palladio, they built rigidly symmetrical mansions with "dependencies," formal gardens, neat rows of slave quarters, and other structures.

By the time of the American Revolution, this new society was several generations old. Just as the laws of primogeniture had driven their ancestors from England, the planters now drove their younger sons westward. By the early 19th century, exhausted soil became another reason for moving west. Over a third of the free population born around 1800 left the Tidewater. The day of the tobacco cash crop was over, and the planter elite was taking the plantation system and cotton south and west.

The architecture of the Chesapeake Bay Tidewater followed the development of the colony over its nearly two centuries of existence. The first shelters at Jamestown had been little more than hovels, crudely constructed from green timber with few tools and fewer skills. The first settlers of St. Marys City—what would become Maryland's capital—purchased an entire village from the native inhabitants, living there until they could put up their own English cottages.

At first the English tried to bring their building styles and construction methods nearly wholesale to the Chesapeake: the Cross House, the Hall-and-Parlor, and the One-Room Cottage were the most common. In Jamestown, even row houses were laid out in the medieval English fashion. But environmental, economic, and social pressures resulted in the development of a distinct regional aesthetic. By 1660 the colony included houses of the Center Passage plan, and by 1700 the move toward Georgian architecture was in full swing along the creeks and rivers of Maryland and Virginia. However, the Tidewater of the 17th and 18th centuries looked very different from what we might imagine today based on the surviving structures, which offer a misleading legacy dominated by sturdy brick houses. Most dwellings were built of wood and, with very few exceptions, have long since vanished.

The necessary (privy), Sotterley Plantation, *St. Marys County, Md., 18th c.*

Reconstruction, *St. Marys City, Md.*

The One-Room English Cottage (1620–1860)

FORM: A simple 1½-story, nearly square, gable-ended structure on a low foundation, with a large external mud or brick chimney at one end and a steeply pitched roof. Front entry opens directly into the "hall" at the end opposite the fireplace.

STYLISTIC DETAIL: Plain, asymmetrical façade. Small, outward-swinging casement windows glazed with diamond-shaped panes.

CONSTRUCTION: Most were timber frame with mud nogging (mud mixed with straw or twigs) between the studs and, often, weatherboard cladding. Only later brick masonry examples survive, however. Roofing evolved from thatch to weatherboards to shingles. Foundations were first wood, later stone.

The Tidewater One-Room English Cottage, also called the Single-Bay or One-Bay, was no doubt the most common house in the region from the first years of settlement. Resembling the New England One-Room English Cottage (see page 9), it continued to be built into the mid-1800s, its popularity ensured by its simplicity and low cost.

Typically, the house was a single rectangular room, ranging from 16 to 20 feet on a side and dominated by a fireplace. A steep stair or ladder led to the sleeping loft. These houses were frequently expanded by adding a room with a fireplace opposite the original chimney, creating in effect a Hall-and-Parlor House.

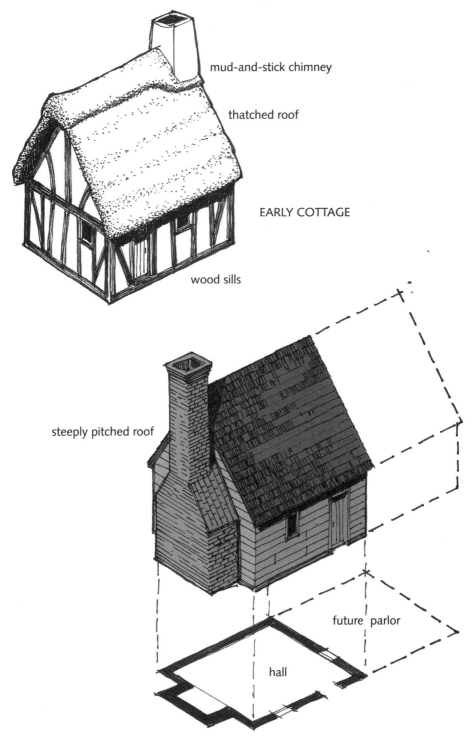

mud-and-stick chimney

thatched roof

EARLY COTTAGE

wood sills

steeply pitched roof

future parlor

hall

Early examples, especially those built before 1650, had steeply pitched roofs of thatch or weatherboards and a "Welsh" chimney of mud and sticks over an open, hooded hearth. The wood frame structure rested on sills set directly on the ground or on puncheons, and the walls were filled with wattle-and-daub or nogging. None of these early houses survives, but reconstructions can be seen at Jamestown National Historic Park and St. Marys City, Maryland.

While similar houses were built throughout the early 17th century, after 1650 more substantial examples were constructed of timber or brick. Typical features of this period included diamond-paned casement windows and, in brick examples, Flemish bond coursing and segmented or flat arches at the door and window openings.

While few, if any, free-standing One-Room English Cottages remain from the late 17th and early 18th centuries, they can sometimes be seen as parts of other houses. Resurrection Manor (c. 1735) in St. Marys County, Maryland, is such an example, where a brick joint in the façade indicates an addition to the original one-room plan. In the late 18th and early 19th centuries, it was common to add a slightly larger space to one end of a small house, sometimes twice, resulting in the aptly named Telescope House. From at least the mid-18th century until the Civil War, stark one- and two-room plans were commonly used as slave quarters on southern plantations.

Slave cabin on Sotterley Plantation,
St. Marys County, Md.

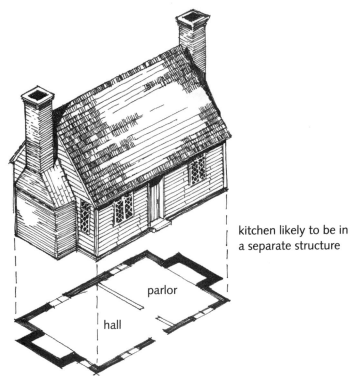

kitchen likely to be in
a separate structure

parlor

hall

EXPANSION OF ONE-ROOM ENGLISH COTTAGE

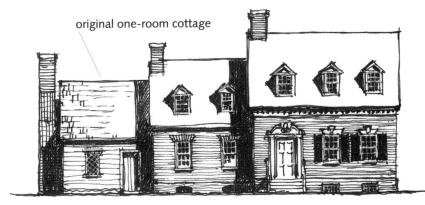

original one-room cottage

MARYLAND TELESCOPE HOUSE

Orem's Delight, *Royal Oak, Md., c. 1725*

The Hall-and-Parlor House (1620–1860)
Hall-and-Chamber

FORM: A 1½-story, 1-room-deep structure on a raised foundation with large, stepped chimneys centered on each gable end. Heavily corniced chimney caps may have T-shaped flues. Steep roof pitch. Later 18th- and 19th-century versions sat on higher foundations and had a gentler roof pitch, occasionally with prominent dormers.

STYLISTIC DETAIL: Brick detailing includes Flemish and English bond, molded brick water table, flat or segmented arches at doors and windows, and diapering (diagonal patterns of dark, glazed bricks) on gable ends. Diamond-paned casement windows are roughly symmetrical on the façade. Later examples may have a more symmetrical façade with sash windows and rectangular chimney flues with corniced caps.

CONSTRUCTION: Brick masonry bearing walls or timber frame covered with weatherboards. Weatherboard or shingle roof.

The simple one-and-a-half-story, two-room Hall-and-Parlor House was common in the late-17th- and early-18th-century Tidewater region. A similar style was common in England from at least the 16th century, but it often had the chimney (or chimneys) placed at the back of the house. The typical Tidewater Hall-and-Parlor had a chimney at each gable, resulting in the familiar one-and-a-half-story, two-chimney form, which by the late 17th century had become the accepted vernacular house

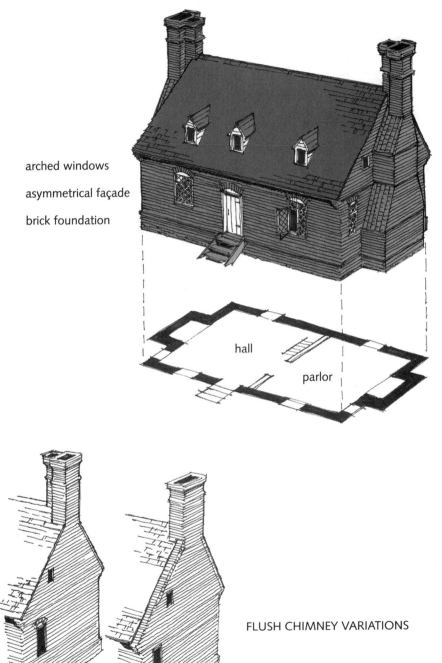

arched windows

asymmetrical façade

brick foundation

hall

parlor

FLUSH CHIMNEY VARIATIONS

The Chesapeake Bay Tidewater Hearth

form in the region. Built by rich and poor of brick or wood, it was at one time so closely identified with the area that it was known as the Virginia house. Its overall dimensions ranged from 16 to 20 feet deep by 20 to 40 feet long.

The multipurpose "hall" included the entry and corner stair and served as dining room, workroom, and kitchen if there was no separate kitchen structure. The parlor or chamber, somewhat smaller and more private, served as a bedroom and guest room. The second floor could be divided into two rooms, separated by a passage, and was used for sleeping or storage.

Though small by today's standards and even by English standards of the time, the Hall-and-Parlor House often served as an early plantation manor house, with a separate kitchen, dairy, barn, servants' and slave quarters, and other outbuildings. Most were modest in their building materials, interior finishes, furnishings, and number of outbuildings. The plan's lack of privacy reflects in part the relatively informal relationship between family members, servants, and slaves in the late 17th and early 18th centuries. Later houses built by prospering landowners, such as the Center-Passage or Four-Room Plan, introduced different floor plans and larger living spaces, but they were usually accommodated within this basic form. The elite turned to other house types in the 18th century, but the Hall-and-Parlor continued to be built as slave housing and by those of lesser means until the Civil War.

Most early Hall-and-Parlor Houses were undoubtedly timber frame and clad in weatherboards. However, most surviving examples are the less typical but more durable brick houses. Though often absorbed by or expanded into a larger house, the Hall-and-Parlor type can still be seen around the Tidewater region.

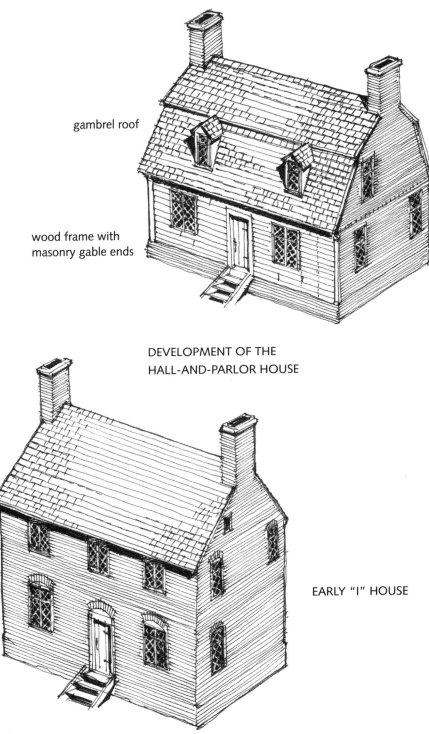

THE HALL-AND-PARLOR HOUSE

gambrel roof

wood frame with
masonry gable ends

DEVELOPMENT OF THE
HALL-AND-PARLOR HOUSE

EARLY "I" HOUSE

The Chesapeake Bay Tidewater Hearth

Smith's Fort Plantation, *Surrey County, Va., 1762*

The Center-Passage House (1700–1860)

FORM: A 1½-story, 1-room-deep house on a raised foundation with large stepped chimneys at each end. Steep roofs and T-shaped chimneys give way to gentler roof pitches with dormers and rectangular chimney caps in the 18th century.

STYLISTIC DETAIL: Decorative brick detailing includes Flemish and English bonds, molded brick water tables, flat or segmented arches above doors and windows, and diapering (diagonal patterns of dark glazed bricks) on the gable ends.

CONSTRUCTION: Brick masonry bearing walls or, less commonly seem today, timber frame clad in weatherboards.

Originally created simply by adding a second partition to the Hall-and-Parlor plan, thus walling off a corridor, the Center-Passage House was built as a distinct type by the late 17th century in Virginia and after 1700 in Maryland and North Carolina, becoming especially popular after 1725. Refinements typically included moving the stair into the passage and adding a rear door.

It has been speculated that this house originated in the 12th- and 13th-century English lords' houses, where screened passages separated the great hall from the kitchen. However, Virginians surely realized that they could gain a little privacy (and social control) by putting up another wall. They also found that with the doors open at either end, the passages created a cool draft in the hot and humid summer, and eventually they were widened, providing space for informal gatherings where one could

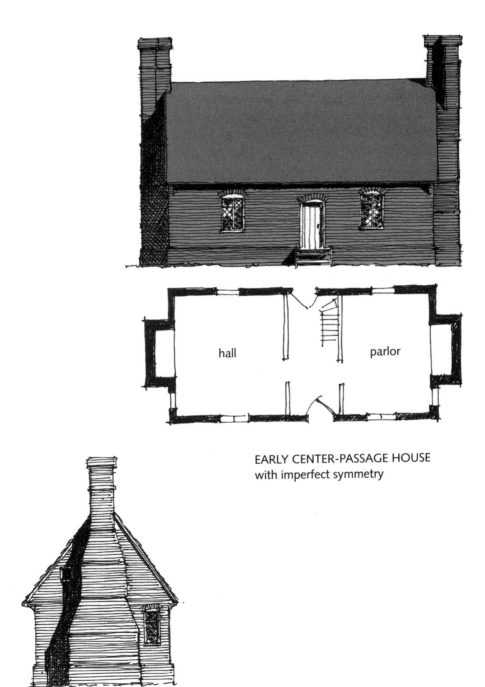

EARLY CENTER-PASSAGE HOUSE
with imperfect symmetry

relax without the formal wig or many-layered gown worn by the gentry even in the Tidewater heat.

The central passage performed a more subtle social function as well, restricting access to other rooms of the house. Whereas in 17th-century homes servants and masters often lived together, in the 18th century masters sought more privacy (and security). The passage was a physical manifestation of the more formal and hierarchical posture that characterized the new, slavery-based society.

Timber frame versions, once the most numerous, were inevitably clad in weatherboards. Brick Center-Passage Houses had masonry details typical of the region, although in Maryland it was not uncommon to combine brick gable ends with wood framing and siding in between. Later versions, called the Advanced Center Passage, tend to be larger, five-bay houses with flush chimneys, prominent dormers, larger sash windows, and symmetrical façades.

The Center-Passage was one of the most popular house types of the Tidewater region in the late 17th and especially the 18th century. Many have survived and can be seen throughout the region.

Belle Air, *Charles City County, Va., c. 1725*

five-bay nonsymmetrical façade

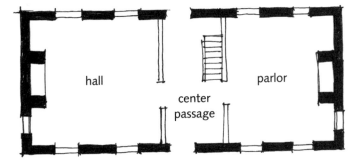

hall

center
passage

parlor

The Chesapeake Bay Tidewater Hearth

Bacon's Castle, *Surrey County, Va., c. 1665*

The Cross House (1665–1700)
Cruciform House

FORM: A 1½- or 2-story end-gabled house with a central full-height tower at the entry. There may be a tower opposite at the rear as well. Large chimneys are at each gable end.

STYLISTIC DETAIL: Variable, but includes the typical features of the time: elaborate chimney caps, diamond-paned casement windows, flat or segmented arches over openings, and raised, molded water tables. Molded "battlements" appear around front entries.

CONSTRUCTION: Timber frame with weatherboard cladding or brick masonry bearing walls.

The imposing Cross (or Cruciform) House is one of several variations on the Hall-and-Parlor and Center-Passage plans, with an enclosed entry porch added to the front or an enclosed stair tower to the rear, or occasionally both. The porch, which led to a hall or center passage, was often two stories high, the room above called the porch chamber. The rear stair tower led to the second story and usually opened into a passage separating the two bedchambers.

The stair tower was used in English manor houses by the 13th century, and the enclosed porch can be traced to at least the 14th. The similarity between the plan of the Cross House and those of churches in England and early Virginia suggests the possibility of church

Christ's Cross or Criss-Cross,
New Kent County, Va., c. 1690

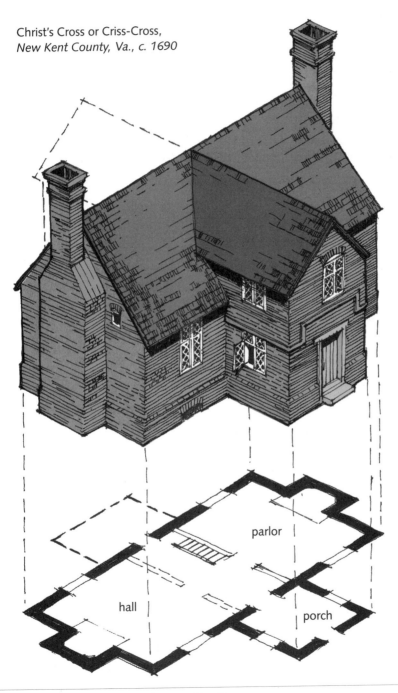

parlor

hall

porch

architecture's influencing house design. More likely, the Cross House in Virginia represented efforts by the planter elite to emulate the English aristocracy. The houses were clearly meant to impress; note the frequent use of "Castle" in their names: Bacon's Castle, Foster's Castle, and Bond Castle, for example.

Partly because of its expense, but perhaps also due to a regional preference for simpler forms, the Cross House was never common. With a distinctly medieval character, it was soon overshadowed by the Georgian aesthetic. Today, only a handful survive: those with stair towers are more common in Maryland; those with porches in Virginia. Most surviving examples are built of brick, with details typical of the region, an indication of their medieval heritage. The grander houses often had additional detailing, such as molded battlements and elaborate chimney caps.

The best-known example is the atypical Bacon's Castle, built by Arthur Allen in 1665 in Surrey County, Virginia. It received its name after 1676, when it was occupied by Colonial rebels during Bacon's Rebellion (although Nat Bacon was not there in person). It is a prime example of the rare Jacobean style in the Colonies, characterized by curvilinear gables and ornate chimneys and seen infrequently in South Carolina (page 139) and occasionally in northern cities.

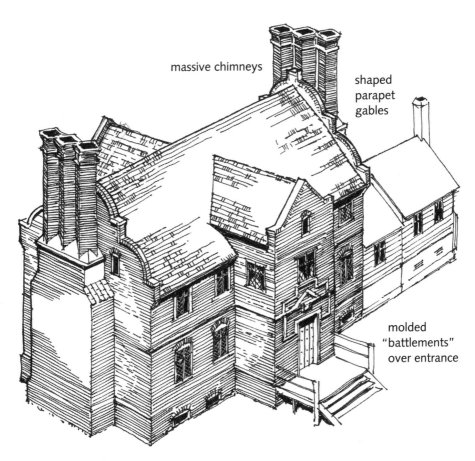

massive chimneys

shaped
parapet
gables

molded
"battlements"
over entrance

Bacon's Castle

Otwell, *Talbot County, Md., early 18th c.*

Three-Room Plan, "L," and "T" Houses (1700–1800)

FORM: Typically a rectangular, 1½-story gable-ended house of 3 or 5 bays on a raised foundation. The moderately pitched roof may have dormers. Large brick chimneys are at each end. "L" and "T" 3-room plans have a wing at the rear.

STYLISTIC DETAIL: Brick detailing includes the molded water table, segmented or flat arches over windows and doors, and diapering (patterns of glazed brick) on the gable ends. Georgian ornament may appear at the entries.

CONSTRUCTION: Timber frame clad in weatherboards or, more commonly seen today, brick masonry bearing walls.

A demand for more comfortable homes and an awareness of English fashions, including interior design and entertaining (particularly dining), resulted in the larger houses built in the 18th century. Traditional builders in the Chesapeake region developed ways to expand familiar forms without disrupting the vernacular aesthetic. Thus arose the Three-Room Plan, which maintained the simple Hall-and-Chamber floor plan and the formal façade. Like the Center-Passage, the Three-Room Plan house reflected the evolving Tidewater society, and the arrangement of a hierarchy of spaces to which access was limited also served as a means of social control.

Built primarily from 1700 to 1800, the Three-Room Plan was created by dividing the chamber of a Hall-and-Chamber or Center-Passage House. Typically, the new back room remained the chamber,

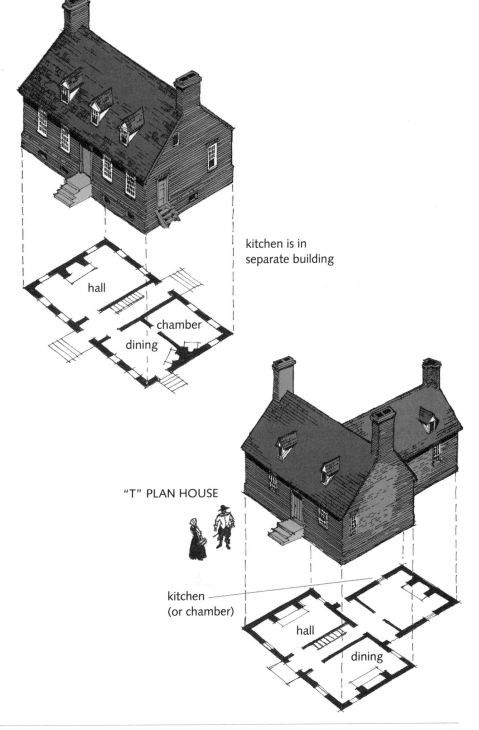

kitchen is in
separate building

hall

chamber

dining

"T" PLAN HOUSE

kitchen
(or chamber)

hall

dining

its privacy enhanced by its being deeper in the house. The new front room was known after 1750 as the dining room. It assumed the informal functions of the hall, serving as a place of work and other family activities besides dining, and it often had an exterior door opening toward a separate kitchen building. The hall, still the most ornate room in the house, remained the center of formal activity and the place to display prominent possessions, such as china, glassware, and other furnishings.

"L" and "T" houses also represent extensions of Hall-and-Chamber and Center-Passage Houses, either in their original construction or by later additions. As in the Three-Room Plan, the rear space was most often used as a chamber, allowing the front room to become a dining room. The "T" plan extension was placed at about the center of the house and reached from the central passage, if present, or the hall. A third chimney served this room. In the "L" plan the new space was on one side, typically opening into the dining room. In some examples of early-18th-century buildings, the addition housed the kitchen. It might also have contained a second stair, a passage, or an additional room plus space upstairs. The logic of the "T" plan, with the addition at the rear of the passage, is obvious, whereas the "L" plan, which could force circulation through a second room, seems less effective.

While it is difficult from the road to tell a Three-Room Plan from a Hall-and-Chamber or Center-Passage House, a glance at the side or rear wing distinguishes it. Look for differences in detail from the house to the wing for indications that the wing was a later addition.

Though not as common as other house types, the Three-Room and "L" and "T" plans were popular alternatives for 18th-century builders, and a number are still scattered around the Chesapeake Bay region. Many of these houses were substantial structures, so they are more likely to have survived. However, these houses varied widely, and surely no two were alike. Although the Tidewater builders of the 18th century were familiar with English pattern books, they commonly strayed from prescribed designs, adjusting to their clients' wishes, local conditions, and their own ingenuity.

"L" PLAN

Otwell, *Talbot County, Md.*

"T" PLAN

Abington Glebe House,
Gloucester County, Va., 1740

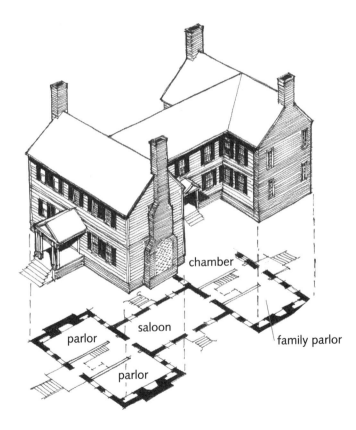

Tuckahoe, *Goochland County, Va., 1733–1740*

Booth House, *Edenton, N.C., c. 1770*

The Catslide, Tidewater Cottage, and Tidewater Gambrel (1750–1860)

FORM: The Catslide is a small, 1½-story house with a shed-roofed extension at the rear. The roof may be a straight slope or "broken" at the addition. Façades are typically and roughly symmetrical. The Tidewater Cottage is similar, with extensions front and rear, the front being a covered porch. Brick chimneys at both gable ends are common.

STYLISTIC DETAIL: Plain with minimal corbeling at chimneys. Brick versions use Flemish or English bond. They may show typical glazed brick patterns (diapering) on gable ends and segmented or flat arches at windows and doors.

CONSTRUCTION: Typically weatherboarded wood frame on low brick foundations. Some examples have brick masonry bearing walls.

A common method of expanding a small house in the Chesapeake Bay region was to add one or several small rooms at the rear. In its simplest form, it is an extension of the rear roof slope of a Hall-and-Chamber or Center-Passage house. The new rooms created serve a variety of purposes but are most often bedchambers. Small, secondary chimneys were frequently added to serve fireplaces in the new space. While the plan, the extended roof, and the name are English in origin, the Catslide in the Tidewater region maintained the traditional vernacular aesthetic of the Chesapeake Bay region.

The Catslide can still occasionally be found, built of brick or timber frame and weatherboarded, some combining a brick main section

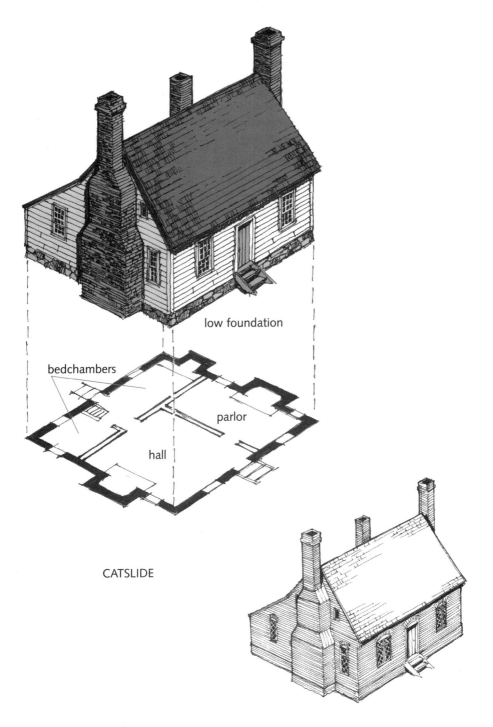

low foundation

bedchambers

parlor

hall

CATSLIDE

with a timber frame addition. Early examples are likely to have a low foundation, a steeply pitched roof, large chimneys with corniced caps, and an asymmetrical façade. The 19th-century examples are more likely to be timber frame, to sit on higher foundations, and to have lower-gabled roofs with prominent dormers, smaller chimneys, and a more symmetrical façade. For a similar silhouette and floor plan adapted to another region, see the New England Saltbox.

By the early 18th century, a new architectural feature had appeared in the southern colonies: a covered but open platform along the front of a house called a porch, piazza, veranda, or *galérie*, depending on the region. When joined to the traditional small houses of the Chesapeake Bay, by 1750 it produced a new house type called the Tidewater Cottage; with a gambrel roof, a Tidewater Gambrel. (The Tidewater Cottage is more common in Virginia, the Gambrel in North Carolina.) Both remained popular vernacular house types well into the 19th century. Variable in plan, they resemble the Catslide, but the front shed roof extends over the porch. The addition of the porch was not only a natural adaptation to the climate but a socially useful, semipublic buffer space as well: a place to greet and deal with visitors (and those of lower social status) without admitting them inside.

Tidewater Cottages were commonly timber frame and clad in weatherboards. Since most were built after 1750, they tend to have small rectangular chimneys, sash windows, and a more symmetrical façade. They follow a simple aesthetic, usually lacking overt Georgian features like the high foundation and the rigid symmetry of more prestigious homes of the time. Their exteriors resemble the Huguenot Southern Tidewater Cottages of South Carolina and Georgia (page 146), but their floor plans eventually evolved toward the Georgian Center-Passage type.

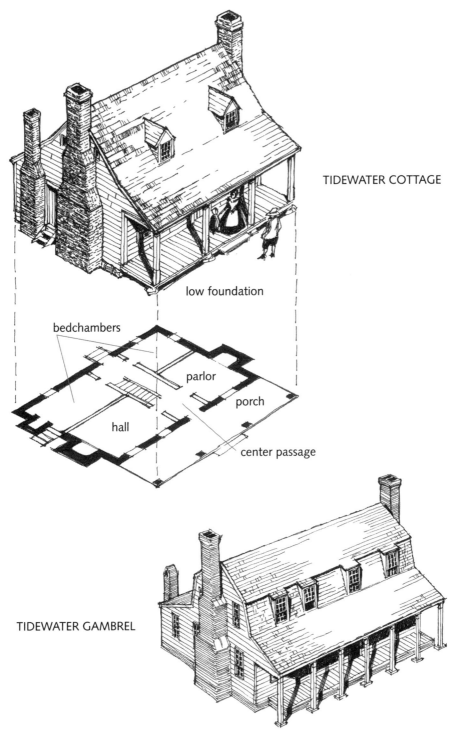

TIDEWATER COTTAGE

low foundation

bedchambers

parlor

porch

hall

center passage

TIDEWATER GAMBREL

Linden Farm, *Richmond County, Va., 1700–1728*

The Four-Room Plan House (1700–1800)

FORM: A symmetrical 1½- or, later, 2½-story, 2-room-deep, end-gabled block on a raised foundation. Twin chimneys at the gable ends. Gabled dormers common.

STYLISTIC DETAIL: A generally symmetrical façade with some loosely interpreted Classical detailing at the entry. Molded water table and rubbed brick detail around windows and doorways. Quoins used only occasionally. Notable was the chimney arrangement: rectangular chimneys with their corniced caps, often doubled at each end, their greater width perhaps including a window or doorway between the flues. Segmented or flat arches over sash windows.

CONSTRUCTION: Brick masonry bearing wall, timber frame, or a combination of the two.

The Four-Room Plan is a logical adaptation of early house forms, reflecting the considerable social changes occurring from the late 17th to the late 18th century. This multiplication of rooms continues the ongoing sorting and separation of social functions combined with the planters' need for control and privacy. Those spaces used for entertaining became showplaces of possessions that denoted status: tea sets, silver plate, ceramics, and wineglasses, for example, items rare in the Tidewater before 1670. Regional Maryland and Virginia architecture and social standards were merging with the Georgian ideals now spreading throughout the Colonies, north and south. There is no doubt that modest versions of this plan were built, but the Four-Room Plan is best

The Chesapeake Bay Tidewater Hearth

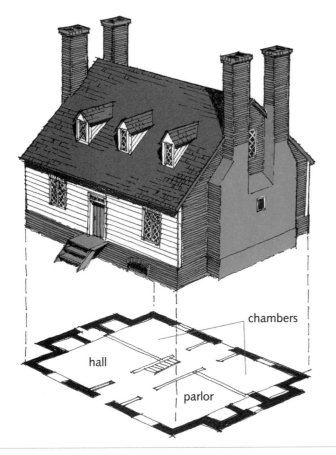

West St. Mary's Manor,
*St. Marys County, Md.,
mid-18th c.*

chambers

hall

parlor

known today as a substantial house of the planter elite. Accompanied by a number of outbuildings — a kitchen, workshops, and slavequarters — it included a hall, dining room, chamber, and passage much like those in a Three-Room House. In the Four-Room, builders added new space, typically behind the hall. While at times it may have been little more than a closet, it usually had its own fireplace and was likely used as a bedchamber. There was considerable variation in the arrangement and relationship of the first-floor rooms as functions and formality evolved.

The new space resulted in a further deepening of the house and a lengthening of the center passage, which was becoming a room in its own right. Initially it was a cooler, informal gathering place in the heat of summer (Center-Passage House, page 94). By the mid-18th century it was often referred to as a hall, leaving a parlor and dining room at the front of the house and two chambers or a chamber and a smaller, less formal children's dining room at the rear. The main dining room had now become a place of formal entertainment and the passage or hall a formal reception area. Classically derived detailing at the entry, and occasionally in the hall, further emphasized a growing Georgian sophistication.

Though the symmetrical double-pile Four-Room Plan represented a significant development in Chesapeake Bay house planning, it maintained the traditional regional aesthetic with just the faintest remnant of a medieval character in its massive brick chimneys. Though not as common now as other Colonial houses of the Chesapeake, a number of especially elegant Four-Room Plan Houses survive, including West St. Mary's Manor in St. Marys County, Maryland, and Gunston Hall in Fairfax County, Virginia.

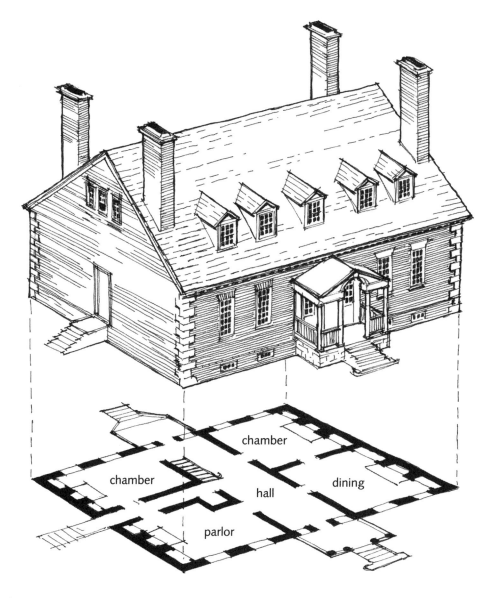

Gunston Hall, *Fairfax County, Va., c. 1758*

Berkeley, *Charles City County, Va., c. 1726*

The Chesapeake Bay Georgian (1700–80)

FORM: Typically a 2-story, 5- or 7-bay rectangular block on a raised foundation. 1½ stories common, 3 stories rare. Steeply sloped hip roofs as well as more gentle pitches are typical; gable ends are not unknown. Dormers common. Façades, center entry, and chimney placement are symmetrically organized. Elegant "three-part" and "five-part" examples include the main house, two outbuildings (dependencies), and connectors (hyphens) in a geometrically symmetrical composition.

STYLISTIC DETAIL: Variable, but symmetry is always paramount. Classical elements and detailing at the main entry may include pediments and pilasters with dentils at the cornice line. Belt courses between stories are typical. Quoins are not common. Rubbed brick patterns are common around windows and doors. Paneled doors, some with transom lights, and sash windows standard. Palladian windows commonly placed over the entry or at stairways. Fanlights and projecting, gabled entry bays appear near the end of the period.

CONSTRUCTION: Brick masonry bearing wall is the standard, but wood frame clad in weatherboards is used as well.

With the founding in 1693 of the College of William and Mary at Middle Plantation, Virginia, the Chesapeake Bay region saw the arrival of English Renaissance architecture in a style generally attributed to the British architect Christopher Wren (1632–1723). Four years later, the city of Williamsburg was laid out around the college and included the first Colonial capitol in North America and the Governor's Palace, both

George Wythe House,
Williamsburg, Va., c. 1750

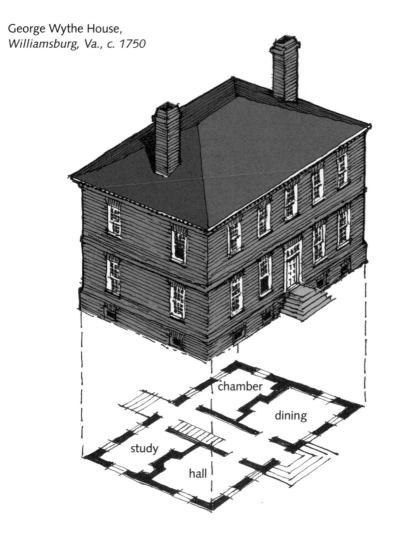

chamber

dining

study

hall

similar in style to the college's Wren Building, as it is now called, and the college president's house. Plans for these structures are thought to have come from England, particularly that of the Wren Building, which may have been conceived by Wren's office if not his own hand.

Despite some provincial adjustments by local craftsmen, the design of these structures contrasted sharply with that of the region's more somber, late medieval architecture. The governor's mansion and college president's house in particular caught the attention of prospering southern planters, eager to show their awareness of fashionable English taste. These "Wrenish" public buildings are often described as the beginning of a Georgian style in the Colonies, though the first King George didn't sit on his throne until 1714. The term is more useful as a description of an interval in our history rather than as a precise aesthetic: the Georgian period is generally accepted as extending from 1700 to the Revolutionary War. In that period, fashionable residential architecture in the Tidewater was largely composed of interpretations of the country villas of the Renaissance architect Andrea Palladio (1508–80).

Wren was relatively free with his baroque applications of Palladian and other Classical influences, and the tastes of local builders further diluted the prescribed aesthetics of pattern books. However, the strictly symmetrical façade was adopted wholesale, becoming de rigueur in new Chesapeake Bay houses. These mansions consisted of a horizontally composed two-and-a-half-story block, but the overall composition retained a vertical aspect, evident in the steep roof pitch, the tall, narrow dormers and sash windows, and the tall chimneys. As time passed, the hipped roofs were lowered, the windows widened, and the horizontal Palladian aspect prevailed.

In many ways the early Georgian houses of the Chesapeake were similar to Georgians elsewhere: the basic four-room concept, not always precisely symmetrical in plan, was organized around a prominent central passage or hall. However, certain characteristics set the Tidewater region's houses apart from the rest, the most obvious being the preference for brick masonry construction with white trim. Next was the arrangement of outbuildings—dependencies—in a symmetrical composition with the main house, a practice not common in New England or the Middle Atlantic. Frequently these dependencies were in the vernacular style of the region's small houses, as at Westover Plantation in Charles City County, Virginia, where the smaller structures even had different roofs—one a gable, the other a gambrel—while the commanding main house had a hipped roof.

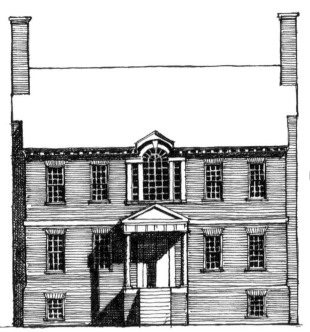

Palladian window

riverside elevation

John Rideout House,
Annapolis, Md., c. 1765

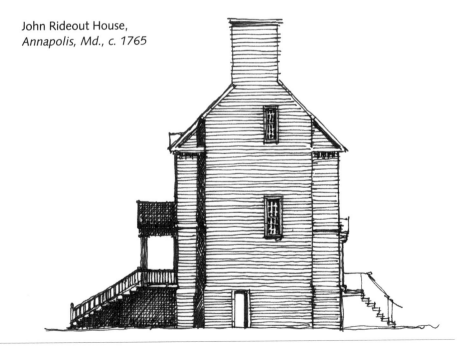

Geometrically relating separate outbuildings to the main house resulted in a "three-part plan." When, as frequently happened, the dependencies were later directly connected to the main house with links, or "hyphens," a five-part plan was created. This configuration continued to develop in Maryland and Virginia, becoming typical of the second phase of Tidewater Georgian architecture, the Palladian country villa.

Wren houses, as Georgian mansions are sometimes called, drew, not on the heritage of the ponderous, aristocratic English country manors, but on the smaller but quite refined detached house popular with the new English middle class. Wren houses usually lacked the details of their successors, such as quoins, imitation stonework, and overt Classical elements. In all, their verticality and modest use of heavy detail gave them a certain reserved elegance when compared with the Palladian houses that would follow. Westover Plantation (1750) is an excellent illustration of the style but is more lavish than most. The Nelson House in Yorktown, Virginia (c. 1729), and the Wythe House at Williamsburg (c. 1750) are fine, less imposing examples.

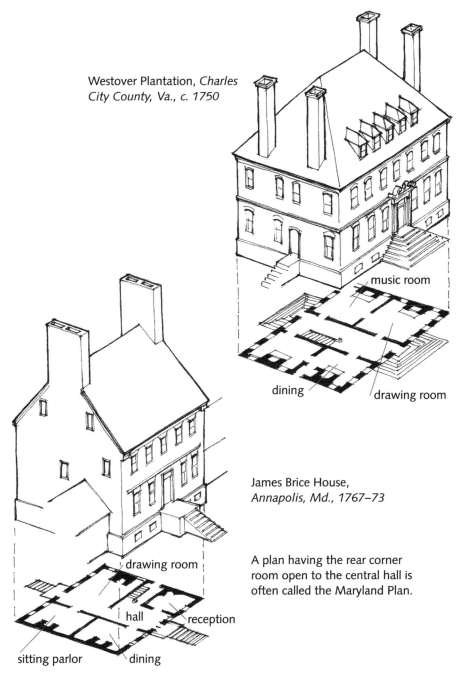

Westover Plantation, *Charles City County, Va., c. 1750*

music room

dining

drawing room

James Brice House, *Annapolis, Md., 1767–73*

A plan having the rear corner room open to the central hall is often called the Maryland Plan.

drawing room

hall

reception

sitting parlor

dining

Mount Airy, *Richmond County, Va., c. 1758*

The Late Chesapeake Bay Georgian (1750–80)

FORM: A symmetrical 5-part composition consisting of a 2-story main house, 2 dependencies, and long connecting arcades, some curved. There may be a projecting, pedimented pavilion at the entry. May also consist of a 3-part temple-form structure with a large main block and separate dependencies on either side. Low-pitched hipped or double-hipped roof, only occasionally gabled. Dormers rare.

STYLISTIC DETAIL: Georgian detailing at porches, entries, and windows includes paneled doors, pediments, pilasters, dentils, transom lights (rectangular and semicircular); double-hung sash windows with segmented or flat arches; and occasionally Palladian windows over entries or at stairways. Classical columns may support pavilion pediments. Swan-neck and broken pediments are less common. Windows and doors are separate and spaced symmetrically in 5- or 7-bay façades. Rubbed brick trim at the windows and doors is not uncommon. Pedimented dormers.

CONSTRUCTION: Brick masonry bearing walls. Stone and timber frame rare.

By 1750, Georgian architecture in the Chesapeake had evolved in a direction that set Maryland, Virginia, and to some extent North Carolina apart from the standard Georgian aesthetic of the New England and Delaware Valley colonies. In *The Four Books of Architecture* (1570), Andrea Palladio laid out standards for building design based on his observations of Roman Classical structures, providing absolute rules and formulas for using Classical orders and illustrating them with his own excellent

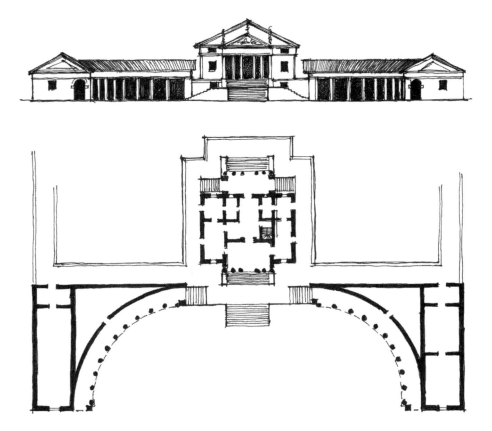

Design for a Venetian Villa
by Andrea Palladio, mid-16th c.

drawings. This book was enormously well received throughout Europe and reached England by way of Inigo Jones (1573–1652) on his return from Italy in 1614, though it was not translated into English until 1716. During the interval, Palladian principles gradually infiltrated the vernacular aesthetic; eventually villas designed in Europe two centuries earlier for Venetian traders and Roman dignitaries had been studied, scaled down, and adapted to the stratified, slavery-bound plantation society of the Tidewater colonies.

A Book of Architecture, by the talented architect James Gibbs, was published in England in 1728 and brought a somewhat scaled-down Palladian sensibility to Tidewater builders and their prosperous clients. Along with typical Wren house illustrations, Gibbs included drawings of relatively modest Palladian-influenced country villas that featured the prominent central mass and symmetrical dependencies connected by curved or straight hyphens. Gibbs's handsome drawings represented buildings in three dimensions with a sensitive use of shadow and line. He retained a baroque interest in decorative texture and ornament (meaning rustication and quoins, for example), which were inconsistent with the high English Palladian style being touted at the time.

Gibbs's manageable Palladian villa form was well suited for large plantations, which were often on commanding sites and accompanied by prominent outbuildings. The Tidewater "villa," reaching out with its hyphens and dependencies to enclose a grassy forecourt, broad steps, and perhaps a loggia, created an impressive axial entry. Mount Airy (c. 1758) in Richmond County, Virginia, is a famous example, taken largely from Gibbs's book, as is George Washington's Mount Vernon in its final form. Annapolis, Maryland, boasts several five-part townhouses, including the Hammond-Harwood House (1774), the James Brice House (1773), and the William Paca House (1765). The North Carolina governor's mansion, Tryon Palace (1767–70), in New Bern is an exceptional example, now rebuilt.

Toward the end of the Georgian period in America, other house plans emerged, also inspired by Palladio and featured in pattern books. Roger Morris, in his *Select Architecture* (1757), illustrated a simpler villa form taken from Palladio's designs for prosperous Romans. Essentially only one room deep, these villas stretched out laterally from a tall central block, adding one, two, or three rooms to either side, always symmetrically. The central passage became a large reception room, shouldering aside parlors, dining rooms, and chambers. The villas' relatively modest size and simplicity appealed to many planters' families,

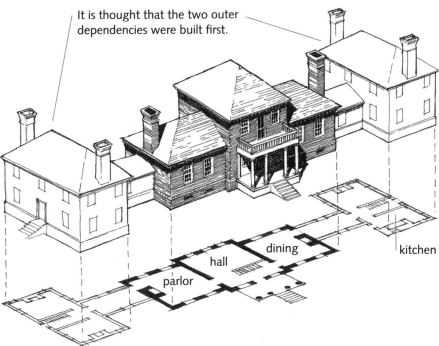

It is thought that the two outer dependencies were built first.

parlor

hall

dining

kitchen

Brandon, *Prince George County, Va., c. 1765*

and quite a few were built, including Brandon (1765) in Prince George County, Virginia, which was taken unashamedly from Morris's book, and the elegant Whitehall (1763), on the Severn River near Annapolis, although the latter has been considerably added to over the years.

Finally, gentry houses were taken apparently straight from Palladio's designs and were therefore more "high" Palladian than the adaptations of Gibbs's and Morris's designs. Squarish in plan and elevation, they resemble the main block of Palladio's sumptuous villas without the arms and thus were suitable for townhouses as well as plantations. The Shirley Plantation house (c. 1738) in Charles City County, Virginia, and the Miles Brewton House (1769) in Charleston, South Carolina, are outstanding examples (page 159). Monumental in character, with two-tier pedimented pavilions, they lead us directly to the first sketches of Monticello by Thomas Jefferson, that great admirer of both Palladio and Classical Roman architecture.

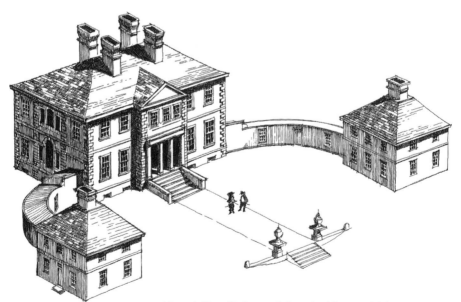

Mount Airy, *Richmond County, Va., c. 1758*

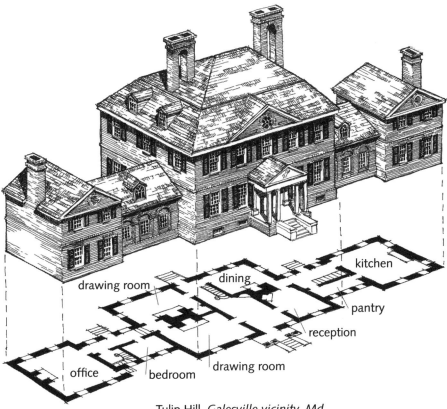

drawing room

dining

kitchen

pantry

reception

drawing room

office

bedroom

Tulip Hill, *Galesville vicinity, Md.,*
main block c. 1756–62, dependencies c. 1790

Andrea Palladio

Andrea Palladio, a 16th-century Italian architect, had an enormous impact on English architecture in the 17th and 18th centuries and, in turn, on residential design in the American colonies, particularly the rural landscapes of Virginia and Maryland. Having carefully studied and measured the Classical proportions of Roman remains and ruins, Palladio devised a set of design principles and presented them in his famous work *The Four Books of Architecture* (1570). He also published his own designs of the monumental country villas commissioned by the wealthy traders of Venice.

It was the combination of new drawing techniques developed during the Italian Renaissance and new printing processes that enabled Palladio to influence architectural style far beyond his Venetian studios. In fact, he did more drawing than building; Venice entered a period of commercial decline following the loss of its monopoly on Eastern trade to the Ottomans, and few clients could afford extravagant villas. However, his designs were distributed throughout Europe and especially admired a century later in England, where architecture was becoming an established profession. English architects were then visiting Italy to study the ancient buildings that were being excavated. Among them was Inigo Jones, who, notably fortunate in having James I as a patron, was able to introduce Palladian concepts to England in several of his projects.

The Palladian movement, along with building in general, was interrupted by the English Civil War (1642–49) and Oliver Cromwell's

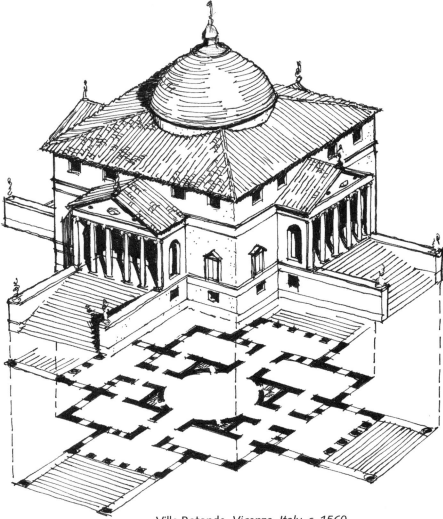

Villa Rotonda, *Vicenza, Italy, c. 1560*

reign (1649–60), but it was revived when the Great Fire of London resulted in the need for many new structures. Christopher Wren, England's most important architect after Jones, adapted Palladian elements to his many ecclesiastical and municipal projects, and his influence on other designers was instrumental in spreading Palladio's ideas over the English countryside. The typical Italian scheme of symmetrically flanking the main structure with outbuildings connected by long arcades was recognized as a way of increasing the architectural presence of a country house by stretching it across the horizon.

A group of enthusiastic English architects, almost a cult, reasserted "pure" Palladian design in the 18th century in what we call the Palladian Revival. Looking back past Wren to Jones and earlier, they shamelessly copied Palladio's ideas and drawings and published them in pattern and design books that eventually found their way to Virginia, along with tradesmen familiar with this new style.

Nowhere was Palladio's notion of prominent country houses more appropriate than on the huge plantations of the 18th-century Virginia Tidewater region. With their burgeoning tobacco wealth, the planters were eager for their homes to dominate the surroundings. A first attempt at Palladian "massing," the Governor's Palace at Williamsburg (1705–6), ensured imitation throughout the colony. It also underscored the increasing influence of "professional" architecture on the vernacular building that had dominated the Tidewater from 1620 until the 18th century.

When applied to English country homes, the monumental Palladian designs too often resulted in difficult (some said unlivable) living conditions. Their scale was well beyond residential, with vast, high-ceilinged, hard-surfaced halls and extravagant exterior façades taking precedence over interior comforts. However, when applied to the relatively modest houses of Virginia, Maryland, and North Carolina, the Palladian ideals produced some very comfortable homes. Many mansions are not only still standing today but in daily use as well.

On page 121 is a plan and elevation from one of Palladio's books for a relatively simple Italian country villa. (Simple for Palladio. Some designs were symmetrical in all four directions.) The principal visual characteristic of this style is clear: order imposed by uncompromising symmetry. Regardless of function, opposite rooms must match with only an occasional exception. Indeed, the floor plans of Palladian villas resemble very tidy Rorschach tests. The second characteristic is the five-part composition: the central block, the dependencies (flankers), and the hyphens (connecting passages).

The more relaxed Colonial plantation houses followed the typical Georgian floor plan. The hyphens occurred in different forms: enclosed or as a colonnade, straight or curving out from the sides of the house, or turning at right angles to enclose a formal approach to the front door. In some cases the dependencies are not connected but still properly lined up. Wherever possible, the plantation houses were set back from a riverfront with the entry hall receiving visitors from either the river or plantation side. Most plantation houses were built of brick, with notable exceptions: Mount Vernon (wood) and Mount Airy (stone). The simple floor plans had a wide entry-stair hall and two rooms on either side, all duplicated on the second floor.

In Richmond County, Virginia, Mount Airy (1758–62) (pages 120 and 124) displays the spreading arms of the arcades that connect the dependencies to the mansion. A projecting two-story pavilion, pedimented and supported by Classical columns, frames the entry. Two Palladian three-piece arched windows, one above the other, light the interior stair at the end of the main house. The massive chimneys (not Palladian) are an accommodation to Virginia winters. Although built of stone and smaller than the similar Mount Vernon, Mount Airy is nonetheless fairly typical of Virginia plantations in layout and size.

The Southern Tidewater Hearth

Before the Revolutionary War, the Carolina "Low Country" (from Cape
Fear to north Florida) developed a culture far different from those of
the Chesapeake Bay Tidewater region and the other English colonies.
Centered primarily around Charleston, it was oriented more toward
the city, with strong economic and social ties to the West Indies and
England. Planters from Barbados, Dutch and English opportunists from
Europe, and French Huguenots escaping the Counter-Reformation
joined others to produce more ethnically varied traditions than those of
the essentially British coastal settlements of the Chesapeake Bay and
New England.

Early in the 16th century, the Florida coast was explored by the
Spanish in an effort to establish military posts and missions, partly to
protect the loaded treasure ships riding the Gulf Stream back to Seville
but also to convert the native inhabitants to Catholicism. The French
attempted to place two Huguenot settlements along what became
the Carolina coast, but they were driven out by the Spaniards, who
maintained fortress missions north of St. Augustine for a time. These
outposts eventually failed, however, with the general decline of Spanish
influence worldwide, the difficulties of defending against hostile Indians
and pirates, disease, and, finally, English incursions from the West Indies
in the late 17th century.

No structures remain from this early period in the southern
Tidewater, although it could be argued that the surviving buildings in
St. Augustine demonstrate Spanish Colonial architecture of the time.
What does remain in the Carolinas are a few Spanish mission names and

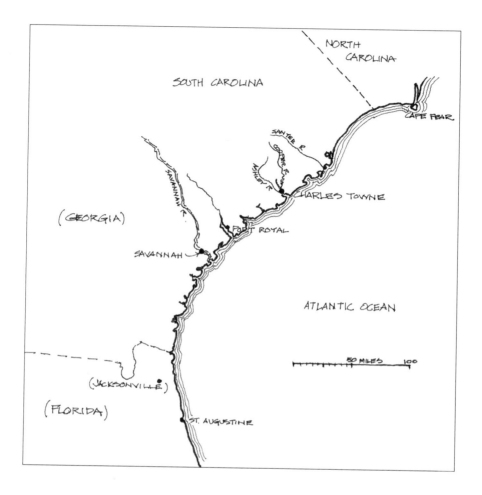

the "tabby" concrete system of construction, which combined crushed seashell, oyster shell lime, sand, and water that was poured into wooden forms. Centuries-old Indian "kitchen-middens," mounds of discarded shells, provided enormous quantities of material for forts, churches, and even some plantations in Georgia as well as the Carolinas. A few tabby buildings exist today in Charleston.

English colonization began in 1670 when Charles II rewarded Sir John Colleton, a Barbadian planter, for loyal service against Oliver Cromwell during the Civil War. Colleton was granted a proprietary charter for a slice of the American continent from what is now Virginia to Florida and extending west into the wilderness. The first outpost near the Cape Fear River struggled and, after Colleton's death, it was Lord Ashley who, with his philosopher friend John Locke, devised a semifeudal society, complete with a constitution and noble titles. Their intention was to attract aristocratic, or at least ambitious, colonists wary of the continuing upheavals in Europe. A new site on the Carolina coast was obtained from the Kiawah Indians in 1670, the future site of Charles Towne. At the convergence of three rivers yet somewhat protected from Atlantic storms and pirates by the Sea Islands, it proved ideal. Under Lord Ashley's direction, plantations were immediately laid out; with a sufficient supply of slave and indentured labor from the West Indies and English debtors' prisons, cotton and indigo were planted while hides from the interior were exported. These social and economic structures would govern the Low Country until the American Civil War.

The 18th century saw an amazing economic growth as the British mercantile system rewarded the colonists' efforts, particularly the exporting of rice, indigo, and deerskins. Absorbing traditional Indian lands, plantations spread along the waterways that provided access to other estates and Charles Towne. Swamps, soft soils, and a lack of stone made building roads difficult, and the many creeks and rivers would have required scores of bridges, so canoes and small boats poled and paddled by slaves became the primary mode of transportation. The river side of the plantation became the principal façade, influencing the siting and relationship of outbuildings as well as the layout of the main house. In contrast to the Chesapeake region, the shallow Carolina rivers and creeks prohibited direct access to the plantations by seagoing vessels, further ensuring Charles Towne's role as the primary southern business center.

The meager early Low Country Colonial architecture that remains displays the contributions of several immigrant traditions. Forms and floor plans evolved that are found only in this area, yet they show French, Dutch, and English traits. An extreme variation in their outward appearance obscures strong common elements, and as the surviving buildings suggest, only a few floor plans were used consistently. For instance, the Huguenot plan noted by many writers underlies a number of houses that vary considerably in other respects. Similarly, the Single- and Double-House plans were repeated in quantity in Charles Towne.

As in Virginia and Massachusetts, rough structures of earth and wood housed the early colonists until more substantial homes could be built. There was reportedly a Low Country log tradition, but no examples remain other than outbuildings. Wood and brick were the basic building materials, with roofs of locally made tile, imported slate, or wood shingles. The early, inferior brick was often plastered over, particularly in Charles Towne, contributing to a distinctly European flavor along the streets. Diamond-paned casement windows were common into the 18th century. Piazzas or long porches, familiar from the West Indies, were eventually added to shade the long sides of the Single House and provide breezy, outdoor living space.

Although the climate was generally agreeable along the coast, lifespans were short for those working in the swampy lowlands, which exposed them to disease-carrying mosquitoes, and infant mortality was high. Prospering planters and their families began spending summers in Charles Towne (renamed Charleston in 1783), building second homes there and leaving the fields to be worked by overseers and slaves. Eventually, some families spent very little time on the plantations, returning for only a few weeks or holiday feasts. These families lived in Charleston or even Newport, Rhode Island, which had become a popular business and banking center for Carolinians. Others made their fortunes and retired to England.

Residential structures that reflect not only the varied backgrounds of the Carolina colonists but, with their increasing wealth, the fashionable trends emanating from England are often omitted from guidebooks written outside the South. Unfortunately, few plantation houses have survived, and the thousands of dwellings of small farmers, laborers, and slaves are virtually nonexistent. These settlers, as well as the more prosperous planters, extended their patterns of settlement on the Southern Tidewater but are hardly represented

Drayton Hall, *Charleston, S.C.*

architecturally. The few surviving mansions are highly individual examples rather than representative of typical house designs. Buildings like Mulberry, Hanover, and Brick House are presented here as individual solutions to the problems facing their owners: environmental shelter, defense from various enemies, and, as always, everywhere, an obvious preoccupation with status.

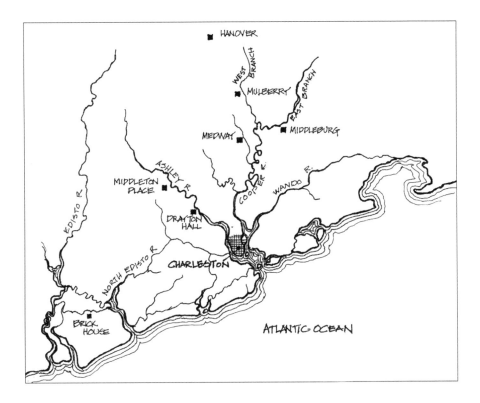

Fortunately, despite extraordinary periodic devastation from the 17th century through the end of the Civil War—fire, war, disease, pirates, angry Native Americans, and even earthquakes—a sampling of the Southern Tidewater's unique Colonial houses can still be observed. It is possible that ongoing archaeological investigations will contribute to a broader and deeper understanding of the region's distinctive architectural and cultural heritage.

Since this chapter focuses primarily on individual houses, more general stylistic field marks are not listed.

Medway with later additions

Medway (1705)

The rich variety of architectural styles found in South Carolina's
Low Country includes numerous Dutch façades; the plantation
house Medway, dating from the 17th century, is one example. The flat
elevations, with their "parapeted gables"—gable ends that rise past the
roof—offered an opportunity for decoration that even the busy Dutch
exploited. Parapet gables had been appearing on buildings in England
since the 16th century, when Henry VIII imported European craftsmen,
including Flemish masons, to construct castles in the new Renaissance
manner. Later, during the reign of James I, the ruling class and wealthy
merchants built vast country homes, such as Blickling Hall in Norfolk,
with large, shaped parapet gables resembling those on Dutch houses.
The style is often called Jacobean (from the Latin for "James"), and it
flourished during the relatively brief period of James's reign (1603–25.)
Other distinguishing features were ornate chimneys, battlements, and
towers. Although built after James's reign, the relatively modest Bacon's
Castle in Surrey County, Virginia (see page 101), is the best-known
surviving example of the Jacobean style in the Colonies, with several
distinctive features. The terms baroque, gothic, medieval, and Tudor are
sometimes used interchangeably, if incorrectly, with Jacobean.

Whether a parapet-gabled house in Charleston and its environs
should be considered true Jacobean or Dutch probably depends on
whether particular examples were conceived by English settlers repeating
English traditions or by Dutch builders arriving directly from the

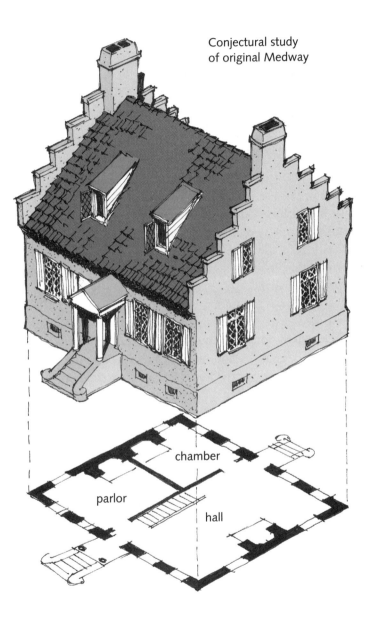

Conjectural study
of original Medway

chamber

parlor

hall

Netherlands. Huguenots, who took refuge in Holland before coming to Carolina, may also have brought Dutch building techniques. Regardless, parapeted gables can be seen on plantation buildings, country churches, and urban structures in Charleston, including outbuildings behind some prominent Double Houses.

Medway is considered the oldest house in South Carolina. Built by Jan Van Arrsens, the leader of a group of ambitious Dutch settlers who came directly from Amsterdam, it recalls designs common along the canals of Holland since at least the 14th century. Medway's very efficient three-room plan is thought by some to have inspired the much-discussed Huguenot plan, common to many of the early dwellings in the Carolina Low Country.

The original structure had the prominent front and rear entries also seen in the French and English plantation houses that soon followed. Its brick construction was consistent with European and West Indian building practices, but the brick was plastered to protect the inferior masonry of the time. It is reported to have had diamond-paned casement windows, even though sash windows were already common in 17th-century Holland.

Medway has undergone many additions and alterations in its three hundred years. While largely preserving its character, they have obscured the original house, although its plan can be discovered within the present layout. The illustration on page 137 is an attempt to visualize the original structure from written descriptions, measurements of the existing building, and informed guesses about details such as dormers and entries.

Perhaps more clearly Jacobean than Medway is the south dependency at Middleton Place, a spectacular plantation that was burned and looted by Federal troops in 1865. Rebuilt on its foundation, it displays traditional English features — a steep roof, shaped parapet gables, and decorative arched chimney caps — rather than Dutch. (Some have attributed this Jacobean flair to overexuberant 19th-century "restorers.") A remaining building, the stable at the site of North Chachan (c. 1760), a former rice plantation along the Cooper River in St. John's Parish, has a similar elevation, as do several early churches near Charleston.

stable at North Chachan, *c. 1760*

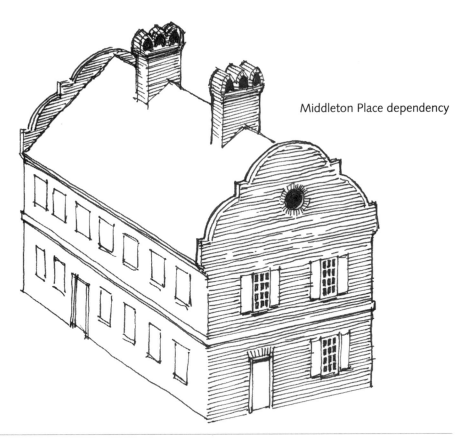

Middleton Place dependency

Middleburg, *Dufer, S.C.*

Middleburg and Mulberry

Until Georgia was tamed and the upland frontier pushed farther west by the influx of settlers coming down the Appalachians from the North, the Low Country remained insecure, threatened by the Spanish, marauding pirates, and angry Indians. In the Yamassee Indian War of 1717, for example, two hundred homes were looted or destroyed and more than a hundred settlers killed. Fires in the pine woods were also common during the dry season. The resulting gaps in the archaeological record leave little to discuss between Medway (page 136) and Mulberry (page 142), a 1714 plantation house overlooking the West Branch of the Cooper River.

Middleburg (1699, traditional date; maybe late 18th century)

Given the difficult times, it is surprising and fortunate that Middleburg, a Huguenot wood frame house, has survived to this day. Middleburg represents an original adaptation to the semitropical climate, with a long, one-room-deep plan and full-length piazzas. It is sometimes seen as the precursor of the Charleston Single House (page 154), but other than being one room deep, it lacks other important features of the Single House: a central stair hall, side-wall fireplaces, and two-story piazzas.

    In its original two-room configuration, when it probably lacked one or both piazzas (uncommon even in Charleston before the Revolutionary War), Middleburg could be viewed as a simple hall-and-parlor or

MIDDLEBURG

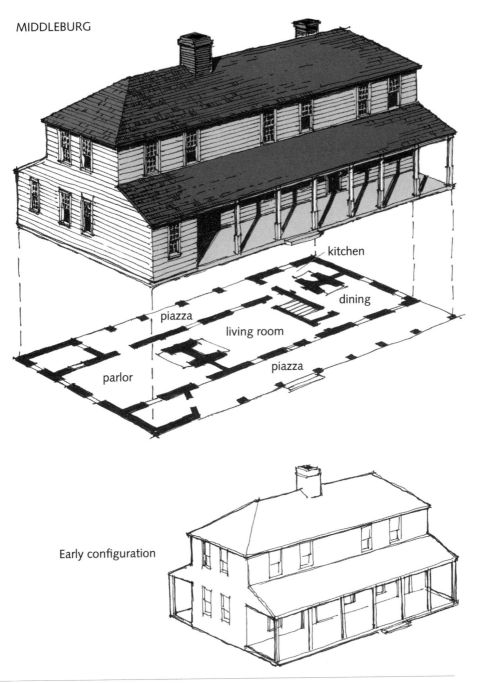

kitchen

dining

piazza

living room

piazza

parlor

Early configuration

hall-and-dining room structure. It is the first house in the South known to use back-to-back interior fireplaces, a practice continued throughout the Low Country well into the 18th century, when it eventually merged with Georgian ideas and pattern books. These interior fireplaces of the Southern Tidewater are in notable contrast to the massive exposed chimneys of the Chesapeake Tidewater. Typical of Huguenot houses at the time, the insides of the exterior walls of Middleburg are plastered, with partitions of vertical siding. In the bedroom, a plaster panel sits above the mantelpiece, laid directly on the face of the chimney.

Mulberry, *Goose Creek, S.C.*

Mulberry (1714)

No one knows why Thomas Broughton, an Englishman, chose a French Huguenot floor plan for his plantation house or why he adorned it with corner pavilions and a sort of gambrel-jerkinhead roof with flared eaves. Like several nearby plantations, Mulberry was intended to produce silk but instead became known for its fertile rice fields along the Cooper River. Built just a few miles north of Charleston, it is noted primarily for the curious corner rooms attached to what has come to be called the typical Huguenot plan. The basic plan, without the pavilions, appears again and again throughout South Carolina in various styles, attesting

MULBERRY

to its comfort and practicality. Usually it is almost square: four rooms with the main entry opening directly into the larger hall. Between the two rear rooms is a stair hall, often with its own dormer to provide the extra headroom needed. Mulberry is the earliest example of this popular layout.

Although it is not a large house, the corner pavilions give it a rambling aspect, and its regular symmetry maintains a certain dignity. The masonry construction suggests permanence and stability, and its layout has led some observers to see it as a kind of fortress; indeed, Mulberry was successfully defended during the Yamassee Indian War. Others have found precedents for the pavilion in large English country houses with corner stair towers. An equally strong case, however, is made for a French influence, for roughly similar house plans published earlier in France were probably known to the Huguenot immigrants.

The dentiled eave moldings, the columned portico, and of course the pavilions with their bell-shaped roofs and weather vanes indicate an awareness of architectural theory not previously seen in the Carolinas and are in striking contrast to the simple practicality of Middleburg. Fortunately, Mulberry has been well maintained since a careful restoration by the British architect Charles Brendon in 1915.

Pond Bluff, *Berkeley County, S.C., c. 1820 (destroyed)*

The Raised Southern Tidewater Cottage (1700–1800)

Common throughout the Southern Tidewater, including the Carolinas and Georgia, this house sat well off the ground on brick walls or piers, sometimes nearly a story high, particularly in Georgia. Similar to the Chesapeake Bay Tidewater Cottage (page 106), the Raised Southern Tidewater Cottage had a Huguenot floor plan, occasionally with two front doors opening into two similar halls. The breaks in the roofline suggest that the piazzas were a later addition. The rear porch was often partially or entirely enclosed to gain more interior space. The typical stair tower or dormer was necessary to provide sufficient headroom at the stair; seen from the outside, it confirms the Huguenot plan.

The 1726 cottage at Sloop Point, North Carolina, is an example of one of the many variations on the cottage form. Initially a simple three-room plan, it was altered not long after its construction by the addition of a deep front porch and additional rooms to the rear, all sheltered by an unbroken gable roof. Note the unusual side entry between two fireplaces.

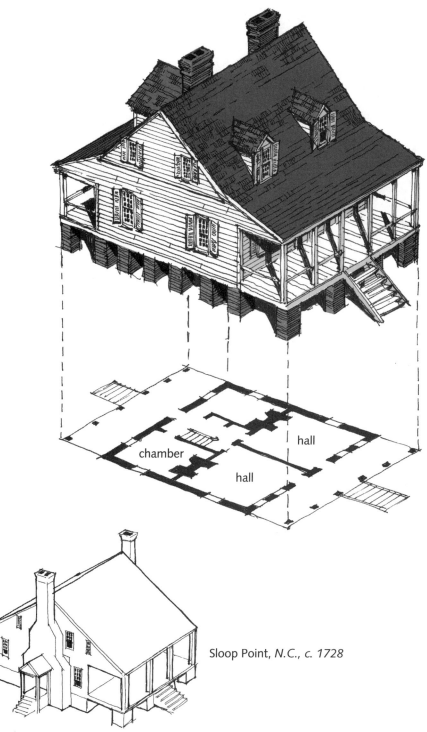

chamber

hall

hall

Sloop Point, *N.C., c. 1728*

Hanover, *Clemson University campus, S.C., c. 1720*

Hanover (1720)

Originally built at St. John's Parish, Berkeley, South Carolina, this plantation was named by Paul de St. Julien for the British royal family that ruled from 1714 to 1901 and allowed Huguenot refugees like himself to settle in the southern colonies, escaping the persecutions of Louis XIV. Unlike any other house in South Carolina, Hanover illustrates the broad variety of styles used with the Huguenot floor plan. The exterior T-shaped chimneys and gambrel (some might say mansard) roof, with nearly flat upper sections and flared eaves, differ considerably from those of the generic Southern Tidewater Cottage just described. The unusual stair configuration apparently allows sufficient headroom without the typical stair tower. Hanover is larger than it appears in photographs, as the 11-foot-high ceilings and 6-foot-tall windows give it the proportions of a squat cottage.

One of several historic buildings threatened by hydroelectric dam projects, Hanover was moved from St. John's Parish, Berkeley, to the Clemson University campus in the northwestern corner of the state, far from its Low Country origins. During its dismantling and reconstruction, it was found to have been built entirely of cypress, which no doubt contributed to its survival.

HANOVER

Brick House, *Edisto Island, S.C., c. 1725*

Brick House (1725)

This two-story house was built for Paul Hamilton, a governor of South Carolina and Secretary of the Navy, and is another indication that the Huguenot plan was freely adopted by other groups as well. It was also evidence of the rising prosperity of the area. Little expense was spared in constructing Brick House: high-quality brick was imported from Boston, and stucco detailing formed the quoins, window trim, and the false window and door panels on the sides. With a French flavor, it is somewhat similar in character to the Place des Vosges (1605) in Paris and also closely resembles a château near Loos-les-Lille, France. The steeply pitched roof with flared eaves was common to the Southern Tidewater, this hipped version appearing also on the handsome Miles Brewton House in Charleston (page 159). Brick House burned in 1929, but the walls still stand, as though waiting for restoration. The dependencies have long since vanished, giving us the misleading impression of an isolated structure in the landscape; in fact, the house had been the center of a thriving plantation.

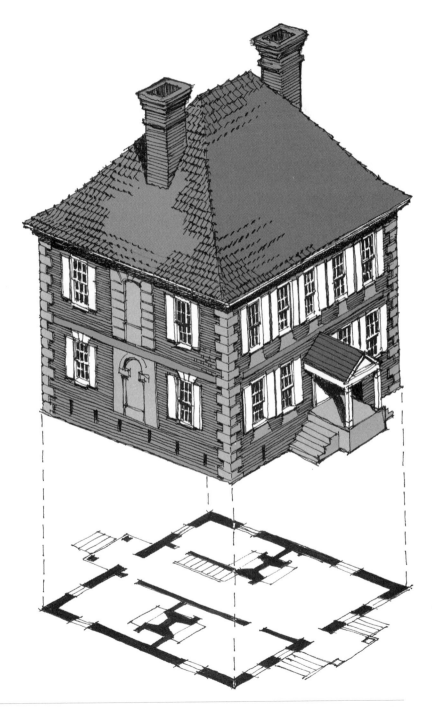

Drayton Hall, *Charleston, S.C., c. 1738–42*

Drayton Hall (1738–42)

Drayton Hall is one of the few plantation mansions in the Carolina Low Country as large and elegant as those in Virginia and Maryland. Its designer remains unknown but its origins are fairly obvious, for it was built after the appearance of several influential architectural books in England. Among them was the translation in 1720 of Palladio's *Four Books of Architecture.*

The wealthy plantation heir John Drayton had his mansion built near the family's enormous plantation on the Ashley River, bringing from England the required carpenters, joiners, and other tradesmen. No doubt a custom design from a Palladian-inspired English architect was brought along as well, for no American-designed mansion could approach Drayton Hall's elegance and style. It was the only plantation house along the river to survive the Civil War, reportedly because the Federal troops were told that it was being used as a yellow fever hospital.

Often called the first Palladian house in America, it stands today largely as it appeared 250 years ago thanks to Drayton's descendants, who did not wish to renovate or restore it. Remarkably, it remained in their hands until 1974, without electricity, gas, or plumbing. The original cypress paneling remains intact, as does a remarkable molded plaster ceiling. The land-side elevation has a two-story portico closely resembling those in Palladio's *Four Books of Architecture.* The dependencies have disappeared over time, giving the false impression of an isolated and serene landscape.

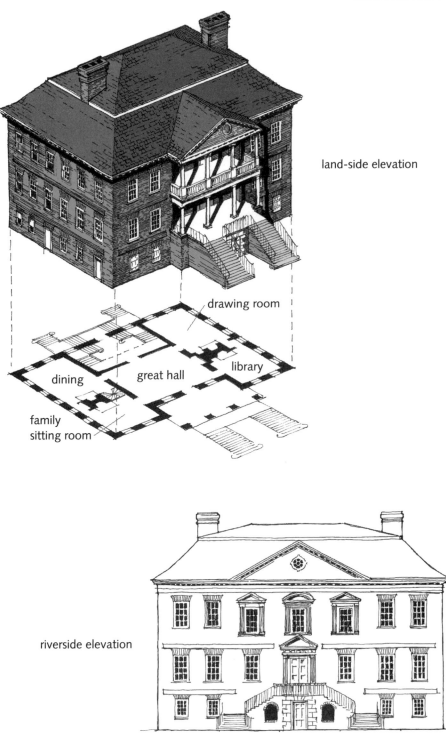

land-side elevation

drawing room

library

great hall

dining

family
sitting room

riverside elevation

The Southern Tidewater Hearth   **153**

Thomas Legare House, *Charleston, S.C., c. 1752*

The Charleston Single House (1750–1863)

The Single House is virtually unique to Charleston, South Carolina. It was designed to accommodate the semitropical climate as well as the city's layout of many narrow but deep house lots. Typically, the two- or three-story structure, often raised high over a basement, shows a three-bay short side to the street, inviting a walk down a longer five-bay façade to reach the central entry hall and stair. Additional structures at the rear, attached or free-standing, include the kitchen, servants' quarters, and a stable.

Single Houses vary considerably in their appearance, but the one-room-deep plan, with the central hall opening to a room on either side, is common to all. There may be a secondary public or business entrance directly off the street. The blank back wall opposite the entry contains the chimneys, usually one for each main room. This wall, with few if any window openings, is believed to have acted also as a firewall, protecting the house from an adjacent burning building—a genuine fear, even with a garden in between. The firewall theory is also consistent with the idea that Single Houses evolved from paired townhouses.

However, it is the two-tiered, full-length piazzas that give the Charleston Single House its relaxed, inviting character. Shading the long south or west walls, they provide comfortable outdoor living and entertaining space high enough to catch the breezes. Not common until after the Revolution, piazzas are believed to have been developed locally as expanded balconies and porches, although they may also have come

The Southern Tidewater Hearth

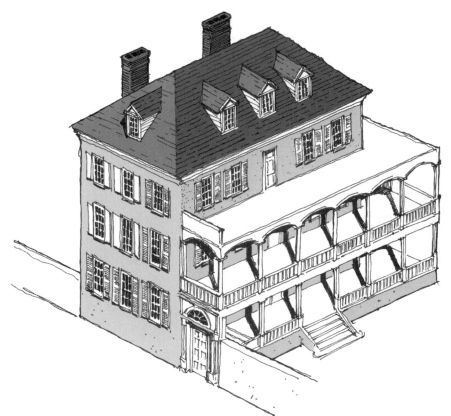

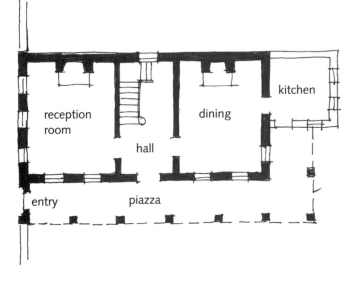

by way of the West Indies. Added to earlier houses, they eventually became part of the original construction of post-Revolutionary and antebellum structures, with Georgian, Federal, and eventually even Greek Revival detailing.

Although builders attempted to follow the 18th-century English architectural fashion, local materials and preferences lent Single Houses, and thus Charleston as well, a Mediterranean flavor, with their worn but colorfully painted stuccoed brick walls and hipped, gabled, or parapet-gabled red tile roofs. Valuable real estate today, they survive as restored elegant townhouses looking down on lavish gardens, recalling an earlier time of great prosperity in the Carolina Low Country.

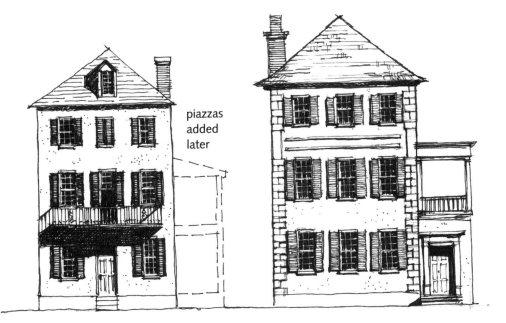

piazzas
added
later

PRE–REVOLUTIONARY WAR
SINGLE HOUSE

PRE–CIVIL WAR
SINGLE HOUSE

John Edwards House, *Charleston, S.C., c. 1770*

The Charleston Double House (1730–1863)

The Double House is not two Single Houses combined but a distinct, much more formal type of townhouse, generally built on a larger lot and perhaps twice the width of a Single House. Also unique to Charleston, it has a definite Palladian flavor, particularly when embellished with a two-tiered, pedimented portico taken straight from English architectural books.

Early Double Houses appear as urban versions of the Huguenot plan houses and were almost square, with the centered entry opening directly into a hall, the largest room in the house. Next to the hall was a dining room, and two or three smaller rooms in the rear served as bedchambers or offices. A stair hall was typically centered at the rear, with its own dormer. While the second floor also had bedchambers in back, the front might contain a large drawing room for entertaining. As with the Single House, the combination of a raised basement and high ceilings helped push the second floor up into the cooling sea breezes, a virtue in South Carolina's climate.

Later Double Houses, built just before or after the Revolution, were more stylish, featuring Adamesque or Federal elements such as quoins, shutters, dentiled cornices, and Palladian windows. Their nearly square plan has an 18th-century Georgian layout, with a wide straight-through hall and two rooms on either side, typically a reception room, dining room, and offices. An elaborate Double House may have dependencies

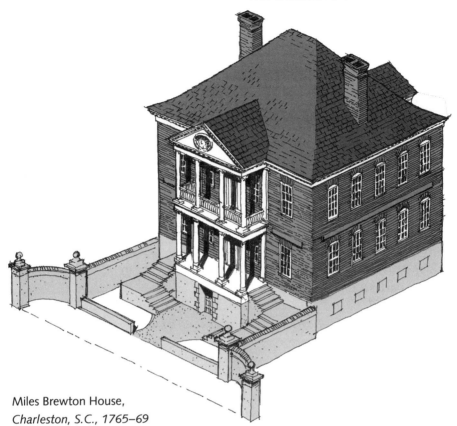

Miles Brewton House,
Charleston, S.C., 1765–69

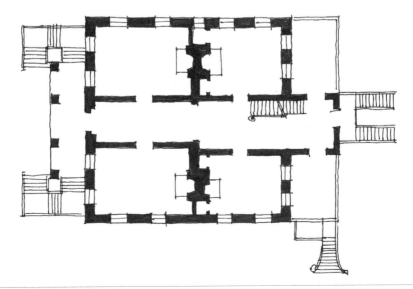

strung out behind or alongside in a walled courtyard behind a wrought-iron gate. Lush gardens thrive in the subtropical climate.

Easily the finest and most celebrated Double House is the Miles Brewton mansion (c. 1769), with a Classically columned and pedimented two-story portico. Its plan resembles that of the Georgian houses of the Chesapeake, but its square footprint and rear stair tower point to its Low Country heritage. The Brewton House represented the height of society in Charleston. Presumably chosen for its stately aspect and elegant interior, it served as headquarters for the British in the Revolutionary War and then for the Federals during the Civil War. Ironically, Miles Brewton, who was responsible for shipping untold numbers of Africans across the Atlantic, drowned at sea with his wife and children in 1775.

The Brewton House, along with Drayton Hall, suggests that Charleston offered a more architecturally refined and style-conscious clientele than the other American colonies. Arriving in the Low Country already rich from their West Indies plantations, the Charleston elite did not hesitate to bring skilled artisans, exclusive materials, and fashionable designs from England, with whose privileged society they maintained close ties. Despite losses due to wars, fires, storms, even earthquakes, many Double Houses, with gardens, outbuildings, and details intact, can be seen in Charleston's historic district.

William Gibbs House, *Charleston, S.C., pre–Revolutionary War*

The French Mississippi Hearth

Architecturally, one of the more innovative early European presences on the North American continent was the French settlement along the Gulf coast and the Mississippi River in the 17th and 18th centuries. These settlers adapted French Colonial home building traditions to the warm, wet environment of southern Louisiana, an area that suffered from floods, hurricanes, and rampant yellow fever. Like so many traditions, French Colonial building styles were fated to be overwhelmed by the westward push of the Anglo-American frontier in the 19th century. Only a few precious examples survive today.

Working inland up the St. Lawrence River during the 17th century, French explorers and fur traders established outposts among the Great Lakes and beyond, eventually reaching the Mississippi. The result was the "French Crescent," a thin line of settlements stretching from maritime Canada to the Louisiana Gulf coast by way of the St. Lawrence, the Great Lakes, and the Mississippi River valley. The area comprised a vast, vaguely defined territory, essentially the drainage basin of the Mississippi River, including the Ohio and Missouri River watersheds and the deltas and bayous of Louisiana.

France's interest in Louisiana was linked to the rapidly growing taste for sugar in Europe. By the 18th century, French colonies dominated the formerly Spanish Caribbean, and French plantations dominated the sugar trade. Seeking further expansion, the French sent an expedition from their stronghold on Saint Domingue in 1699 to begin colonizing the Gulf coast. Landing first in what is now Biloxi Bay, Mississippi, and moving on to the future site of Mobile, Alabama, they established

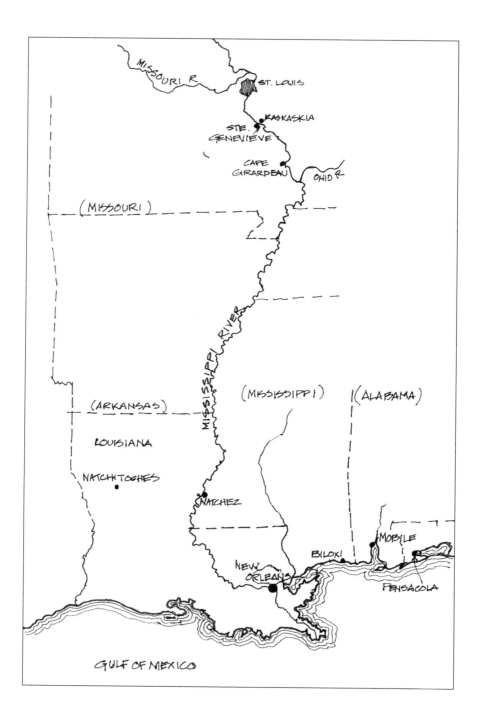

MISSOURI R

ST. LOUIS

KASKASKIA

STE. GENEVIEVE

CAPE GIRARDEAU

OHIO R

(MISSOURI)

MISSISSIPPI RIVER

(ARKANSAS)

(MISSISSIPPI)

(ALABAMA)

LOUISIANA

NATCHITOCHES

NATCHEZ

MOBILE

BILOXI

NEW ORLEANS

PENSACOLA

GULF OF MEXICO

outposts along rivers as far inland as St. Louis on the Mississippi, Natchitoches on the Red River, and Fort Toulouse on the Alabama River. A number of French Canadians settled along Bayou St. John near the site of New Orleans twenty years later. These Acadian settlers may have brought their building tradition of steep pavilion roofs with them, although no examples remain.

In 1718 a French trading company founded the walled town of New Orleans and modeled its new plantations on those of the French sugar islands. As only the well-drained natural levees along the Mississippi and principal bayous could support intensive cultivation, a riverine settlement pattern was established, with each property having frontage on the waterway, the primary transportation route. Unsuccessful attempts were made to bring much-needed labor from Europe by inducement, indentured servitude, kidnapping, and sentencing of French convicts to the new territory. Instead, slaves in considerable number were imported to work on the plantations, and by 1731 the four thousand white settlers along the lower Mississippi were already outnumbered by Africans.

Other nationalities and cultures were represented as well, with some settlers coming directly from Europe or the American colonies. But it was the three distinct peoples from Haiti that dominated the culture and landscape of Louisiana: the Creoles (a cultural amalgam of French, Spanish, African, English, and Native American languages and societies), the Acadians, and the former slaves from Saint Domingue. Each brought building traditions that they would adapt to the new environment.

During the Seven Years' War with England (1756–63), many French settlers in Acadia, now Nova Scotia, were deported by the British, some ending up in the American colonies, France, or, in considerable numbers, Haiti, where they strove to reestablish their culture. Resettling in southern Louisiana between 1765 and 1785, the Acadians contributed greatly to the already diverse population. Welcomed by the Spanish, who had retaken the territory in 1763, at the end of the war they were granted land and established farms along the bayous west of New Orleans. Although remaining largely separate from the French Creoles, they blended with other new arrivals, including Anglo-Americans, Spanish, Germans, and Scots-Irish as well as Native Americans, eventually becoming Cajuns, an English distortion of "Acadians."

West African slaves had been brought to French sugar plantations in the West Indies as early as 1650. Their growing number and harsh treatment by the French planters, overseers, and church officials, as well as inspiration from the French Revolution, led to uprisings in Saint

Domingue. Eventually, the French were ejected in the long Haitian revolution. In the confusion during and after the struggle, many former slaves immigrated to New Orleans, resulting in a sizable free black population atypical of that in other American cities, particularly in the South. Many brought useful skills and contributed significantly to the remarkable society forming in the lowlands around New Orleans.

In Louisiana, new settlers immediately built the primitive huts and cabins common to all new settlements. Once established, however, they began erecting more substantial houses, each culture adapting its own familiar forms and layouts to the unique environment. Early construction was always of local materials: soft brick, mud, plaster, and especially the tough cypress wood used for framing members, posts, boards, and shingles. Foundations were originally posts in the ground, then sills laid on the ground, and finally cypress blocks or piers and walls of improved brick. Structures were timber frame, like Haitian huts and French farmhouses, filled in with brick or mud, then plastered or weatherboarded for protection. Roofs were shingled or, later, occasionally covered with imported tile. High ceilings, wide paired doors, and full-height casement windows provided ventilation. Along the rivers and bayous, extended roofs sheltered wide *galéries* (porches), and houses were raised to a second story for better ventilation and protection from flooding, as well as additional space.

Socially and commercially, New Orleans dominated the Louisiana lowlands as Charleston did the Southern Tidewater lowlands, in time becoming the most active port in North America. Except for a few French towns, Louisiana remained entirely rural outside New Orleans as late as the Civil War.

After Jefferson purchased the Louisiana Territory from Napoleon in 1803 and urged Americans to exploit it, Easterners by the thousands descended on the lower Mississippi, bringing with them English tastes and influences. Georgian detailing began to appear around now symmetrically arranged doors and sash windows. Supporting posts became Classical columns. Still, the French flavor prevailed, as it had through the period of Spanish administration, the comfortable Creole house retaining much of its character, especially in the countryside.

New Orleans's influence and commerce reached north along the Mississippi to other French communities at least as far as St. Louis but most significantly to Kaskaskia (now in Illinois) and Ste. Genevieve in Missouri. Although settled by French Canadians, these towns did business to the south; seeing Louisiana's architecture on trips to

New Orleans, Ste. Genevieve's merchants adopted Creole forms and techniques for their own homes. Remarkably, distant Ste. Genevieve, on the Mississippi hundreds of miles from New Orleans, somehow survived the Anglo-American cultural juggernaut and today displays many valuable, well-kept examples of Creole residential architecture.

The great fires of 1788 and 1794 destroyed New Orleans's earliest buildings. Subsequent demolitions consumed much of what followed; urban growth and suburban sprawl have taken over the nearby Creole landscape. Still, a few urban cottages from the early 19th century remain. The French Quarter's familiar two- and three-story townhouses, built after the fires in a sort of French-Spanish style, remain but have been much altered (and expanded) by the 19th-century addition of elaborate wrought-iron balconies and *galéries*. Nevertheless, these structures represent Old New Orleans to many people, and the introduction of wrought-iron work, in the interests of comfort and ventilation, seems in keeping with the earlier improvisations on Creole architecture.

Bolduc House, *Ste. Genevieve, Mo., c. 1770*

The Creole Cottage (1700–1830)

FORM: A 1- or 1½-story, rectangular, 1-room-deep house on a low foundation. The roof may be gabled or a pavilion type with a single or broken pitch. Covered *galéries* appear at the front but more often at both front and rear or on all sides. The small chimney is off center at the roof peak.

STYLISTIC DETAIL: Little decoration. *Galérie* posts and railings are generally plain.

CONSTRUCTION: Initially, walls were of *poteaux-en-terre* (posts in the earth) and filled with *bousillage* (mud). Roofs were timber frame and thatched with palmetto leaves (very early examples) or covered with wood shingles.

The origins of the Creole cottage are much debated. Nova Scotia, Haiti, Normandy, and even West Africa are often cited, along with such varied peoples as the Acadians, French settlers, buccaneers, and various American Indians, including the Arawaks and the Iroquois. Certainly West Indian Creoles contributed to the cottage's unique character with shaded *galéries*, stucco surfaces, and, particularly in Louisiana, the raised foundations. While undoubtedly some early construction details were borrowed from the Gulf coast Indians—palmetto thatching and Spanish moss in the walls, for example—the pavilion-roofed Normandy longhouse provides a basis for the theory that the two-room cottage came to Louisiana from France by way of the West Indies or Canada. It was then modified by Creole builders to suit local conditions. Early drawings of French settlements on the Gulf coast show traditional

WEST INDIES
CREOLE HUT

EARLY CREOLE COTTAGE
without *galéries, c. 1720*

half-timbered, pavilion-roofed buildings looking somewhat out of place among primitive, palmetto-thatched huts. Shortly afterward, West Indian Africans and Creoles from Haiti drew on their own experience to build houses more suited to the warm and wet semitropical environment, houses with Spanish Creole antecedents in Cuba and Hispaniola.

Early floor plans included two different-size rooms side by side, the *salle-chambre* or Hall-and-Chamber layout. Further development of this plan produced one-room-deep three- and four-room houses. A squarish four-room plan with two smaller rooms behind was more common eastward along the Gulf coast. All the rooms opened directly onto the *galéries* and usually not to one another. A center chimney was typical of two-room Creole cottages, and chimneys were not necessarily added when rooms were added. Despite considerable variation, Creole cottages generally had center chimneys, high ceilings, and at least one *galérie* in front but, more likely, at the rear and sides as well.

The construction technique, *poteaux-en-terre* (posts in the earth), used cypress posts, hewn flat, planted vertically and closely spaced in shallow trenches and stabilized with a top plate. The spaces between the posts were filled with *bousillage*, a mixture of clay, lime, and Spanish moss, or with a porous brick infill plastered or covered with weatherboards for protection. Upriver, in Missouri and Illinois, cedar was used for the posts with a *bousillage* of mud and grass and even deer hair. The origin of *poteaux-en-terre* is unclear, but it has precedents in the early French settlements to the north as well as in Native American practices.

Bequette-Ribault House, *Ste. Genevieve, Mo., c. 1790*

It was also known in Saint Domingue, in the West Indies.

By the 1720s, stone or brick piers were used to support a wood sill on which a timber frame was erected (the *poteaux-sur-sole*, post-on-sole, method), with obvious benefits in longevity. This replaced *poteaux-en-terre* as the primary rural construction technique for the Creole Cottage. In New Orleans and elsewhere, however, sills were often placed directly on the ground. Urban versions were typically two rooms deep but sometimes quite narrow, usually with

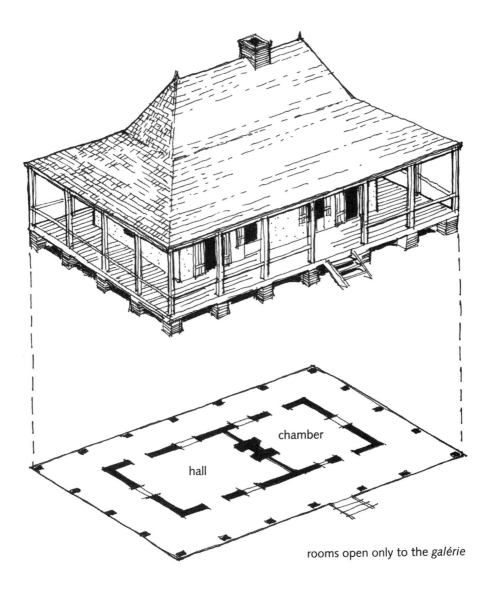

chamber

hall

rooms open only to the *galérie*

a small front *galérie* and gable ends. Smooth parapeted gables were also fairly common.

When the Creole Cottage was expanded, it grew upward as well as out, whether by adding to existing houses or by building larger houses. Brick piers became brick walls a story high, enclosing storage and service areas below the main floor. Rooftop dormers indicated a growing use of attic space. Horizontally, the three- and four-room configurations added rooms by enclosing *galéries*, particularly at the rear corners. The two concepts merged as the three-room plan became two rooms deep and the four-room plan grew longer.

In the early 19th century, an appetite for symmetry in floor plan and elevation arose, reflecting the English influence brought by the increasing number of Americans from the North and East. Despite these Anglo contributions, the distinctive Creole house remained less dominating and more inviting than the harder-edged, unshaded Georgian plantation houses of Virginia and Maryland. Several fine, well-preserved examples can be seen at Ste. Genevieve, Missouri.

One-room structure awaits restoration, *Ste. Genevieve, Mo.*

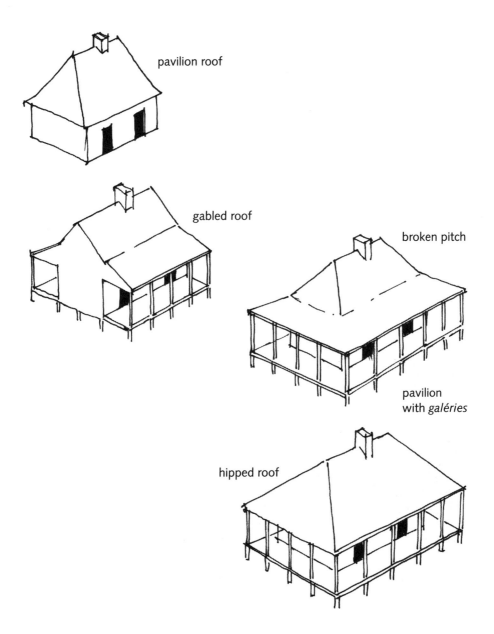

pavilion roof

gabled roof

broken pitch

pavilion
with *galéries*

hipped roof

Homeplace Plantation, *Hahnville, La., c. 1801*

The Creole Plantation House (1765–1830)

FORM: A 1- or 1½-story house over a high basement. Deep *galéries* present at least on the front and probably on the rear and sides as well. Floor plan may be linear or 2 rooms deep. Dormers are seen on larger houses. Roof may be gabled or pavilion type with single pitch umbrella roof or broken pitch with an occasional flare at the eaves.

STYLISTIC DETAIL: Little ornament on early examples, although *galérie* posts may be turned with square bases, or chamfered. Plain-barred *galérie* railings. Full-height paired casement windows. Classical detailing and sash windows more frequent after 1800.

CONSTRUCTION: Timber frame structure with Norman roof trusses on brick masonry foundations, piers, and basement walls. *Bousillage* of plaster and lath or brick in exterior walls, sheathed in clapboards. Roofing of oak or cedar shingles.

The distinction between a Creole Cottage and a Creole Plantation House is not always clear. One seems to have grown from the other, although many plantation houses were quite modest. When the Louisiana farmer, black or white, had sufficient acreage and enough slaves to grow a single crop intensively for a specific market (in this case, sugar or cotton), he became a plantation owner and his home a plantation house. Larger houses were visually imposing, often with eight or more rooms on the main floor, and the overall dimensions were exaggerated by the surrounding *galéries*. Later, in the 18th and 19th centuries, larger, more

SMALL PLANTATION HOUSE

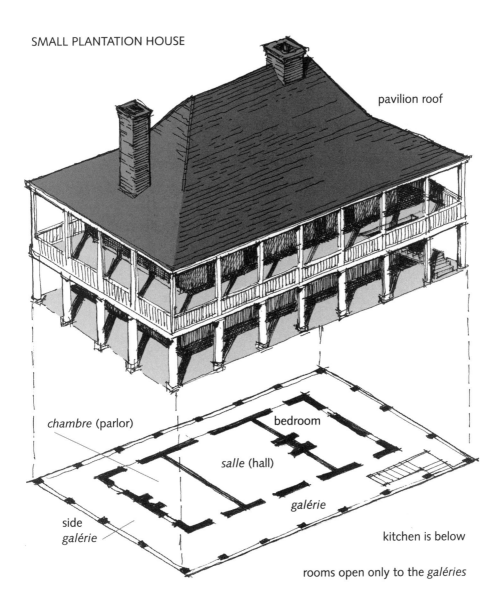

pavilion roof

chambre (parlor)

bedroom

salle (hall)

galérie

side
galérie

kitchen is below

rooms open only to the *galéries*

elegant rural mansions were built with formal gardens and outbuildings geometrically set in the landscape.

Even more than the design of the house, it was the number and placement of the outbuildings that identified the operation as a plantation. As in the Tidewater regions, the planter's house was the most substantial structure and on typical sites is the only building left standing today, giving a false impression of isolation. In fact, the plantation was a scene of intense industry that involved scores, perhaps hundreds, of workers, mostly slaves, laboring in the fields and dozens of nearby outbuildings. These structures might include a sugar house and sugar mill on sugar plantations as well as the blacksmith and cooper's shop, slave cabins, and overseer's house. There were also the smokehouse, dairy, stables, barns, offices, and, unique to Creole settlements, *pigeonniers* (dovecotes) and *garçonnières* (young men's dormitories). With growing prosperity and the increasing Anglo-American influence, these layouts became more geometrically formal, with the offices and *pigeonniers* flanking the main house symmetrically. The slave cabins and work buildings were then grouped some distance away.

The Creole vernacular gave way to the Georgian and Adamesque influences preferred by stylish Americans, who came to dominate the formerly French and Spanish colony. Yankee architects and builders brought fashionable designs to southern cities, leaving a marked effect on gentry house façades. Husky Greek and Roman colonnades wrapped plantation floor plans, obscuring their Creole origin, and *galéries* blended into pedimented porticoes. Plantation house architecture soon crept down the dead-end road of antebellum mansions, which were able to exist only under a system of slave labor. Louisiana plantation architecture ended abruptly with the Civil War.

Parlange, near the Mississippi at New Roads in Pointe Coupee Parish, Louisiana, is a classic example of a mid-18th-century plantation house, its slender columns not yet fattened by the Anglo-American passion for Classical ornament. Not quite symmetrical, it nevertheless has a quiet dignity, all in white with the tall, shuttered French doors topped with fan transoms. It was built of traditional materials: all brick below, with sturdy brick columns and a paved floor and timber frame above with plastered *bousillage*. Parlange was the home of French nobility who eventually renounced their royal titles to become ordinary Louisiana citizens, albeit wealthy ones.

The floor plan shows its descent from the two- and three-room cottage. Sacrificing some cross ventilation, the house is now two rooms

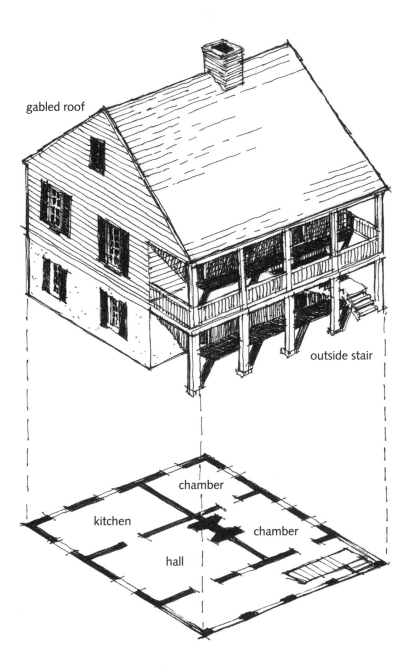

gabled roof

outside stair

chamber

kitchen

chamber

hall

deep but still without corridors. Access to all spaces is from the *galéries*, though some rooms now open to one another. Ceilings are nearly 10 feet high. The lower level has a similar layout, with rooms for the laundry and storage, including a sizable wine cellar. Cooking was done in a separate kitchen, a typical southern practice.

The front stair is thought to have replaced a more traditional one under the front *galérie*, although the present stair "bay" is smaller than the others. Except for the stair and some space added at the rear, the house appears to be quite original.

Parlange, *Pointe Coupee Parish, La., c. 1757*

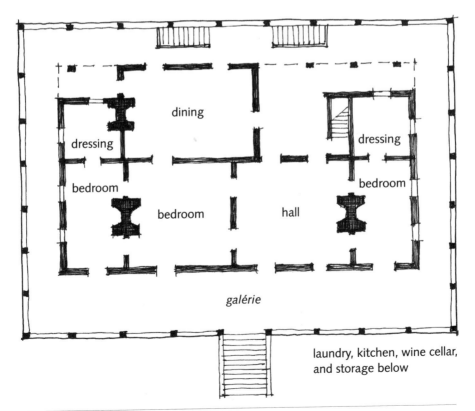

dining

dressing

dressing

bedroom

bedroom

bedroom

hall

galérie

laundry, kitchen, wine cellar, and storage below

Cajun House, *Baton Rouge, La.*

The Cajun House (1790–1850)

FORM: A 1½-story, nearly square, end-gabled house. The single pitched roof extends over a full-width *galérie* in front and often, at the rear, a small *galérie* between corner rooms.

STYLISTIC DETAIL: Generally without ornament. Overall finish is untreated cypress, but façade may be whitewashed or left exposed, without siding. Amenities such as *galérie* railings and shutters may have been added.

CONSTRUCTION: Wood frame with *bousillage* of plaster and wood lath for the exterior walls, covered by clapboards. Brick or cypress block foundations. Roof covered with exceptionally long cypress shingles.

In the mid-17th century in Acadia (now parts of Nova Scotia and New Brunswick along the Bay of Fundy), the first continental European settlers in North America created a culture that would separate itself gradually from its French origins. A strong sense of community developed in Acadia over a hundred years, despite contentious, alternating French and English domination. The Acadians resisted English control after the French defeat at nearby Fort Beausejour in 1755, and many were deported to the Carolinas and Georgia shortly thereafter. Others dispersed into outlying areas, including the American colonies, and even to France. Some who remained were interned at Halifax, where eventually two thousand agreed to move to Saint Domingue during 1764 and 1765, resettling in Louisiana within the decade.

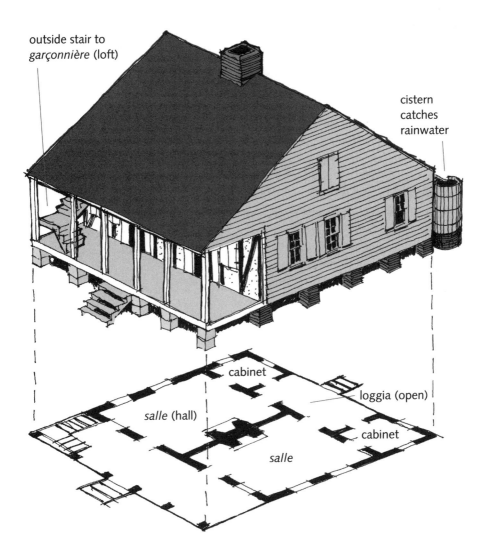

outside stair to
garçonnière (loft)

cistern
catches
rainwater

cabinet

loggia (open)

salle (hall)

cabinet

salle

A few Acadian exiles arrived in New Orleans in April 1774 by way of Mobile, Alabama, on the Gulf coast, but the larger migrations began the following year as Louisiana was being transferred from French to Spanish control. Other groups followed from the American colonies and directly from France. Generally welcomed by the Spanish, who saw them as apolitical, productive settlers, they were given rudimentary tools and plots of land to farm and, ideally, to supply the growing center of New Orleans.

Early Acadian Americans settled along the Mississippi River and the bayous feeding into it, principally the Bayou Teche in the prairie to the west and Bayou Lafoureche, southwest of New Orleans. Later immigrants settled in the woods and grasslands farther west. Homesteads were built along the major streams and creeks, which provided transportation routes for skiffs and bateaux. The Spanish, and after 1803, the American authorities, followed the French practice of dividing land into long, narrow strips facing the water and stretching back into swamps or woodlands, giving a special character to the landscape that is still apparent.

In addition to bringing their own building traditions, the Acadians found an established Creole vernacular, also with French origins but already well adapted to local conditions. First inclined to reproduce the simple hall-and-parlor cottages of Nova Scotia, by the 1790s the Acadians had adopted some Creole building techniques, resulting in small, gable-roofed structures similar to the two-room Creole Cottage (page 168). The Cajun House included a loft, reached by a steep stair directly from the porch, and often small additions at the rear for kitchens or extra bedrooms. Space permitting, there were two shuttered front doors and windows on the front façade. A one-room version with a mud-and-stick, gable-end chimney has been restored at the Acadian Museum in the Evangeline State Park, in St. Martin Parish.

Common by the early 19th century, Cajun Houses were built on raised sills supported by brick piers or blocks of cypress. Varying in depth from 10 to 17 feet and in length from 20 to 35 feet, their proportions were remarkably consistent. The structure was of timber frame, the walls typically filled with *bousillage* and protected by weatherboards. Cypress was used throughout, from large framing members to the exceptionally long roof shingles. Single-pitch roofs extended over a full-width front *galérie*. The central chimney indicates back-to-back fireplaces, each serving a main room. As the Cajuns prospered and had larger families, the typical Cajun House expanded: small rooms,

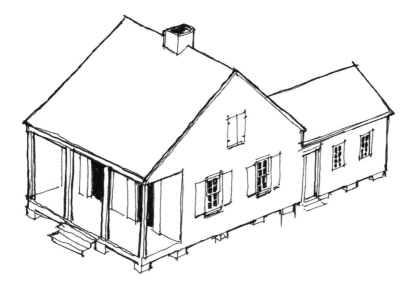

TYPICAL SMALL HOUSES

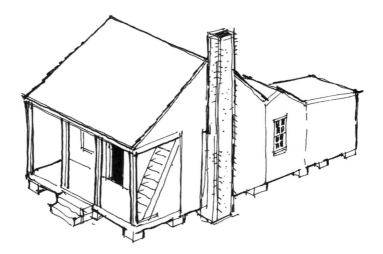

reconstruction at the Acadian Museum

cabinets, were occasionally added at each rear corner, with a loggia (open porch) between them. Unlike the Creoles, who used the loft mainly for storage, the Cajuns used it as a sleeping space, usually for young men, the *garçonnières*. In the eastern settlements, it was typically reached by an outside stair from the *galérie*, a feature also seen in Haiti.

The exterior was not painted, allowing the cypress boards to become a handsome deep gray. However, the front gallery wall under the roof was often whitewashed or even left with the timber frame and white-washed *bousillage* exposed. The well-known Louis Arceneaux House (opposite), also at the Acadian Museum, is an example of a Cajun House raised high on piers and masonry walls to provide space below the main floor.

Most authentic Cajun Houses have long disappeared from the bayou country and been replaced by slab ranches and mobile homes. However, their legacy remains with the appearance of modern "Cajun-style" builders' houses, structures with the general proportions of the original plan under a deep, single-pitch roof and with an inviting, full-width gallery.

Cajun House, *Pointe Coupee Parish, La., 1811*

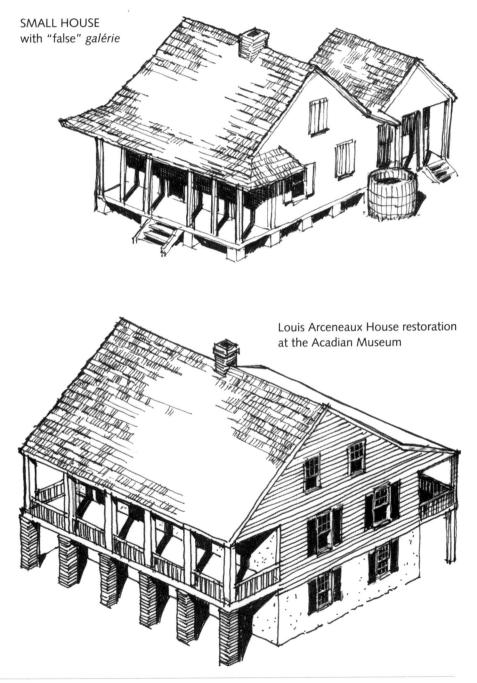

SMALL HOUSE
with "false" *galérie*

Louis Arceneaux House restoration
at the Acadian Museum

The New Orleans Urban House (1788–1850)

Southern Louisiana remained a rural landscape, with few village settlements outside New Orleans. Farms and plantations devised their own solutions for domestic shelter, guided by hard-earned experience and Creole tradition. The development of residential architecture in the city took its own direction, tempered by a disastrous history of floods, disease, war, hurricanes, and, most destructive, fire. Many ethnic groups contributed their vernacular traditions as well.

New Orleans was founded in 1718 as a commercial venture and laid out on a grid pattern around a main square facing the Mississippi River. However, its visible architectural history goes back only to 1788, when the first of two monstrous fires devastated the city, virtually destroying the Vieux Carré (French Quarter), the oldest part of the city. Aside from the Ursuline convent, no French Colonial buildings survived the second fire, in 1794.

French techniques were used to rebuild the city in a sort of Spanish-Mediterranean style, strongly influenced by new, fire-conscious building codes. Tile roofs were mandated, and structures taller than one story had to be of brick masonry construction or wood frame, with masonry infill covered by stucco. With the addition of Mexican wrought-iron ornament, fences, and balcony railings, the special character of the present French Quarter was established.

New Orleans at the turn of the 18th century was a city like no other in North America, with a population of Spanish and French Creoles,

Germans, Irish laborers, American frontiersmen, black slaves, free blacks, and black slaveowners as well as white. The river carried lumber, produce, and furs from the interior to be shipped across oceans. A relatively light-handed Colonial administration showed considerable social tolerance, and there was great prosperity.

After Jefferson's Louisiana Purchase (1803), American social, political, and economic institutions began to infiltrate the worldly culture of New Orleans. Swarms of "barbaric" Americans descended on the city, seemingly determined to smother Creole traditions. New suburbs (*faubourgs*), Creole as well as American, were being built outside the French Quarter. There, Creoles who resented the Anglo onslaught and the few Americans who preferred the more "civilized" Creole values continued the Colonial architectural heritage for a time. In addition to the typical Creole Cottage and plantation houses, new urban cottages and townhouses had a French flavor but floor plans common to northeastern cities. The Shotgun House (page 192) proliferated in a variety of styles but retained its distinctive plan.

However, beginning in 1820, eastern American architecture gradually supplanted the Creole styles. Influenced by professional architects from Philadelphia and New York, local designers dressed townhouses and even Shotgun Houses in white temple façades and Classical trim. Then, at midcentury, the Gothic Revival and Italianate styles brought the Victorian era to New Orleans.

double-pitch roof

front directly on street

French door with plank shutters

stuccoed brick

Madame John's Legacy, *New Orleans, La., 1788*

Latour and Laclotte's atelier, *New Orleans, La., 1811*

The Urban Creole Cottage (1790–1850)

FORM: Typically 1½-story, 4-bay, gable-ended small house, square or deeper than wide, slightly raised and opening directly onto the sidewalk. Sometimes 2½ stories, on raised foundations. Hipped roofs, gable on hip, or parapeted gables acting as firewalls common. A pair of dormers may indicate sleeping space upstairs. Twin front doors open to the two front rooms. The 4-room plan likely to have 2 chimneys on a center line, one behind the other. Usually a roof overhang at the street side, either a sturdy flat awning supported on wrought-iron brackets or an extension of the roof, either at a second pitch or integral with the roof slope.

STYLISTIC DETAIL: Typically unadorned, although early houses (late 18th century) may have stucco moldings around doors and windows and stucco pilasters. Openings may be arched. The 2½-story houses may have front *galéries* with wood railings and turned colonettes (slim columns) supporting porch roofs. Classical details were often added during the Greek Revival. Batten-type shutters are standard at French doors and first-floor windows. Dormers typically had casement windows in round-topped or segmented arched openings; today, they usually have 6-over-6 sash windows. Stucco and brick surfaces were painted in pastel shades.

CONSTRUCTION: Early cottages were timber frame and peg, with a brick infill and stucco finish. Later houses used brick masonry construction either painted or stuccoed to protect the soft brick. Horizontal board siding was also used. Shingled roofs may well have been tile or slate.

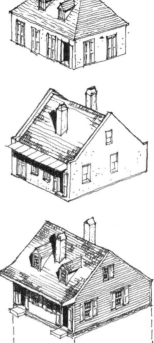

HALF COTTAGE, *1830*

COTTAGE, *1825*

DOUBLE COTTAGE
with passthrough, *1825*

Louis Lanoix House, *New Orleans, La., c. 1820*

The Creole Townhouse (1795–1850)

FORM: A 2- or 3-story structure, parapet-gabled, with a steep roof slope and 1 or 2 dormers. Upper floors may have balconies. One room wide and 2 main rooms deep, with a narrow side passage leading to a courtyard and stairs. Second-floor rooms are typically full width. Small service rooms are often attached at the rear. Townhouses may be attached, as in row housing. A porte-cochere version was wider, with a side passage able to handle carriages. Curiously, the *entresol* type has a middle floor at the base of the fanlights, creating a 3-story house with the appearance of 2 stories. Twin chimneys were in the side wall opposite the passage.

STYLISTIC DETAIL: Tall, arched openings at the ground level, one with a paneled door as the main entry and the other two with shuttered, full-height casements or French doors with fanlights. Shutters were batten type or louvered. Decorative wrought-iron balconies appear at the second floor and possibly the third. Classical detailing arrived with the Greek Revival style.

CONSTRUCTION: Brick masonry, either exposed or stuccoed. Roofs are slate or tile.

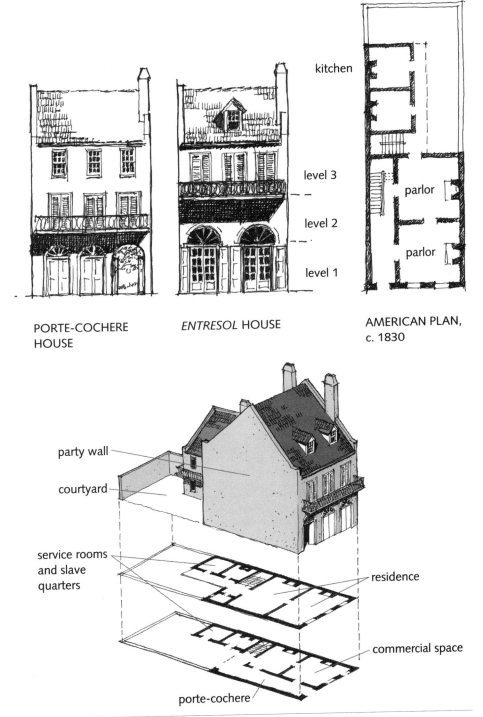

PORTE-COCHERE
HOUSE

ENTRESOL HOUSE

AMERICAN PLAN,
c. 1830

kitchen

level 3

level 2

level 1

parlor

parlor

party wall

courtyard

service rooms
and slave
quarters

residence

commercial space

porte-cochere

The French Mississippi Hearth

John Eckert House, *Madison, Ind., c. 1872*

The Shotgun House (1830–1930)

FORM: Typically a 1-story, 1-room-wide house, 2 or more rooms deep, with a gable end perpendicular to the street or a hipped roof at the front only. There is usually a shallow porch across the front under a shed roof. Chimney location varies. There are double-shotgun variations (two homes attached side by side) and "camel backs," with a second story at the rear, as well as L-shaped versions.

STYLISTIC DETAIL: Variable, from exceedingly plain (most common) to Classically ornamented.

CONSTRUCTION: Wood frame is most common, with a few masonry examples, particularly in New Orleans.

Although the Shotgun is not a French Colonial house, it is closely associated with New Orleans and Creole culture. Originating as housing built by and for slaves in the West Indies, quite possibly with roots in West Africa, it may be our one significant example of African-inspired architecture. Modest versions were built in great numbers to house Haitian Creole immigrants. Highly styled models were also common. Obviously adaptable to narrow city lots, the Shotgun's simple but efficient floor plan was easy to build, and it was a natural success on urban streets, particularly through the last half of the 19th century. The Shotgun also became a common sight in the countryside, in towns along the Gulf coast, and along rivers and, eventually, railroad tracks, but it was never common outside the South.

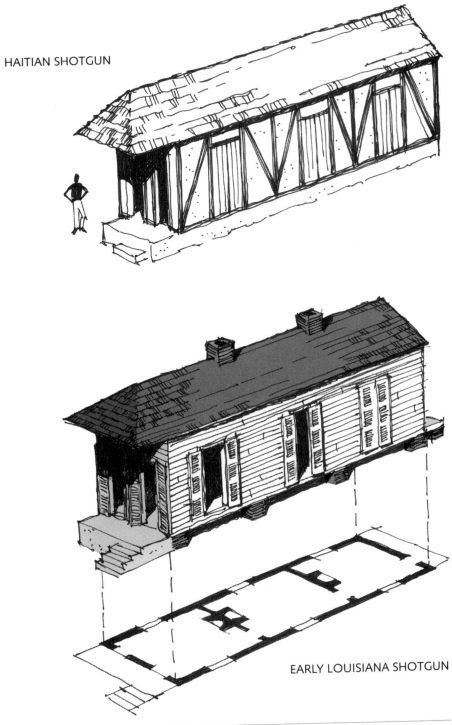

HAITIAN SHOTGUN

EARLY LOUISIANA SHOTGUN

The house is named for its plan: with the doors lined up, it was said that a shotgun could be fired straight through from end to end without hitting anything. Aligning the doors to one side eliminates the need for a passage but allows traffic to flow with minimal disruption while keeping the house narrow and enabling good cross ventilation. The rooms are typically 12 or 14 feet wide and roughly square. Originally the ceilings were high, and two front doors were common in Haitian Shotguns, but "modern" versions appear more as ordinary builders' houses. A front porch is typically shaded by either a cantilevered extension of the roof or a shed roof supported by posts. Some houses have a porch along one side leading to an entry into a middle room. A few have porches on both sides and the front, considerably obscuring the typical Shotgun character.

The Shotgun House is generally associated with blue-collar neighborhoods, but some startling examples of highly styled Greek Revival and Italianate Shotguns can be found in New Orleans and elsewhere.

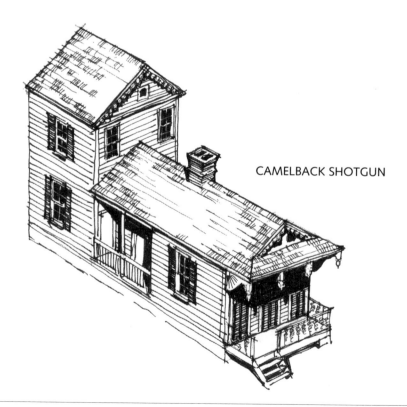

CAMELBACK SHOTGUN

THE SHOTGUN HOUSE

EARLY 20TH C.

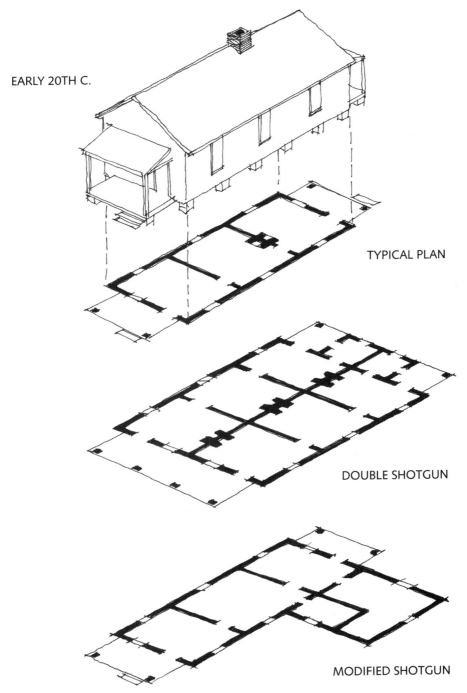

TYPICAL PLAN

DOUBLE SHOTGUN

MODIFIED SHOTGUN

The Spanish Colonial Hearths

From the late 16th through the early 19th century, Spanish explorers had energetically pushed northward in two directions. First, they sailed from the Caribbean to Florida, both west along the Gulf coast and north along the Atlantic coast. Second, they advanced from Mexico overland into the future American Southwest and California, reaching as far as what is now the Oregon coast. Spanish explorers crossed the continent through southeastern forests as well as western plains and deserts, establishing outposts and making contact with the native inhabitants. Always treasure hunters, the Spanish had a missionary purpose as well: converting the native population to Catholicism and turning them into loyal, hard-working subjects of the Spanish crown. This Hispanic colonization, including that of Florida and the Gulf coast, persisted in North America from 1565 to 1846, almost twice as long as the English Colonial period.

In 1513, only twenty-one years after Columbus's first contact with the New World, Ponce de León and a small force explored and attempted to found a settlement in Florida near what was eventually St. Augustine. The colony failed within months, but a vast area was claimed for the Spanish crown and named Florida. In 1565 the Spanish returned in force to protect their Caribbean treasure fleets from English raiders and to rout a colony of French Huguenots that had settled near Ponce de León's original site. The Spanish contingent proceeded to build fortifications to use as a base camp for their operations against the French, founding St. Augustine, now the oldest continuous settlement in North America. In 1593 the Spanish began to establish missions along the Atlantic coast from what is now Port Royal, South Carolina, south to the future site

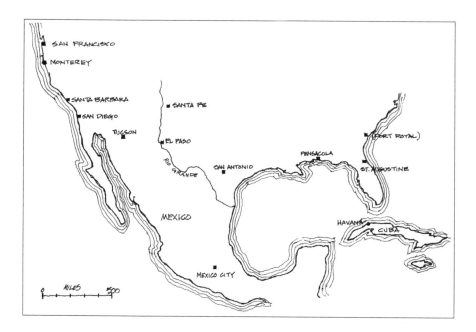

of Miami and inland to Tampa Bay and Pensacola. Little remains of these structures except at St. Augustine, and even there only the massive 17th-century fortress, the cathedral, and a few *coquina* (porous limestone) houses from the 18th century are standing.

In northern New Mexico, permanent settlements were developed as early as 1610 at Santa Fe in a strategic move designed to protect Spanish interests in Mexico from any English threats to the north and east. Similarly, California was occupied to trump Russian interests reaching south along the Pacific coast. In California, as in Florida and New Mexico, outposts were established that comprised both Catholic missions and military *presidios* (forts). These architecturally simple structures inspired California's architecture long after the Spanish Colonial ambitions had faded.

In each of the main settlement regions in the Southwest—Texas, New Mexico, Arizona, and California—missions and the few *presidios* also served as homes. Soldiers and missionaries lived within the walls, usually in a string of rooms along one long side, each room opening directly onto a *portale* (covered walkway) looking toward the main plaza. The church was either open to both the outside and the inner plaza or built entirely outside the walls, but always connected to the main plaza. Later, when individual houses were built, they tended to follow this

Fernandez-Llambias House, *St. Augustine, Fla., mid-18th c.*

pattern, with rooms grouped around a courtyard in single file.

In the 18th century, as settlers were induced to join outlying communities such as Santa Fe, simple houses of adobe blocks plastered with mud were built just outside the mission or military compound. Originally an African technique used by the Moors, adobe construction was brought to Mexico by the Spanish. None of these first dwellings survive, but houses from the early 19th century can be found along the northern Rio Grande, representing earlier examples despite later stylistic "improvements" or the ravages of nature. In most areas, the missions are the only original structures remaining.

Although generally laid out according to established Spanish practice, mission architecture varied regionally according to the ideas of individual *padres* and the availability of skilled labor. The most architecturally sophisticated missions were built in Texas. Somewhat closer to Mexico City and with easier access to skilled workers, San Antonio has magnificent mission architecture. Along the northern Rio Grande Valley in New Mexico and in Alta (upper) California, native labor was used with a more rustic result. Laid out by military officers and priests, the missions there were charmingly innocent of formal decor and precise geometry. This uncultivated character formed the basis of southwestern architectural styles, derivatives of which are still in vogue today.

Don Raimundo House, *St. Augustine, Fla., c. 1770*

New Mexico House, *Tuba, Ariz., mid-19th c.*

The Spanish New Mexico House (1600–1846)

FORM: Low, flat-roofed, 1-story building, 1 room deep, often extending to form L- or U-shaped floor plan or entirely enclosing a *placita* (courtyard). *Portales* (arcades) may shade the inner *placita* walls.

STYLISTIC DETAIL: Little applied trim or decoration before 1850. Character is created by softly rounded adobe walls broken only by a few (if any) small openings to the outside and a single entryway. Color is determined by the local adobe. *Canales* (scuppers) protrude from the parapet at roof level. The few windows are not glazed but may have wooden bars and shutters. Plain wood lintels span openings. Heavy wood doors may be attractively carved. *Portale* posts are plain but may have decoratively sawn corbel brackets (*zapatas*). Log roof *vigas* (joists) may protrude through the wall but are usually sawn off and plastered over on houses.

CONSTRUCTION: Adobe brick walls up to 2 feet thick, built on shallow stone footings and plastered with a mixture of straw, sand, and wet mud. Wood *vigas* support a composite roof made of sticks (*latillas*) laid across the *vigas*, followed by a layer of brush and a thick surface of mud. Floors are of packed earth, often cured with a mixture of oxblood and ashes or later covered with wood planks.

Spanish planning and Pueblo Indian labor produced a Colonial architecture in northern New Mexico distinct from that of the Spanish settlements in California, despite their similar intentions and similar building materials. Remote from the skilled artisans and tradesmen of Mexico, limited to basic building materials, and without Spanish or

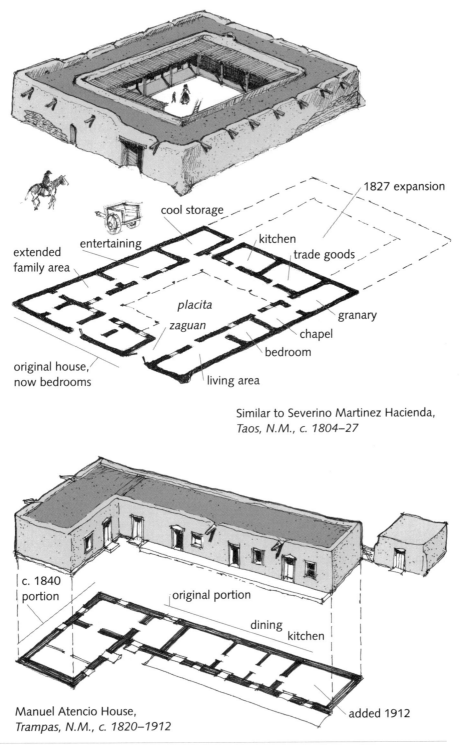

1827 expansion

cool storage

kitchen

entertaining

extended
family area

trade goods

placita

zaguan

granary

chapel

bedroom

original house,
now bedrooms

living area

Similar to Severino Martinez Hacienda,
Taos, N.M., c. 1804–27

c. 1840
portion

original portion

dining
kitchen

Manuel Atencio House,
Trampas, N.M., c. 1820–1912

added 1912

The Spanish Colonial Hearths

Mexican laborers, the missionaries still preferred to build with adobe blocks rather than use the "puddling" method of the Pueblo Indians—a process of building walls with thick layers of mud.

Thousands of Spanish New Mexico Houses have been lost; unless regularly maintained and protected from water damage, adobe soon reverts to its original state—mud. Thus only a few examples survive from the early 19th century to suggest the early architecture. Furthermore, these artifacts have endured numerous modifications over the years. A handful have been rescued, however, and some even rebuilt to their original form.

Garcia House, *Santa Fe, N.M., c. 1838*

Adobe dwellings of the 17th and 18th centuries ranged from the simplest one-room, dirt-floored structures to large haciendas enclosing *placitas* (courtyards). Typical rooms were about 13–15 feet wide, limited by the usable length of the available logs for *vigas*. A major function of these houses was to defend against marauding Apaches, Comanches, Navahos, and Plains Indians. Windowless exterior walls and rooftop battlements were part of the architecture until the mid-1850s, particularly for the large haciendas far from Spanish fortifications. In villages, smaller houses huddled around central squares for protection.

Taos, New Mexico, is a good place to see authentic pre-Territorial houses, particularly the Severino Martinez Hacienda (c. 1804), which has been properly restored and is open to the public.

The Spanish Colonial Hearths

Garcia House, *Santa Fe, N.M., c. 1838*

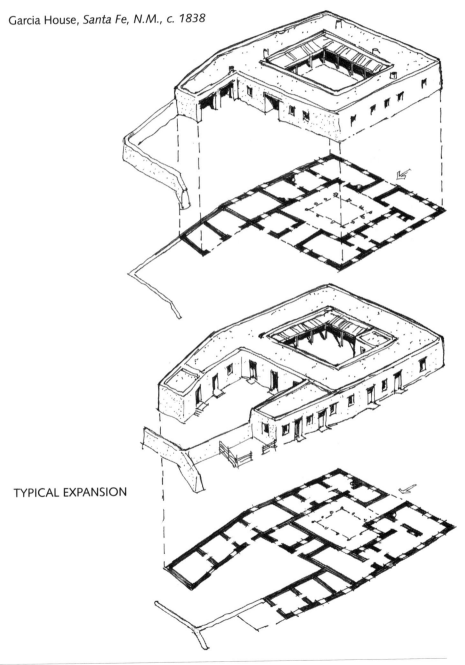

TYPICAL EXPANSION

The Spanish Colonial Hearths

Borrego House, *Santa Fe, N.M., c. 1842*

The New Mexican Territorial House (1848–1912)

FORM: Based on Spanish New Mexico Houses, usually 1 story, 1 room deep, L- or U-shaped or may fully enclose a central placita (courtyard).

STYLISTIC DETAIL: Similar to Spanish New Mexico style, with the addition of simplified Greek Revival detailing at wood-trimmed windows, doorways, and porches. Sash windows usually glazed. A peculiar but frequent detail is the dentiled brick coping along the top of adobe walls.

CONSTRUCTION: Traditional adobe brick building techniques combined with the innovations of sawn lumber and manufactured windows.

With increasing traffic along the Santa Fe Trail and the arrival of Anglo-Americans in the second quarter of the 19th century, new materials became available, and the rough, rudimentary character of much New Mexican architecture was refined into what is known as the Territorial Style. After the Civil War, East Coast style elements were imported in the form of Greek Revival detailing for windows and doors. Sawn lumber was also becoming available from local Anglo sawmills, and with the opening of the railroad, affordable glazed windows and other innovations could be brought from Kansas and Missouri. Houses were even built with gabled roofs and front porches. No longer fearing attack, the settlers added sizable windows to the outside walls, and inevitably new center-hall floor plans appeared, reflecting the increasing Anglo presence and an interest in Classical architectural features.

Commanding officer's quarters, *Fort Union, N.M., c. 1870*

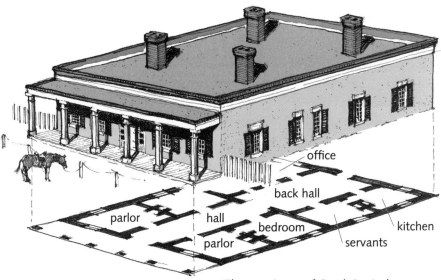

office

back hall

parlor | hall

bedroom

parlor | servants | kitchen

The army's use of Greek Revival
detailing on new structures was a major
factor in creating the Territorial style in
the Southwest.

Surprisingly compatible with the brown adobe vernacular, the Territorial Style's wood trim, usually painted white, brought a level of delicate sophistication that pleased the growing population, and it remained in vogue through the turn of the 20th century, lasting somewhat longer in remote areas. Adding to the charm of the style, adherence to the academically "correct" Classical details and proportions attempted back East was quite relaxed in New Mexico, where local craftsmen and builders added their own interpretations, often with delightful if irreverent results.

Borrego House, *Santa Fe, N.M.*

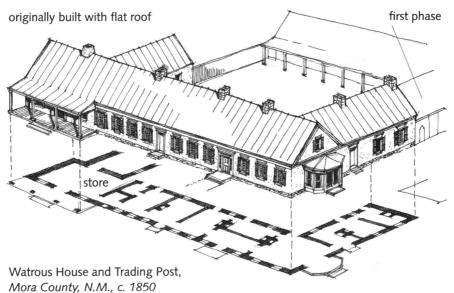

originally built with flat roof

first phase

store

Watrous House and Trading Post,
Mora County, N.M., c. 1850

simplified Greek
Revival detailing

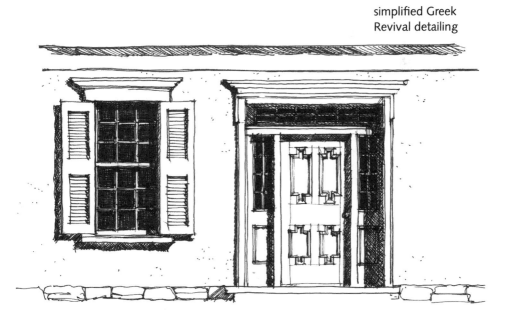

WINDOW AND MAIN ENTRY
detail of Watrous House

Casa Abrego, *Monterey, Calif., c. 1835*

The Spanish California House (1769–1848)

FORM: Typically low, 1-story, 1-room-deep house forming three sides of a high-walled courtyard, but may be L-shaped or single file. The floor level is nearly at grade. Shed and gabled roofs are gently sloped; some are flat. Eaves may extend to shade walls. A continuous *portale* (porch) roof supported on posts faces the courtyard. No towers. Some 2-story houses were built in the north.

STYLISTIC DETAIL: Very plain, although posts along the portale may be carved and painted. Small punched windows are spaced along the outside walls, usually one to a room. Stucco walls were often whitewashed. Sash windows (typically 6-over-6) are an Anglo feature appearing after 1830.

CONSTRUCTION: Usually thick, plastered, adobe brick walls on a loose stone foundation. Roofs were covered with locally made clay tiles on a framework of wood beams tied together with rawhide strips.

The surviving architecture from the Spanish era of Alta (upper) California consists almost entirely of well-known late-18th- and early-19th-century missions. Functioning as small villages, the missions initially included dwellings within their walls as well as churches, storerooms, barracks, and various other workshops and service spaces wrapped around a large courtyard or plaza. Settlement was very sparse, with only a few missionaries; the military contingent never numbered more than a few hundred soldiers along the entire coastline, and few settlers made the trek from Mexico, let alone farther away.

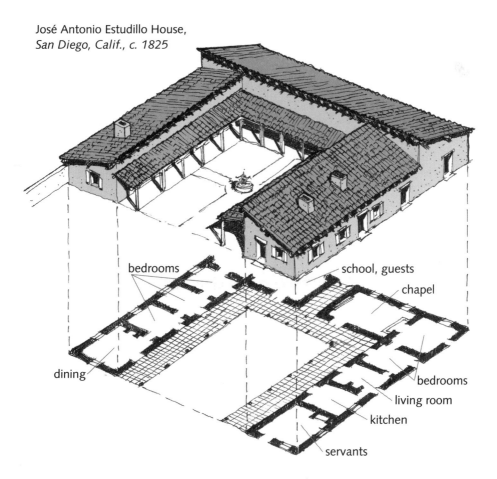

José Antonio Estudillo House,
San Diego, Calif., c. 1825

bedrooms

school, guests

chapel

dining

bedrooms

living room

kitchen

servants

Little has been written about early detached houses in California, although some historians refer to one- and two-room dwellings (made of adobe), a configuration that, as in every Colonial settlement hearth, preceded more substantial homes. As the Spanish and missionary influence waned, the land was given over to large farms and ranches, and the region grew more prosperous. More permanent *casas* (houses) were built; most of the survivors seen today date from the 1830s and '40s.

The first free-standing houses of note (ancestors of the omnipresent American ranch house) had extended floor plans of several rooms in a line, bending to form an L or a U shape enclosing a courtyard in the familiar Spanish style. A typical *casa poblador* (townhouse) might have as many as twelve or more rooms, all opening directly onto a continuous *coreodor* (veranda) overlooking gardens and fruit trees in the courtyard. Like the missions, it featured a chapel, kitchen, dining room, bedrooms, and a guest room, as well as a servant's room. Finer homes included libraries and wine rooms. The shaded *portales* or *coreodors* and other outdoor areas served as living spaces, the distinction between indoors and outdoors less obvious than in English-derived homes or even those in other Spanish colonies, such as New Mexico.

Spanish California Colonial houses were extremely plain and rustic, almost crude, this period being one of the very few in American history when a landowner's worth was not judged by the appearance of his house. The settlers did not seem to need conspicuous architectural ornament, Classical or otherwise, to assure others (or themselves) of their worth as citizens. Other customs served that purpose, with generous hospitality being particularly important, as well as more personal displays of wealth in the form of silver- and gold-trimmed clothes and accessories and fine saddles and horses. While household amenities common in the eastern United States were absent in California, the more relaxed, comfortable lifestyle had its own rewards.

Sherwood Ranch (Old Adobe), *Salinas, Calif., c. 1824*

Stokes House, *Monterey, Calif., c. 1835*

The Monterey House (1835–80)

FORM: Typically a rectangular 2-story house with a full-length second-floor porch along the street side. Porch may be cantilevered or supported on posts, forming a first-level porch. Low-pitched gabled roof or, less common, a hipped roof.

STYLISTIC DETAIL: Simple unadorned, whitewashed adobe walls. Carved or beveled porch columns and plain balusters at porch railings. The symmetrical arrangement of windows and doors arrived with the American settlers, as did the attempt at Greek Revival porch columns.

CONSTRUCTION: Plastered adobe brick or exposed rough stone.

Sparsely settled by the Spanish and Mexicans, by 1848–49 central California was full of Americans drawn to the gold rush. Settlers flooded into Monterey and San Francisco, bringing their eastern building traditions with them. In the haste to build new communities, Spanish casas and ranchos were generally ignored as models, and, with a ready supply of wood, midcoastal towns took on a simplified eastern Colonial flavor, with two-story, clapboard houses, including Saltboxes. Soon whole knocked-down houses were being ordered from Maine, Massachusetts, and even the Far East.

The few professional architects, who were mostly from the East, favored the fashionable Italian and French Renaissance styles for finer homes. The casas, haciendas, and the gracious Hispanic style of living were slipping away. However, as early as 1835 a few settlers, recognizing

Larkin House,
Monterey, Calif., 1835

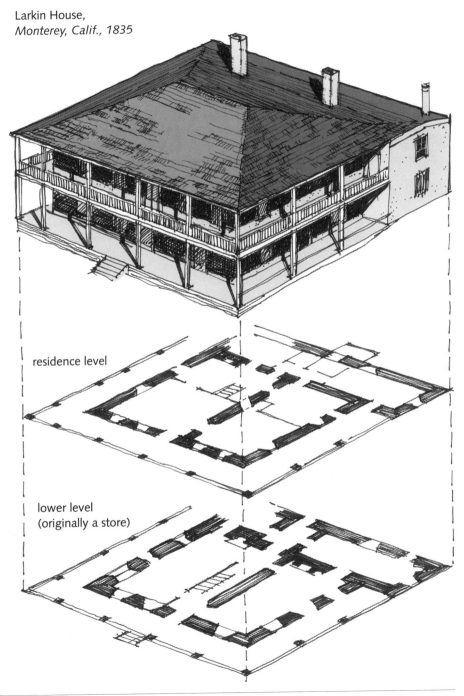

residence level

lower level
(originally a store)

the comfort and practicality of the local building practices, combined Hispanic and Anglo traditions to produce what is now called the Monterey style. A wood-shingled, gable-ended roof stretching over a cantilevered upstairs porch, shading whitewashed adobe walls, is the essence of the original style, although red tile roofs and porches supported on posts were also common. The style faded through the 19th century but appeared as a "revival" in the early 20th. With the explosive growth of suburbs across the nation, there was renewed interest in a pseudo-Monterey style from about 1920 to midcentury. Assorted interpretations appeared nearly everywhere, most sharing with the originals an upstairs balcony, white stucco imitating adobe, and little else.

Historians cite the Boston merchant Thomas Larkin as having launched the style with an innovative home built in Monterey in 1835. His two-story, hipped-roof house stood out among the single-story Spanish casas, resembling a Mississippi Creole plantation house as much as anything, and it was much imitated. Its most distinguishing feature, the second-level porch, had plenty of precedents in Spain and Mexico. Although the squarish form may appear to have East Coast origins, it may simply have followed the footprint of Larkin's store on the first floor. The style can, in any case, be regarded as a Mexican-Californian style (rather than Spanish-Californian), since it appeared between Mexico's independence from Spain (1821) and the American flag-raising at Monterey (1846). Many homes in the Monterey style were built along the coast from San Diego to Sonoma. Few remain today, victims of neglect as well as overly ambitious restoration.

Larkin House, *Monterey, Calif., c. 1835*

Ortega House, *Monterey, Calif., c. 1835*

Part Two
19th-Century Styles

The Early Classical Revival
Neoclassicism, Neoclassical Revival, Classical Revival

Architecturally, the period between the Georgian and Victorian eras, from 1780 to about 1830, was a time of searching for forms and elements suitable for the new republic. During the Colonial period, there were few if any professional architects, and few of the early settlers had much grasp of Classical architecture. No masons were available to lay up a vaulted ceiling, let alone engineers to design one. Although there was a general lack of enthusiasm for the very English Georgian façades—particularly after the Revolution—many builders still looked to England for direction. Others, like Thomas Jefferson, turned to the Greek and Roman classicism then in vogue in France, and a steadily increasing flow of publications from Europe featured drawings and interpretations of Renaissance architecture.

A few English architects visited Athens, returning with misty, romantic images of the Greek origins of democracy. In 1796 the talented Benjamin Henry Latrobe (1764–1820) and several other British architects came to America and virtually founded the profession of architecture here, bringing with them a knowledge of engineering and training in professional design in the English manner. The amateur architect Charles Bulfinch (1763–1844) returned to Boston in 1787 after a European tour that included an exposure to the designs of Robert Adam (1728–92), the prominent London architect and Classical scholar.

This mix of influences led to America's first national architectural expression—what some now call the Early Classical Revival period. Despite its European roots, it produced some uniquely American styles:

Federal-Adamesque, Jeffersonian Classicism, and the pervasive Greek Revival. They were the first architectural symbols of the country's somewhat tenuous but hopeful experiment with democracy.

In addition to building a capital city in the feverish swamps of the Potomac River, the nation also needed to provide structures for a fledgling banking system, religious activities, colleges, and other public functions. The affluent politicians, planters, financiers, and their architects — collectively the executors of aesthetic affairs in the new United States — tried not to take inspiration from their own Colonial buildings. They reached into the past beyond the recent Age of Enlightenment, the glowing Renaissance, and the dimmer Gothic ages back to the dusty, vine-covered ruins of ancient Rome and Athens, seeking legitimacy among what they believed to be the origins of republican ideals.

In the 18th century, Georgian houses and table manners had helped contribute to the distinction between a prosperous elite and those aspiring to prosperity. The Federal period after the Revolution continued that tradition, providing even more stylish homes for thriving traders of fish, rum, and other goods often related to the slave trade. The refinement of Classical detail during the Federal period, influenced by the scholarly Robert Adam, led directly to the American Classical Revival. The Federal-Adamesque Style can be seen as either the last gasp of Georgian geometry or a refinement of it. Whereas the Federal was largely a residential style, the more recognizably Roman and Greek styles that followed were intended for important public buildings and monuments. The Greco-Roman character did find its way into the design of homes, however, first in elegant homes (as always), but eventually in the simpler American vernacular as well.

Thomas Jefferson, as ambassador to France during the Revolutionary War, came into close contact with ancient Roman architecture and French aesthetic ideals. At the same time, archaeology was providing new insights into antiquity. In contrast to crumbling ruins, newly excavated sites provided a richer, more detailed view of Roman culture. The resulting study of the many Roman building types other than temples enhanced Jefferson's appreciation and confirmed, at least to him, that Roman architecture was an ideal model for American buildings: monumental in scale, inspirational, and permanent. Returning to America, Jefferson, as both statesman and architect, promoted this architecture aggressively as an appropriately "official" aesthetic, particularly for the new capitol. Jeffersonian Classicism was meant to revive what was, in Jefferson's view, the highest form yet of human society, that of republican Rome. His penchant for a scholarly approach to the use of Classical Roman orders contributed to their acceptance among architects and builders in the first quarter of the 19th century, particularly in the South.

Archaeologists also descended on Greece, of course, and with the spread of new information on its culture, including architecture, a remarkable affinity for ancient Greece developed in the United States. Jefferson himself avoided the Greek Revival Style on aesthetic and philosophical grounds, but his own Roman Revival found its finest expression in his magnificent Monticello and the University of Virginia campus. However, there was no one to carry his ideas forth in the face of the Hellenistic wave, and the builders' guides for the Roman orders were neglected until the American Classical Revival at the end of the century. Beginning around 1820, a decisive shift to the Greek orders of architecture made Greek Classical Revival America's own peculiar aesthetic for thirty years, not only for public buildings but for homes across all social classes (even, although rarely, for slave quarters) and far into the frontier. This devotion was based partly on the simple direct beauty of Greek forms, as well as on an idealized notion of Greek culture as being ancestral to American democracy. In addition, Americans felt a great empathy with the Greeks' struggle for independence from the Turks then in progress. Replicas of Greek temples did appear in Europe, particularly in England, as part of institutional buildings. But as residential architecture, they were generally restricted to garden gazebos and such, never achieving the wide popularity found in the United States.

Vernacular building traditions continued, of course, following the settlers along the trails and river valleys west to the remote frontier. But the settlers took with them a spreading stylistic awareness, and farmhouses and other buildings often included some element of Classical styles, if only in a touch of detail applied to a doorway or a pair of Doric columns supporting a porch roof.

Dodge-Shreve House, *Salem, Mass.*

The Federal-Adamesque Style (1780–1820)
Adam Style

FORM: Typically, a 5-bay symmetrical block of 2 or 3 stories, slightly wider than deep, on a raised basement. Often has a very low pitched hipped roof that can appear nearly flat from the street or may be side-gabled with a gentle roof pitch. Less common, steeply pitched roofs may show dormers, original or added. Chimneys are at either end or interior but not necessarily prominent or symmetrically arranged. High ceilings except at the third floor. Bowed or polygonal window bays are common. Townhouses proliferate.

STYLISTIC DETAIL: Simple flat walls; evenly spaced tall sash windows with flat or pedimented lintels, sometimes ornamented. Keystone lintels are common in masonry walls. Tall, double-hung windows (occasionally triple-hung) at the first level, where they reach nearly to the floor. Shorter windows on the highest floor. Large panes with slim muntins, typically 6-over-6. In brick masonry, windows may be set in the recesses of blind arches. Palladian windows are common above the entry. Louvered shutters. Belt courses are occasional in masonry, while inset panels are found under second-story windows in both wood and masonry façades, sometimes decorated with low-relief swags and cartouches. The ornamental entry with paneled doors is sometimes recessed. Sidelights and fanlights incorporate a delicate tracery in wood or lead. The entry porch is typically 1 story and often semicircular, with slim, widely spaced Classical columns and pilasters. Balustrades along the eaves conceal the roofline. Decorative cornices may have dentils.

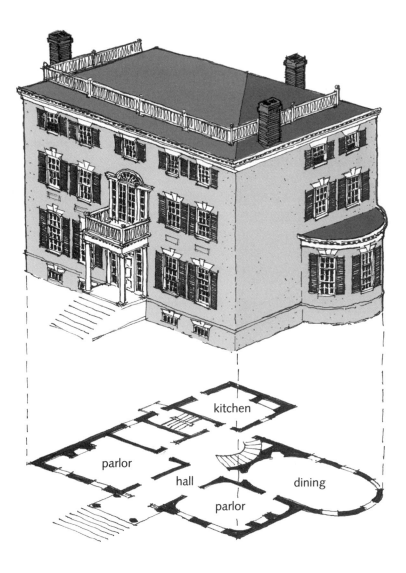

CONSTRUCTION: With notable exceptions, generally wood frame and weatherboard siding in the North, stone and brick masonry in the mid-Atlantic, and brick in the South. Stucco is less common but found in all regions.

A refinement of the ubiquitous Georgian style, Federal-Adamesque residences became fashionable in the prosperous seaports along the Atlantic coast after the Revolutionary War. Some have called it the first American style, although its origins are certainly British, with elements derived from the Classical orders. While superficially resembling Georgian architecture, Federalist architecture looks more to Rome, with its emphasis on Classical detail. It is not coincidental that professional architects found their place in this period. Their pattern books played an important role in promoting the Federal Style and in successive architectural developments throughout the 19th century.

Although varying somewhat due to regional preferences for brick, stone, or wood, all versions of the Federal-Adamesque Style show a certain restrained elegance in contrast to the more ponderous Georgian. This relatively light and delicate character combined understated façades with lacy, decorative motifs interpreted from the work of Robert Adam (1728–92), the prominent British architect. A serious student of Classical antiquity and archaeological sites, Adam's personal innovations had, by the 1770s, vanquished the more rigid Palladian fashion that had dominated English design for decades.

The Boston architect Charles Bulfinch (1763–1844) discovered Adam's work on his European tour and is generally credited with bringing Adamesque design to the United States. Here, Asher Benjamin's famous pattern books brought Bulfinch's less flamboyant interpretations of Adamesque detail to thousands of American carpenters and housewrights. Federal-Adamesque architecture was used for churches and institutional buildings, most notably Bulfinch's Massachusetts State House in Boston, but it was primarily a residential style. Interiors were a significant aspect, often showing more innovation than the somewhat static exteriors. Gracefully curved open stairways were typical, as were elaborate window, door, and fireplace surrounds that included Classically decorated pediments and pilasters. The dining room ceiling at George Washington's Mount Vernon plantation is often cited as the first example of Federal design in the United States; more important than the decorative touches were the creative developments in floor planning, with elliptical, rounded rooms and domed or arched ceilings.

Gardner-Pingree House,
Salem, Mass., c. 1805

Magwood House,
Charleston, S.C., 1827

Samuel Hermann House,
New Orleans, La., 1832

The Early Classical Revival

Federal-Adamesque was an architecture not of farmhouses but of urban prosperity. It reflected a growing wealth in the new republic, at least among the "triangular traders" in the expanding cities along the East Coast. Not surprisingly, their homes featured much crafting of decorative detail, and their elegant interiors and floor plans accompanied the growing emphasis on entertaining and individual privacy, as well as Classical architecture.

Swept aside in the rush to the Greek Revival, which it fostered, Federal-Adamesque design didn't last long enough to be a significant part of the westward expansion. Still, well-preserved Federal houses can be found today from Maine to Georgia, with particularly good examples in Salem, Massachusetts; Providence, Rhode Island; the environs of Washington, D.C.; and Charleston, South Carolina.

Nathaniel Russell House,
Charleston, S.C., 1809

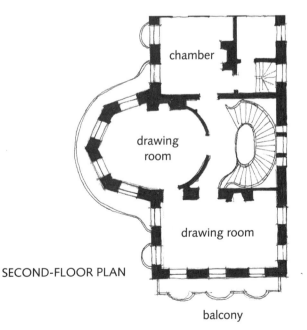

chamber

drawing
room

drawing room

SECOND-FLOOR PLAN

balcony

Monticello, *Charlottesville, Va., c. 1772–1809*

Jeffersonian Classicism (1770–1830)
Roman Revival

FORM: Typically either a symmetrical 1- to 2-story Georgian block or a gable-fronted, 3-part temple form with wings. The 5-part Palladian plan was rare. A full-height columned and pedimented portico is common. There may be a second-story porch over the entry behind the columns. Low-sloped hip or gable roof. Any dormers were probably added. Windows are arranged symmetrically. A raised foundation is typical.

STYLISTIC DETAIL: Classical columns and entablature, especially Tuscan and Doric, less frequently Ionian and Corinthian. Plain entablature. Windows, doors, sidelights, and trim are variable but likely to follow Federal-Adamesque example. Semicircular or elliptical fanlights over paneled single or double doors and semicircular, round, or oval windows in pediments are common. Note that Classical detailing was frequently added to earlier Georgian houses, thereby confusing their histories.

CONSTRUCTION: Typically red brick with white trim, occasionally timber frame with clapboard or stucco finish or sometimes stone masonry.

A relatively short-lived residential style inspired by Roman public buildings rather than country houses or villas, Jeffersonian Classicism closely resembles the Greek Revival that followed it. Primarily a southeastern style, it is centered in Virginia but seen also in Maryland, North Carolina, and occasionally as far west as Kentucky and Missouri. In its simplest block form, it is distinguished from Maryland and

Arlington, *Natchez, Miss., 1819–20*

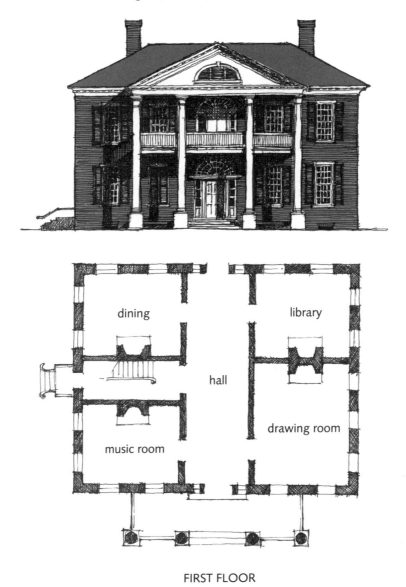

FIRST FLOOR

Virginia Georgian by the full-height Classical porticoes. It is an applied architecture rather than a new fundamental concept, with floor plans retained from the Georgian period. The temple form's three- or five-part plan was generally a one-room-deep, single-pile layout reflecting a continuing interest in Palladio's designs.

Thomas Jefferson saw Rome's architecture, as well as its republican form of government, as a model for the United States, for it offered a wide range of building types compared to other styles. Already an admirer of Palladio's, Jefferson became convinced of the possibilities of Classical design when, as ambassador to France (1785–89), he personally visited the remains of Roman structures and was particularly impressed by the Maison Carrée at Nîmes. The University of Virginia, the Virginia capitol at Richmond, dozens of county courthouses and banks, and much of official Washington, D.C., were built in an American image of Roman temples and government buildings.

Ridgeway, *St. Matthews, Ky., c. 1804–5*

The best-known example of residential Jeffersonian Classicism is Jefferson's own home, Monticello, which he designed and modified over several decades. Not wholly typical of the style, it is a unique and personal architectural statement that nevertheless reveals Roman and Palladian roots with its Roman orders, its temple form, and its composition in the landscape. Jeffersonian Classicism is often lumped with the Federal-Adamesque Style or the Greek Revival into one Neoclassical Style, and the differences between them are somewhat blurred. Some examples show Federal tendencies, and others lean toward the Greek, while Monticello seems nearly to exist on its own.

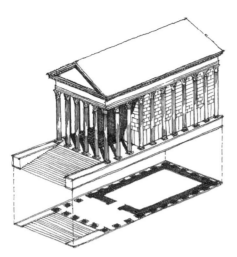

Maison Carrée, *Nîmes, France, c. A.D. 1–10,* Jefferson's inspiration

Monticello

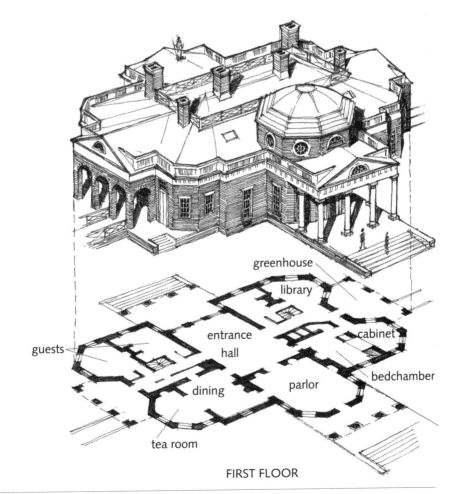

greenhouse

library

entrance hall

cabinet

guests

bedchamber

dining

parlor

tea room

FIRST FLOOR

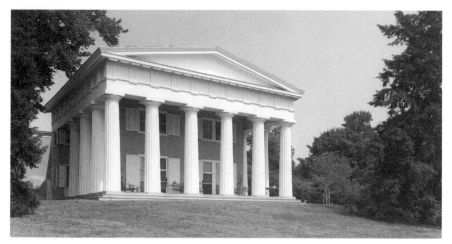

Andalusia, *Bucks County, Pa., portico c. 1836–38*

The Greek Revival (1825–60)
Grecian Style

FORM: Highly variable, but typically a formal 1- or 2-story house with full-height columns supporting a front pediment gable. Heavy entablature and cornices. Gentle roof pitch. Generally symmetrical façade, but entry may be to one side. No arches or domes. Chimneys are not prominent. The temple variant will have lower wings to each side. Vernacular versions are often a simple gable-front or gable-front-and-wings composition with applied Greek Revival features on the façade.

STYLISTIC DETAIL: Classical Greek orders with Ionic and occasionally Doric columns or pilasters and entablature. Columns may be square. Paneled doors, sometimes recessed, can have elaborate frames and trim with rectangular sidelights and transoms. Large double- or triple-hung windows. Small horizontal windows occasionally mounted in the frieze may be decoratively screened. Houses were nearly always painted white.

CONSTRUCTION: Variable, though not particularly innovative. Structure was commonly of timber frame or, less frequently, masonry. Classical columns were sometimes of brick, plastered.

Irresistible to the country's first crop of young architects and their prospering clients, Grecian Style (as it was known) swept through all the states and westward with the expansion. Although the Greek Revival eventually took many shapes, it was the classic form of the Parthenon that inspired the design of a prominent Philadelphia bank (and an

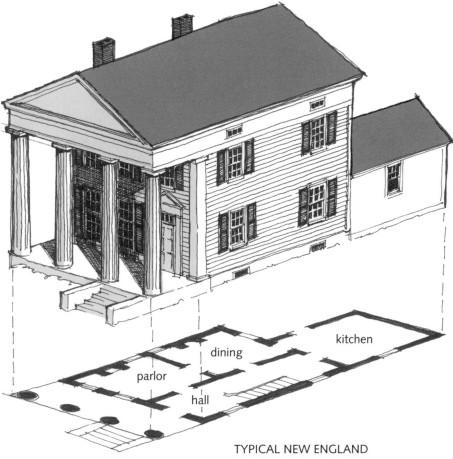

TYPICAL NEW ENGLAND
GREEK REVIVAL HOUSE, *c. 1840*

addition to the house, Andalusia, of the noted financier Nicholas Biddle). Banks sporting columns and entablature soon sprouted everywhere, thereby identifying Hellenistic architecture with economic security. Sweeping aside the Federal and Roman forms, the new style became nearly universal fashion for public buildings and churches as well as financial houses and town halls.

As a building type, the Greek temple was spatially ill suited to all but the most determined residential adaptation, so stylistic detail in the form of columns and pediments was applied to Georgian houses and other rectangular floor plans. The Greek Revival style is often credited for introducing the side-passage, gable-fronted house that flourished throughout American settlements in the 19th century. Structural integrity was no problem for these new front porches with their massive columns. Originally designed to support heavy, short-span stone blocks in ancient Greece, the columns were far more than was needed to carry a wood entablature. A real problem was the difficulty in fitting the growing variation of household activities into a rectangular box, shown by the frequent addition of a wing at the rear to accommodate service functions and additional bedrooms while preserving the "temple" in front.

Mayfield, *West Chester, Pa., c. 1848–51*

In the South, the Greek Revival took different forms and persisted longer than in other regions. Screens of two-story columns were wrapped around shaded Creole plantation house galéries, creating the familiar brooding character of antebellum mansions in Alabama, Louisiana, and Mississippi, with less attention paid to "correct" Classical proportions than in the North.

Approximations of Greek Revival detailing also found their way to the thousands of vernacular village homes and farmhouses quickly going up across the expanding Midwest. Doorway moldings, window frames, and the columns supporting porch roofs were carved and milled to suggest Classical details. Otherwise simple dwellings were often adorned with pediments and friezes. This ubiquity underlines the surprisingly broad appeal of a style representing a distant, idealized culture that few of the rural populace understood. What the Philadelphia bankers had envisioned was enthusiastically accepted and followed across the country.

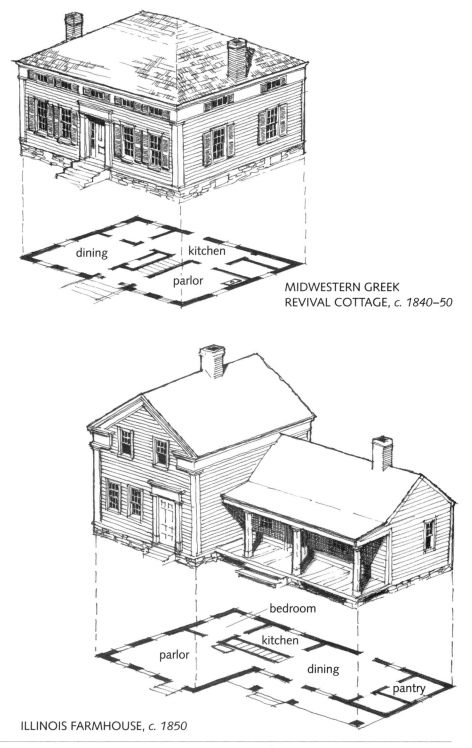

MIDWESTERN GREEK
REVIVAL COTTAGE, *c. 1840–50*

dining

kitchen

parlor

bedroom

kitchen

parlor

dining

pantry

ILLINOIS FARMHOUSE, *c. 1850*

Early Victorian Styles

The dozen or so architectural styles commonly considered Victorian were built from as early as 1820 until the Second World War, but they reached their peak during Queen Victoria's reign, from 1837 to 1901. The rich variety of styles ranges from the moody Gothic Revival to the fanciful, highly decorative Queen Anne and Second Empire and includes such remarkable digressions as Orson Squire Fowler's Octagon houses and H. H. Richardson's Romanesque Revival.

What these seemingly disparate styles have in common are their roots in the 18th-century English "picturesque" movement. Inspired partly by romantic French landscape painters like Claude Lorraine and Nicolas Poussin, English landscapers sought to create a "natural" environment for their clients rather than tightly controlled geometric gardens, and architects designed country houses that could rest gracefully in these more relaxed surroundings. Many chose the Gothic style's expressive detailing to complement this naturalistic setting rather than the restrained Classical design associated with formal gardens.

This choice had a considerable impact on the design of 19th-century houses in the United States. By the 1840s, the Classical orders that had been so entwined with early republican ideals were being replaced by more innovative styles. Population growth and expansion, not only westward along the frontier but from crowded town centers to more spacious outlying areas, were creating a demand for more comfortable homes. Farming became a more solidly market-oriented business rather than a near-subsistence occupation, and farm families wanted better houses. In the large cities, mass immigrations from Europe drove growing numbers of earlier residents out to new suburbs. There they found more room for large homes in "picturesque" surroundings, which not only provided space and comfort but advertised their higher social standing.

Meanwhile, technical innovations allowed homes to be built and maintained more efficiently and economically. The availability of milled lumber in standard dimensions, cheap manufactured nails, and power tools enabled more families to build sizable homes. Workmen with steam-driven scroll saws and shapers could create Gothic flourishes without the expense of special tradesmen or artisans. The revolutionary balloon frame method, which used smaller, lighter, more manageable framing members, quickly became the standard structural system, replacing the heavy timber frame. Abandoning the rigid rectangular form freed up restrictive floor plans, and far more efficient cast iron stoves replaced open fireplaces, allowing larger rooms that could be placed farther from the heat source. Outside, the new mechanical mower allowed ordinary homes to have lawns, a luxury previously enjoyed only by the gentry.

The expansion of industry and commerce was also having a growing impact on family life. The new sources of wealth — factories, banks, railroads, and other businesses — were increasingly distant, requiring the male breadwinners (and perhaps older children as well) to spend their entire days away from home. In this sharper separation of domestic life and public profession, the care of the home and the raising of children became ever more firmly the wife's domain. This division of labor eroded the pyramidal, agrarian model of the family, where work was often shared. Women did gain authority in the house but became isolated from the burgeoning male world of business and commerce.

With no cultural model for this new form of family life, reformers of various stripes, including architects and other house designers, stepped forward to suggest ideal standards of domestic behavior. Architectural pattern and detail books that once taught carpenters how to apply Classical features to Colonial façades were being supplanted by books of house plans and magazines aimed directly at homeowners and housekeepers, offering idealized philosophies of domestic life. Included were detailed renderings of houses in romantic rural landscapes.

Early Victorian residential architecture was a release from the Classical confines of earlier styles, placing more emphasis on the needs of families than on abstract historical design principles. It was an architecture of domestic prosperity for many if not all Americans. With its generous spaces and decorative innovations, it became the American standard.

William Rotch House, *New Bedford, Mass., c. 1846*

The Gothic Revival (1840–60)

FORM: Highly variable but with a strong emphasis on the vertical. A common type is the symmetrical, 2-story, center-entry, side-gabled house, with a steeply sloping roof and deep overhangs. A centered cross gable or paired cross gables are common. Similar houses with irregular massing and floor plans are also typical. Broad porches almost always included. Brick chimneys are tall and slim, sometimes medieval in character. Rare, large castle-style mansions show battlements, towers, turrets, and parapeted gables, stepped and shaped, on irregular, complex building forms.

STYLISTIC DETAIL: Signature pointed arches at prominent windows and, less frequently, doors. Square-topped windows with hood molds are common, as is the false shaping of windows using wood panels and trim. Early examples have ornamental carved or sawn barge boards at gables, occasionally with decorative trusses. Typical also are finials at gable peaks, window tracery, leaded stained glass, and vertical, full-height, uninterrupted board-and-batten siding.

CONSTRUCTION: Stucco on brick or various wood sidings on balloon frame structure. Rarely stone or exposed brick.

The original Gothic architecture, primarily an ecclesiastical style, began to evolve from the Romanesque style in northern France about the middle of the 12th century and lasted until the 16th. Gothic builders invented variations in structure and lighting never before seen, as shown by the remarkable cathedrals of medieval France and England. The

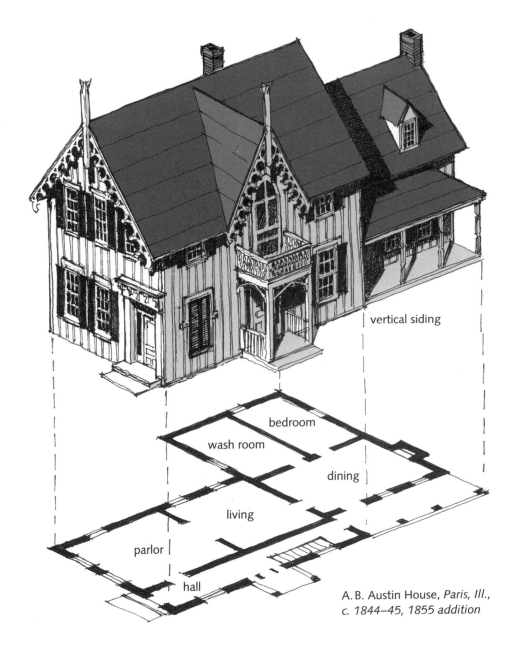

vertical siding

bedroom

wash room

dining

living

parlor

hall

A. B. Austin House, *Paris, Ill.,*
c. 1844–45, 1855 addition

term Gothic originated later in the 17th century as a term of derision suggesting that the style was as primitive as the Goths, who were said to have caused the Dark Ages by destroying Classical civilization.

In 18th- and 19th-century England, however, the Gothic came to be admired for its asymmetrical variety, which especially suited the informal landscaping of the picturesque movement. The signature pointed arch could be scaled up or down and adapted to wide or narrow openings, allowing it to serve country manors as well as churches. For the English, the Gothic Revival represented a virtuous, chaste, and medieval past, in contrast to the materialism of the noisy and egalitarian Industrial Age.

Americans in the early 19th century still looked to England for cultural guidance. The American landscape gardener Andrew Jackson Downing, impressed with the Gothic Revival, published books featuring Gothic designs by the architect Alexander Jackson Davis, his friend. These books had an enormous effect on American tastes, steering prospective middle-class homeowners away from the Greek orders toward the less academic but more practical picturesque.

A few Gothic Revival houses in the United States were rambling, castle-like stone mansions, some designed by Davis for wealthy clients, and show a looser grasp of medieval architecture than their English predecessors. Generally unfamiliar with the original Gothic style, American architects (except when designing churches) showed little concern for academic "correctness." Instead, they adapted Gothic detail to light wood frame construction, resulting in a decorative originality that was purely American. Early examples attempted to imitate the stone construction of the European originals, but American designers and builders soon used the wood vernacular to emphasize the Gothic character with vertical siding and wide, ornamental porches. Steam-driven scroll saws and lathes helped create the derivative Carpenter Gothic and Steamboat Gothic styles, which emphasized intricately sawn railings, crenelated moldings, and inventive window trim. Patterned barge boards and decorative trusses cast complex shadows under deep gable overhangs.

Downing's writings and Davis's designs also encouraged the building of picturesque cottages, which Downing defined as dwellings "so small that the household duties may all be performed by the family." These homes generally lacked the extravagant detail of Carpenter Gothic but displayed the familiar extended overhangs, the vertical board-and-batten siding, and other picturesque characteristics.

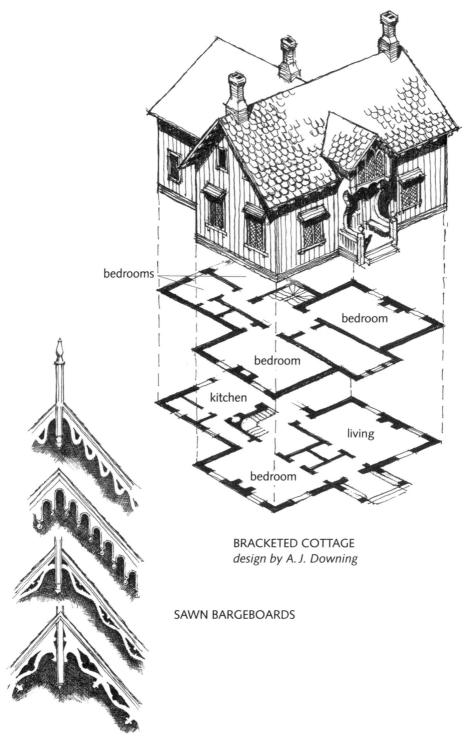

bedrooms

bedroom

bedroom

kitchen

living

bedroom

BRACKETED COTTAGE
design by A. J. Downing

SAWN BARGEBOARDS

Although symmetrical designs were common, irregular composition made a house more picturesque. The Gothic Revival's main contribution to the American house—large or small—was the loosening of the rigid floor plans of strictly rectangular Classical houses. Balloon framing allowed irregular building footprints that provided more useful spaces for a variety of family activities, as well as more privacy. Rooms were bumped out, and ells, turrets, and towers added.

Gothic Revival architecture appeared all across the country, though less often in the South. Essentially a rural or suburban style, it was associated with intellectual and literary pursuits. Owners of Gothic Revival homes were often considered unconventional if not eccentric. Interest in the Gothic style waned after the Civil War but revived again briefly as High Victorian Gothic later in the century.

GOTHIC REVIVAL WINDOWS

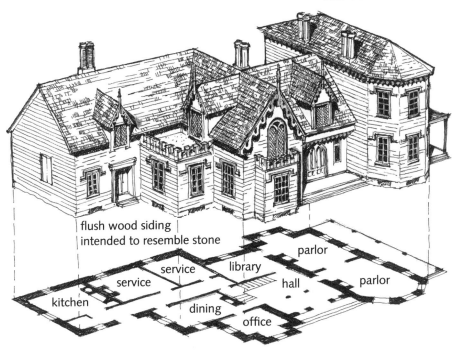

flush wood siding
intended to resemble stone

Kingscote, *Newport, R.I., 1839–41*

DOORWAYS

John Pitkin Norton House, *New Haven, Conn., c. 1849*

The Italian Villa (1830–80)
Country Italian

FORM: Typically an irregular, asymmetrical, 2-story L- or T-shaped house with a 3-story square (or, infrequently, octagonal) tower or campanile. Gently pitched hipped or, less often, gabled roof, both with extended eaves. Balconies, porches, and arcades connecting tower and base are common.

STYLISTIC DETAIL: Accent is on the vertical. Plain cornices under wide eaves have large, scrolled brackets, paired or single—the first consistent use of brackets in the United States. Tall windows, flat-topped or with round arches, may have heavy crown moldings or pediments. Frequently 1-over-1 glazing. Windows are often grouped in pairs or tripled. Early examples lack window trim. Bay windows are common. Smooth exterior finish, often in stucco. Corners are occasionally quoined. Arched openings along verandas. Balconies are balustraded.

CONSTRUCTION: Typically stucco on wood frame or brick. Smooth stone, exposed brick, and, rarely, clapboard or board-and-batten wood siding were also used. Tin or clay tile roofing was common.

The irregular massing of the Gothic Revival continued with the Italian Villa and came to dominate American taste in house design at midcentury. Though often grouped with Italianate, Italian Villa is a more rural style, while the former is more symmetrical and better suited to suburban building lots. Both, however, were inspired by the Renaissance villas and manors on the hilly, irregular ground of northern Italy.

ITALIAN VILLA,
design by A. J. Downing, 1850

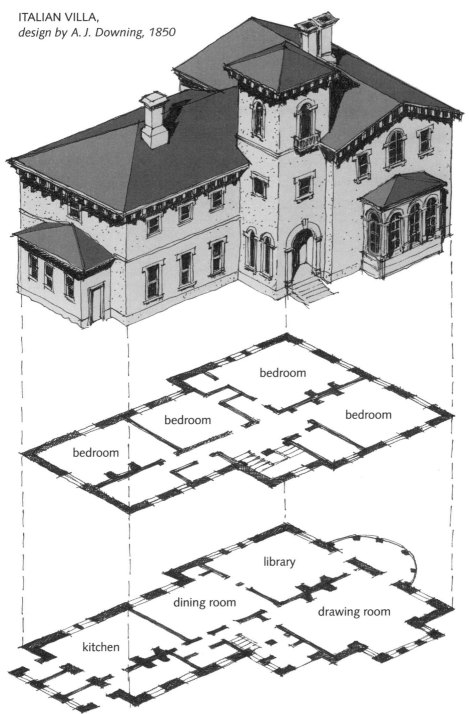

bedroom

bedroom

bedroom

bedroom

library

dining room

drawing room

kitchen

Filtered through the 18th-century English picturesque movement, the Italian Villa had an "irregular outline from every point of view," according to Samuel Sloan in *The Model Architect* (1852), a noted house plan book. Sloan notes slyly that the style "speaks of the inhabitant as a man of wealth ... as a person of educated and refined tastes ... who, accustomed to all the ease and luxury of a city life, is now enjoying the more pure and elevating pleasures of the country." Even so, Italian Villa was enthusiastically adopted by all levels of American society. Brackets and double windows (but not campaniles) were part of even modest midwestern farmhouses.

The campanile (tower), though not always present, tends to define this style, but its principal characteristic is the irregular structure enclosing an open, relaxed floor plan. Seen by some as a transition from the Gothic Revival to the Italianate Style, Italian Villa is clearly its own style, with roots easily traced to Italy rather than to medieval churches.

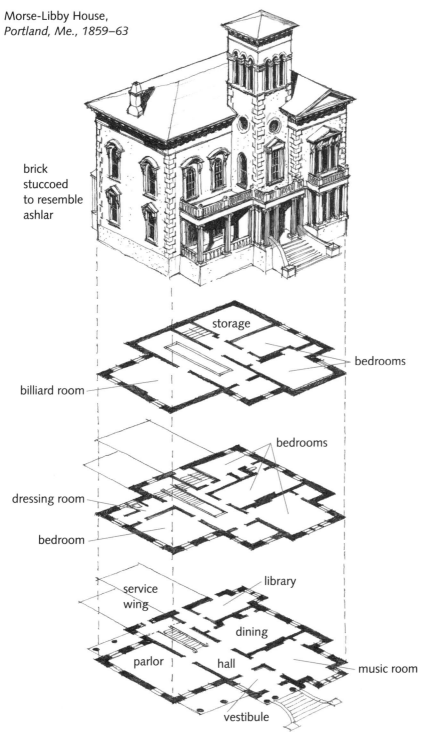

Morse-Libby House,
Portland, Me., 1859–63

brick
stuccoed
to resemble
ashlar

storage

bedrooms

billiard room

bedrooms

dressing room

bedroom

library

service
wing

dining

parlor

hall

music room

vestibule

Wyeth-Allyn House, *Cambridge, Mass., c. 1851*

The Italianate Style (1845–80)
American, Bracketed, Round, Tuscan, Lombard

FORM: Typically symmetrical, nearly square 2- or 3-story box with a gently sloping pyramidal roof, overhanging eaves, and a centered cupola. Asymmetrical examples not uncommon. A 1-story porch, centered or full width, is typical, as are balconies.

STYLISTIC DETAIL: Smoothly finished 3- or 5-bay façade. Decorative brackets, often paired, appear to support wide eaves. Tall, slim windows are usually larger on first floor than on upper levels. Windows may be round-topped, flat-arched, or squared off with elaborate decoration, including hood moldings. Occasionally, horizontal windows are mounted in a decorative cornice. Doors are often paired. May show quoins and string course. Lacy wrought-iron railings on balconies.

CONSTRUCTION: Conventional wood frame with stucco, or smooth masonry bearing walls. Tile roofs are common.

Unlike the Italian Villa style, the Italianate Style maintains the tighter, symmetrical floor planning of an earlier time and is an example of the recurring contests between formal symmetry and irregular massing. Whereas the Victorian Italian Villa (page 246) was a distinct, designed building form, the Italianate Style was more an ornamental variation on a smooth, familiar box. The frequent practice of adding Italianate detailing to various house forms and its widespread use in apartment buildings and row housing contributed to its wide visibility. Its relative simplicity of construction was also an advantage, and the decorative, bracketed

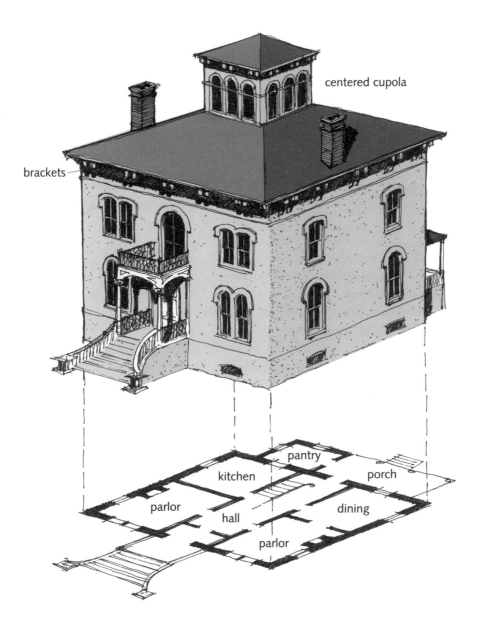

centered cupola

brackets

kitchen

pantry

porch

parlor

hall

dining

parlor

cornice under wide overhangs offered an aesthetically pleasing solution to the always difficult design problem of finishing off a nearly flat-roofed building. This combination of the familiar form and the "picturesque" decoration helped the Italianate Style maintain its dominance throughout the third quarter of the 19th century.

Another recognized and related Italian architectural style of the time was the severe Italian Renaissance Revival (1840–60), yet another English import. Frequently lumped with Italianate, it was rarely used for free-standing houses. Derived from Roman and Florentine Renaissance palazzi rather than country villas, the Italian Renaissance Revival was more tightly formal than the Italianate Style. Popular for public buildings and storefronts, it was also used for hundreds of brownstones and elegant townhouses after the Civil War, nearly always built of smooth ashlar stone. The later Second Italian Renaissance Revival (1890–1935) is similar in character and produced several notable homes (page 298).

Oddly, despite its great popularity, architectural books today devote less attention to the Italianate than to other midcentury styles. Perhaps because of its simplicity, it was susceptible to the public's later application of other styles' features, thus diluting the "pure" Italianate. When carpenters could build directly from plan books and substitute whole elevations or roof configurations at the client's whim, there was less need for architects, and the desire for unsullied "picturesque" architectural qualities began to fade.

ITALIANATE WINDOW SHAPES

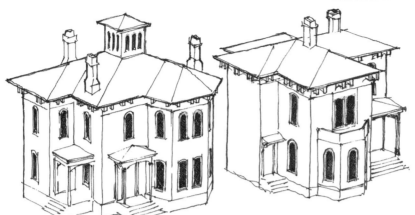

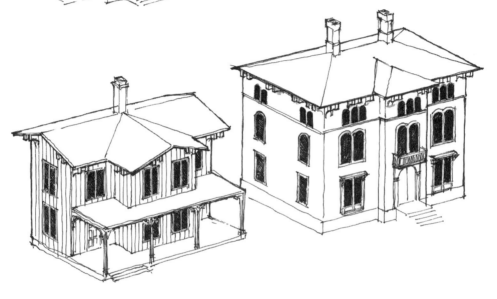

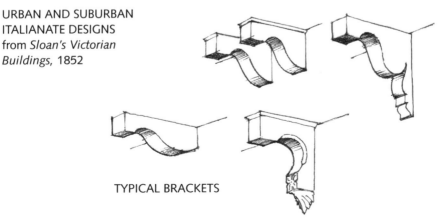

URBAN AND SUBURBAN
ITALIANATE DESIGNS
from *Sloan's Victorian
Buildings*, 1852

TYPICAL BRACKETS

McElroy Octagon, *San Francisco, Calif., c. 1860–61*

The Octagon (1850–60)

FORM: Octagonal floor plan. Typical examples are 2- or 3-story houses on raised basements, topped with an octagonal cupola or belvedere. A porch wrapping all or partway around the first floor is common. Overall mass varies considerably with the decorative style applied.

STYLISTIC DETAIL: Originally a simple, unstyled vernacular character; later examples ornamented in a variety of styles. Italianate bracketed versions dominated. A few architects' examples were dressed in Gothic Revival style.

CONSTRUCTION: Variable: wood, brick, or stone, but occasionally (and remarkably) of cast-in-place concrete.

Easily identified by its shape, the Octagon was not a style but a floor plan. It appeared in the 1850s at the high point of the Italian styles' popularity, and most of the survivors are Italianate in character. Although often considered a reaction to professionally designed and overdecorated Victorian houses, the Octagon accommodated the various decorative styles of the time. A spectacular surviving example, Longwood, in Natchez, Mississippi, is essentially Italianate but has Moorish trim topped by an onion dome.

Octagonal floor plans were not unknown in the early 19th century. The Octagon House (1800) in Washington, D.C., presently the headquarters of the American Institute of Architects, is a partial octagon, and Poplar Forest, Thomas Jefferson's second home, was

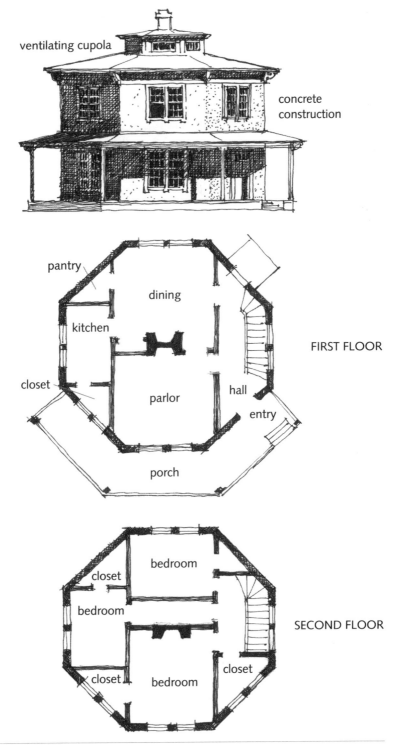

ventilating cupola

concrete
construction

pantry

dining

kitchen

FIRST FLOOR

closet

parlor

hall

entry

porch

bedroom

closet

bedroom

SECOND FLOOR

closet

closet

bedroom

started in 1806 on an octagonal plan. However, it was Orson Squire Fowler's architectural handbook *A Home for All* (1848) that established the residential octagon as a popular topic for discussion, if not always for construction. Fowler (1809–87) was smitten by what he felt was the

Octagon House, *Mendota, Ill., c. 1853*

geometric purity of the octagon. He prized the form not only for its beauty but for its efficiency and practicality, promoting it as the optimal shelter for the working-class family.

Fowler made a good case. He discovered that an octagonal perimeter enclosed 20 percent more space than a rectangular perimeter of the same length. Natural lighting was improved, with more rooms receiving sunlight than those in a conventional plan, while the cupola over the central stair provided healthy ventilation, a major concern of Fowler's. Corridors were minimized, and oddly shaped corners provided ample closet space while, in Fowler's view, the freer circulation encouraged family communication. He was also an early champion of "pebble dash" and "gravel wall" construction, 19th-century terms for cast-in-place concrete with stone aggregate, which was used for some octagon houses. He also promoted indoor plumbing and central heating.

Octagonal houses became something of a fad in the 1850s, mainly in the Northeast and upper Midwest, including a few flamboyant examples by noted architects for eccentric but affluent clients. Interest faded rapidly by the Civil War, however, and, aside from a few contemporary efforts, only a few hundred Octagons remain of the thousands Fowler inspired.

Armour-Steiner House,
Irvington, N.Y., c. 1860

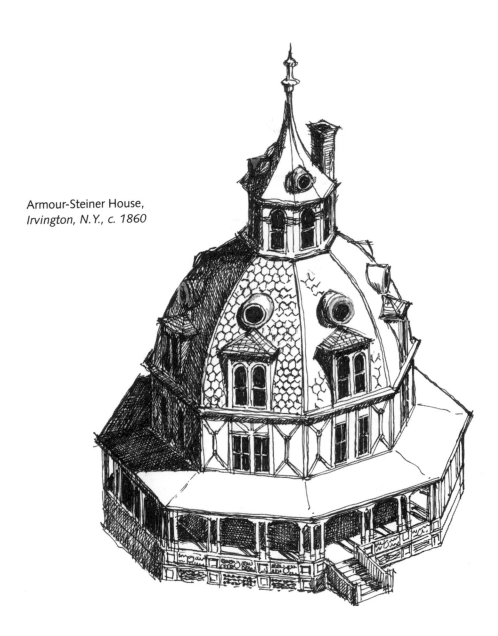

Late Victorian Styles

The houses that were built in this country from 1865 to 1900 in and around the cities and towns of the North and West were like no others in the world. The urban population explosion after the Civil War led to a huge demand for new housing in cities and towns while social reformers, preachers, and, of course, the house building industry espoused the ideal of "home and family." As house design books and building parts catalogues became available nationally, regionalism in residential design faded. Streetcars and trains brought newer, more distant suburbs within commuting distance—suburbs with space for large houses and available financing.

This postwar industrial, economic, and social energy resulted in a variety of architectural expressions that, as always, trickled down from the affluent strata of society, eventually reaching nearly everyone. Several distinct styles arose during this period: Second Empire, Stick, and Queen Anne are well known. The Shingle Style and H. H. Richardson's Romanesque, although not as prevalent in their pure form, were important in influencing later designers such as Frank Lloyd Wright and Louis Sullivan.

Yet houses built in the latter 19th century are not always easy to categorize. As floor plans were liberated and overall forms became more varied and complex, styles were increasingly defined by the shapes of openings and decorative trim around windows, doors, and porches, particularly at the front entry. Catalogues displayed varieties of readily available ornamentation in all styles, overriding the traditional authority of craftsmen and architects. The profession of architecture changed as members sought out the new class of the extremely wealthy, for whom they created lavish new styles. Some looked to the past for imagined prewar stability and wispy romance, then returned to the present for innovation and new technology. House architecture reflected this mingling of aesthetic decisions, often resulting in architectural cartoons still obvious today.

For the middle class, plan books now offered a wide choice of homes in several styles, each with an irregular floor plan. (This marked a change from the first half of the century, when architects like A.J. Downing promoted specific styles for the middle class.) By the time the mansard-roofed Second Empire Style became widely accepted, coherent distinctions between styles, such as those between Federal, Greek Revival, and Italian Villa, were no longer so obvious. Façades and interiors were built in any of the contemporary fashions, frequently in combination, while the mansard roof floated independently above the mélange of styles beneath. The practice of linking style to floor plan was rapidly eroding.

As the period wore on, the desire for still more opulent ornamentation resulted in an architecture of astounding exaggeration. Multifaceted shells enclosed dark, cluttered interiors filled with clashing wallpaper, paint, and fabrics. For many, this gluttony of consumption defines late Victorian house design; its ambiguities continued virtually unchallenged into the 20th century.

William Watts Sherman House, *Newport, R.I., c. 1875–76*

Captain Edward Penniman House, *Eastham, Mass., c. 1867–68*

Second Empire Style (1855–80)

FORM: Typically symmetrical 2-, 3-, or 4-story, square or L-shaped block. A double-pitched mansard roof forms a full additional story. Frequently a centered, full-height pavilion or taller tower is placed at the front entry, often with a different style of mansard roof. The outer roof pitch, almost always with dormers, is very steep; the rooftop is nearly flat. Centered cupolas are typical. Across the front or side, 1- or 2-story bay windows and full porches are common. Tall chimneys. Less imposing rural cottages may have only 1 story.

STYLISTIC DETAIL: May have any of several styles, from Federal to Shingle, but Italianate is most common. Mansard profiles can be straight, flared, or curved, varying even on the same building. Colored roof shingles and slate or tin tiles form decorative patterns. Ornate cast-iron cresting often lines perimeter roof ridges and towers. A full, bracketed cornice supports wide eaves. Windows can be very elaborate: arched, hooded, pedimented, and dentiled. First-floor windows are tall. Windows may be paired or tripled. Decorative chimney caps.

CONSTRUCTION: Typically stone but also brick or conventional wood frame with clapboard siding.

A further expression of 19th-century America's continuing interest in the "picturesque," the flamboyant Second Empire Style represented an escape from historic revivals. The mansard roof, which first appeared on 17th-century buildings designed by the French architect François Mansart, was revived during the reign of Napoleon III (1848–71). His ambitious

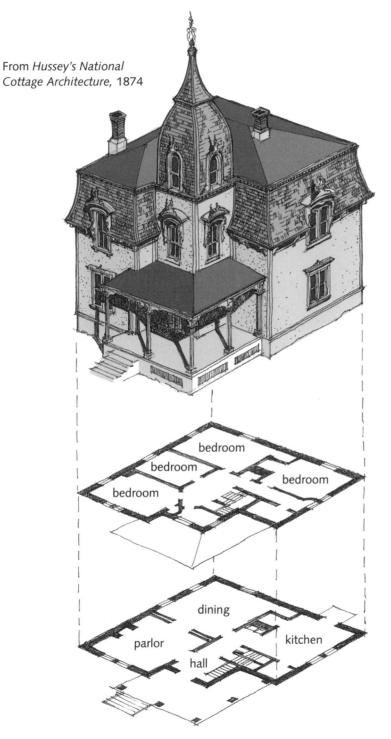

From *Hussey's National Cottage Architecture*, 1874

bedroom

bedroom

bedroom

bedroom

dining

parlor

kitchen

hall

revitalization of Paris from 1852 to 1865 (60,000 new buildings!) and the important Paris exhibitions of 1855 and 1867 displayed French prosperity and exposed international visitors to the new style.

As a result, in the 1860s and '70s American architects and builders began topping off Italianate houses with the fashionable mansard roofs, allowing room for a full extra floor rather than low-ceilinged attic space. This addition was useful, particularly for the rowhouses common in crowded urban areas. Its practicality soon led the Second Empire Style to be adapted to all sorts of buildings, from playful cottages to monumental institutional structures, giving them an ornate, if often haunting, dignity.

Domestic Second Empire is essentially a style of roof more than a style of house. Although any house of the period with a mansard roof may be identified as Second Empire, the term says little else about a house's character, which might reflect any of several fashions or even combinations of them. This less formal approach to design resulted in architectural ambiguities that defy classification, homes so encrusted with ornament that new terms had to be created to describe them.

Elliot House,
Petersburg, Va., 1880

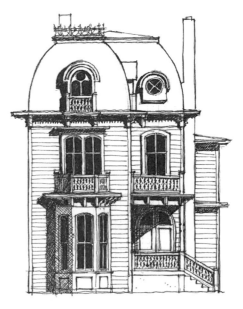

McDreary House,
Cape May, N.J., 1873

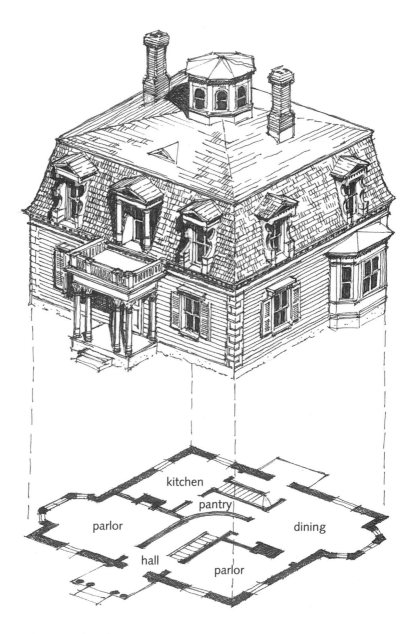

Captain Edward Penniman House,
Eastham, Mass., 1867–68

John N. A. Griswold House, *Newport, R.I., 1863–64*

Stick Style (1855–75)

FORM: An asymmetrical 2- or 3-story house, with an emphasis on the vertical. Articulated towers and projecting pavilions are common. Steep gable roofs have multiple intersecting forms. Projecting gables and eaves are occasionally flared. Jerkinhead gables not uncommon. Extensive porches and verandas.

STYLISTIC DETAIL: Textured wall surfaces of shingle, clapboard, or vertical board-and-batten panels, outlined with flat, projecting wood trim of vertical, horizontal, and diagonal "bracing." Windows, often doubled, are tied into the geometry of the façade. Large window panes; 1-over-1 or 2-over-2 are common. Husky, simple detailing uses shadowing to good effect, such as at the decorative trusswork at gable ends. Trim is usually straight-edged, not carved or turned. Porch supports are commonly simple, square posts diagonally braced. Large brick chimneys swell or "corbel out" near the top.

CONSTRUCTION: Balloon frame. All wood surfaces. Masonry foundations.

Stick Style is an interesting but relatively uncommon fashion, seen by some as a link between Gothic and Queen Anne. Its detailing somewhat resembles that of Gothic Revival, though its huskier scale and sturdy members foreshadow the coming Queen Anne. The "sticks" resemble medieval half-timbering, but they are not structural, and the use of straight, flat boards gives a more precise, geometric quality to the elevations. The undecorated, milled lumber is allowed to set the character of the house, indicating an acceptance of machined components straight

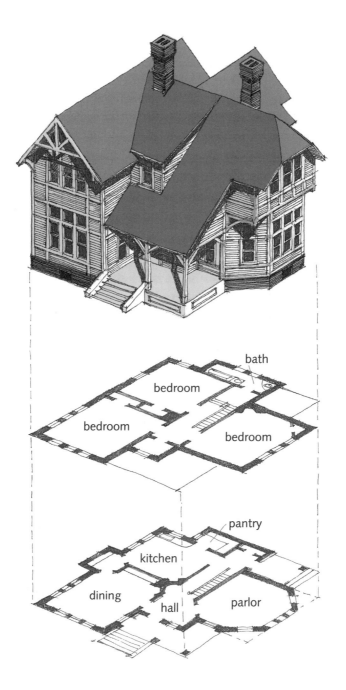

bath

bedroom

bedroom

bedroom

pantry

kitchen

dining

hall

parlor

from the mill and a rejection of style-parts catalogues — no imitation stone quoins here.

Each elevation is a composition of elements — dormers, corners, windows, doors, porches, and balconies — visually tied together with lines of boards, the "sticks." The resulting framed panels of shingle and siding textures are a deliberate part of the composition as well. In this sense, Stick may be said to have anticipated the Prairie Style and the Craftsman or "Western Stick" Style. Its advocates liked its supposed "truthfulness" in expressing the balloon frame structure within, though that honesty is a little strained, for the "sticks" are obviously applied trim, not structural members. Nevertheless, Stick exalts wood construction and is quite pleasing in houses large enough to display its patterns and textures.

Surviving examples are found mainly in the Northeast. The well-preserved Griswold House (1863) in Newport, Rhode Island, is a prime example of Stick Style and shows what a prominent architect (Richard Morris Hunt) could do with it. However, many good-sized Stick Style homes were built from mail-order plans, an increasingly common practice with all types of homes in the late 19th century. In the 1890s Stick Style traveled to California, becoming popular for townhouses, notably in San Francisco. There, with increasingly elaborate, lighthearted ornamentation, Stick homes took on their own special character. As was typical of the later Victorian period, the Stick motif was affixed to other house styles, and, like their contemporaries, Stick houses may occasionally display an eclectic range of ornament belonging to other styles as well.

Vincent Scully, the 20th-century art historian, gave Stick Style its name. In the prominent 1878 plan book *Paliser's American Cottage Homes*, no distinction is made between Stick and other Victorian styles.

Emlen Physick House, *Cape May, N.J., c. 1879*

Theophilus Conrad House, *Louisville, Ky., c. 1892–95*

Richardson Romanesque (1870–1900)
Romanesque, Romanesque Revival

FORM: Typically an asymmetrical, irregular, 3- or 4-story house under a hipped or gabled roof with cross gables. Round or sometimes octagonal corner towers (or both) with conical roofs. Wide, shaded porches and arcades, some recessed. Variable chimneys. A few urban houses were simple rectangles.

STYLISTIC DETAIL: Rough stone texture, or rusticated ashlar, decoratively arranged in contrasting natural hues. Round, semicircular arches are wide relative to their height and typically set on pairs or triplets of short sturdy columns or piers with cushion capitals. Floor lines and cornices provide strong horizontal elements. Gable ends may be parapeted. Deeply recessed, round-arched entries are typical. Heavy lintels over recessed, flat-topped or round-arched windows. These two shapes are often combined, appearing in groups of three. Windows are likely to have single-pane transoms. Eyebrow dormers. Flowery ornament is carved in stone or cast in terracotta panel inserts. Chimneys are usually not emphasized, but quasi-medieval chimneys, when present, are extensively corbeled and decorative.

CONSTRUCTION: Always masonry bearing walls, characteristically of stone but occasionally brick or brick trimmed with stone. Roof is usually slate or tile.

The Romanesque Revival is rooted in the early architecture of Catholic Europe. A spate of new churches after the turn of the first millennium gave birth to a style that reflected several influences, including Roman, Byzantine, and Carolingian. The style flourished in Italy, France,

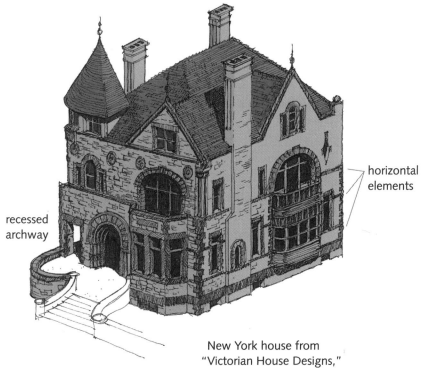

horizontal elements

recessed archway

New York house from "Victorian House Designs," *Scientific American*, 1885–94

FIRST FLOOR

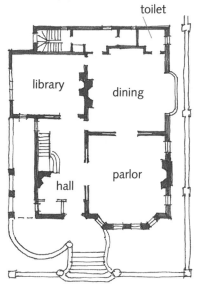

toilet

library

dining

hall

parlor

SECOND FLOOR

bath

bedroom

bedroom

bath

bedroom

bedroom

Germany, and even England until the rise of Gothic architecture began around 1200. Mainly a church and monastery architecture, its few secular examples — mostly fortified towns and castles — rarely survived the incessant wars, fires, and Gothic remodeling of the Middle Ages. The original European style varied regionally, and it was the Romanesque of southern France, with its emphasis on Roman rather than Byzantine character, that attracted American designers.

In the early 19th century, a few American churches and institutional buildings were built in the Romanesque style, but it was Henry Hobson Richardson's interpretation of the style that truly revived it. Indeed, Richardson virtually created the American Romanesque, designing mostly public buildings of rough stone with wide, low arches, thick walls, and deep openings that manifested strength and permanence. His typical designs appear weightier and more massive even than those of the original 11th-century churches (making them more Richardson than Romanesque). Used for railroad stations, jails, libraries, and most notably for Boston's Trinity Church (1872–77), the Richardson Romanesque was far too expensive for the typical homeowner, and the relatively few examples are scattered across the country. However, a wealthy client wishing to project an image of solidity and importance did occasionally commission Richardson or one of his followers to design a mansion. Richardson's short-lived personal interpretation of the Romanesque has left its mark, thanks largely to the prominent siting of his buildings and their enduring, fortress-like construction.

There was a duality in Richardson's work: on the one hand, his Romanesque seemed to grow out of the Victorian picturesque and Gothic traditions and included archaeologically "correct" elements from Classical eras, as exemplified by Trinity Church. But he also developed a more forward-looking, cleaner style that seems to anticipate the Chicago School of Louis Sullivan and Frank Lloyd Wright. This is evident in the Marshall Field Warehouse (1885–87) and the Glessner House (1886), both in Chicago, and in his Shingle Style houses, which had a deeper effect on residential design than his Romanesque Revival.

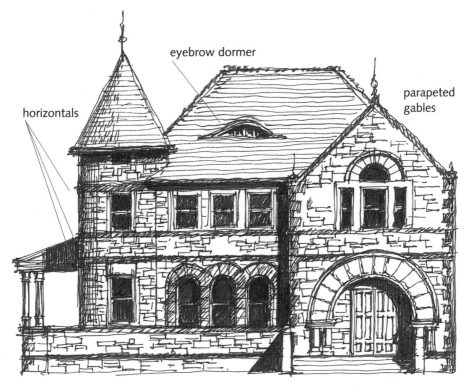

eyebrow dormer

parapeted gables

horizontals

arched recessed entry

Conrad House, *Louisville, Ky., 1892–95*

Sandanwede, *Nantucket, Mass., c. 1881*

Shingle Style (1880–1900)

FORM: A large 2- or 3-story house with an irregular floor plan. Moderately sloped, multigabled, hipped or gambrel roof. Rounded towers and turrets. Single-story porches may nearly surround the house. Rounded or occasionally angular projecting bays. Modest eave overhangs. Tall chimneys.

STYLISTIC DETAIL: Little, if any, ornament; restrained Classical detailing is not typical but does occur. Shingles used throughout, even on porch posts. Romanesque arches at porch entries are typical. Plain wood trim is usually painted a dark color, with window frames and mullions a contrasting light color. Large windows with small panes (8-over-8) and with small-paned sash above single- or double-pane sash (6-over-1 or 2). Windows may be combined in bands. Palladian windows not unknown. Eyebrow dormers. Prominent chimneys are corbeled but not decorated.

CONSTRUCTION: Ordinarily wood frame clad in shingles on heavy stone masonry foundation, although in several examples masonry continues past the first floor. Roofs were originally wood shingle as well.

Shingle Style was a reaction to the jaunty mail-order architecture that dominated American house design in the 1880s. It is not coincidental that the decade or so of the style's popularity coincides with the rise of the English Arts and Crafts Movement, which promoted, among other things, the "honest" use of building materials. The architects who created the Shingle Style were consciously creating a genuine American form,

Isaac Bell House, *Newport, R.I., c. 1882–83*

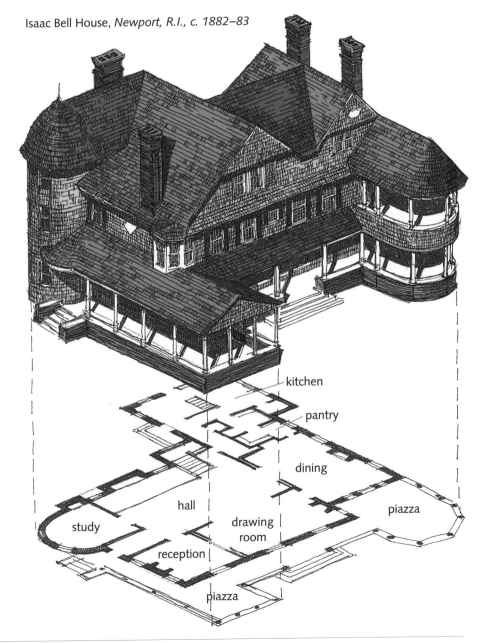

kitchen

pantry

dining

hall

study

piazza

drawing
room

reception

piazza

something American designers had aspired to since Andrew Jackson Downing and Thomas Jefferson. Many early Shingle Style houses were designed by H.H. Richardson or his associates, which has led some to see Shingle as his residential Romanesque: the wood construction and finish were more practical than massive stone for houses. However, aside from the uniformity of materials and finish, the two styles have little in common. Others find a kinship to the spare New England Colonial vernacular, despite the Shingle Style's very un-Colonial, open floor plan.

Named in the 1950s by the historian Vincent Scully, Shingle is the only 19th-century style that regularly finds its way into books on "modern" architecture, mainly because of its clean, unadorned character. The small units of wooden shingles are a far better material for sheathing the complex, irregular footprint and the curved shapes of the evolving open floor plan than traditional horizontal siding. Vertical board-and-batten could suffice, but Shingle's shadow lines provide the uniformly seamless, horizontal texture characteristic of Richardson.

Unlike his Romanesque, which had only a single proponent (at least until his death, whereupon others felt freer to adopt his theme), many noted architects contributed to the success of the Shingle Style. Beginning with seaside vacation homes, Shingle houses were built from New England to California, including several important homes in Chicago and St. Louis. Curiously, the Shingle style stayed mainly in the hands of professional architects, like Richardson, Charles McKim, and Frank Lloyd Wright, and didn't translate into vernacular architecture despite its relatively simple materials and comfortable floor plans. Another style for large suburban lots, Shingle was unsuited to urban streetscapes, as much for its flammability as for its expansive presence. As usual, less pedigreed examples of the style will—especially after a hundred years—show scraps of other styles, particularly around porches and entries.

Gardener's Cottage, *Dedham, Mass., c. 1908*

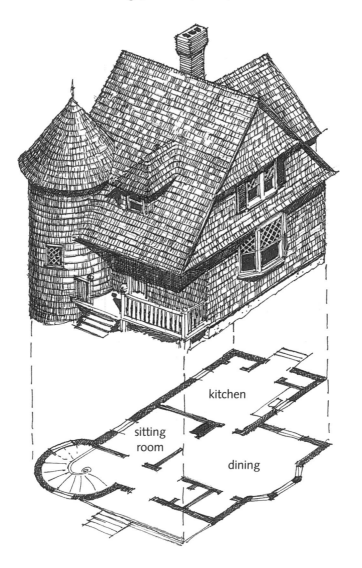

kitchen

sitting
room

dining

Hudson, Mass., c. 1893

Queen Anne Style (1880–1910)

FORM: A 2- or 3-story, multifaceted composition of tall, intersecting, gabled or occasionally hipped roof forms, displaying towers, turrets, and dormers. A vertical emphasis, but strong horizontals hold together diverse architectural elements as well. Very tall, slim chimneys. Projecting upper floors and bay windows. Extensive porches and verandas. Asymmetrical, irregular floor plan.

STYLISTIC DETAIL: A multitude of features, including brackets, roof cresting, ornamental chimneys, turned porch posts and balustrade spindles. There may be Classical columns grouped in pairs or threes. Except for the Gothic arch, no historical detail goes unused, and many are combined regardless of tradition. Textured wall patterning of all types, including decorative shingle patterns, is typical. Some examples feature copious amounts of lacy ornament around porches, entries, and on gable ends. Windows are large, with 1-over-1 glazing common, and upper panes often edged with leaded or colored glass. Rich paint color schemes were and are common.

CONSTRUCTION: Entirely wood frame, or first floor of brick or stone masonry with wood frame above covered in decorative wood siding or wood shingles.

The quintessential Victorian house, symbolic to Americans of the entire period, originated in England with the noted architect Richard Norman Shaw (1831–1912) and his followers, successful designers of rambling, semimedieval, half-timbered country homes. Reacting to the industrial and urban squalor of 19th-century England, Shaw published plans in the

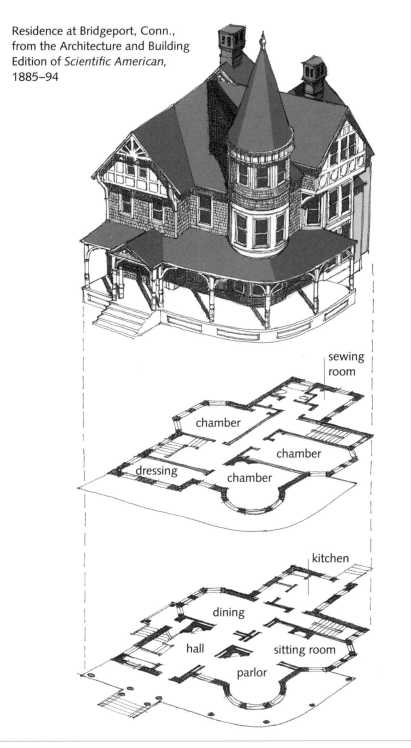

Residence at Bridgeport, Conn., from the Architecture and Building Edition of *Scientific American*, 1885–94

sewing room

chamber

chamber

dressing

chamber

kitchen

dining

hall

sitting room

parlor

"Old English" vernacular, inspired by Elizabethan cottages. His designs allowed unrestrained planning but without the religious connotations of Gothic Revival. Oddly, though his manor houses were rooted in the Elizabethan era, Shaw's movement was named for the 18th-century Queen Anne.

The American architect H. H. Richardson, aware of Shaw's work, designed the first American Queen Anne home at Newport, Rhode Island, in 1874. The style was more widely introduced at the 1876 Centennial Exposition in Philadelphia, where two brick-and-half-timbered houses were built as quarters for the British exhibitors. The buildings were well received, and American designers were soon at work on new plan books, which were sold by mail order nationwide along with whole houses in prefabricated sections. Every town of any size at all, particularly west of the Appalachians, seems to have a Queen Anne house or two along some once prominent avenue. Californians in particular, from San Diego to San Francisco, delighted in the style, and many of the most exuberant examples are found in both townhouses and free-standing homes.

Richard Shaw envisioned the Queen Anne as a brick masonry architecture, but in the United States it was quickly reinterpreted in wood, at least above the first story. While the remarkably tall, ornate chimneys were retained from the British model, the half-timbered structure was discarded in favor of the balloon frame. A multitude of styling treatments were applied, both from established fashions and new cut shapes and forms. The resulting visual clamor evolved into the most elaborately decorative residential architecture the United States has known, which bore little resemblance to Shaw's "Old English" motif.

Cheerful, inviting, and uniquely American, Queen Anne houses stand out against the also irregular, but somber and churchy, Gothic Revival, as well as the relatively unembellished Italianate—in spite of occasionally borrowing details from both. The façades, not only the street side, are an orchestration of light and shadow with their recesses, projections, and textures. Color is a critical part of the design and was applied in patterns of shingles and brick as well as complex paint schemes. Inside was a large entry hall, which typically included both a grand stair and a large fireplace. It led to other spaces through sliding doors and wide openings, encouraging free movement within the house.

Full Queen Annes, larger houses for upper-middle-class families, display more of the features that define the style. Notable examples sport the elaborate "spindle work" associated with the richly ornamented

Greenman House (a catalog house), *Cortland, N.Y., 1896*

Eastlake Style, named for an English architect and furniture designer. Scraps of Victorian detail were also added to farmhouses and the modest vernacular of small town homes, demonstrating an awareness of the fashion through all social levels.

First scorned by classicists decrying the abandonment of all standards and restraint, Queen Anne Style was then ridiculed by austere 20th-century modernists, who saw it as symbolic of the design decadence of the 1890s. Queen Anne is presently experiencing a rebirth of interest and respect. Intricate and costly paint jobs on restored "Painted Ladies" have brought wide attention to this relatively brief turn-of-the-century vogue.

Haas-Lilienthal House, *San Francisco, Calif., 1886*

Thorpe House, *Cambridge, Mass., c. 1887*

The Colonial Revival (1880–1950)
Georgian Revival

FORM: Symmetrically arranged 2- or 3-story block, with side-gabled, hipped, or gambrel roof. Dutch gambrels may have extended eaves on one or both sides. A garrison projection (jetty) is common.

STYLISTIC DETAIL: Georgian or Federal features, including doorways, window treatments, cornices (decorated or plain), corner pilasters, and roof balustrades. Pedimented entrances and entry porches are typical. A Palladian or arched window above the entry is common. Windows are commonly paired. Eclectic decorative dormers. Precise, machine-made wood detailing.

CONSTRUCTION: Usually wood frame with clapboard finish, occasionally a masonry veneer of stone, or, on larger houses, brick. Stone veneer often used on the first floor of "Dutch" colonials, and a brick or stone first-floor façade under the jetty on garrisons is common.

The Centennial celebration of 1876 reminded many Americans of their Colonial heritage, resulting in a surge of interest in Colonial architecture even among prominent Classical and "picturesque" architects. The following year, the noted New York architectural firm of McKim, Mead and White toured New England, observing and recording examples of Georgian and Federal houses. While still executing mansions in the Beaux-Arts (see page 310) or other styles, they designed several significant houses that freely interpreted Colonial traditions using

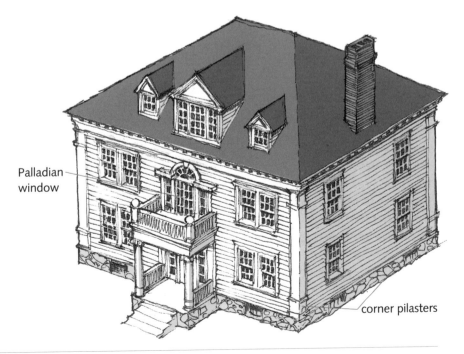

Palladian
window

corner pilasters

Georgian and Federal detail. This Colonial Revival went on to become the most prominent residential style in America, and it continues to be popular a century after "modern" architecture entered the landscape.

Along with pride in our past, simplicity and an "honest" use of materials made Colonial Revival appealing. The Georgian box could also be more economical than the multifaceted Victorian houses with their complex floor plans and roofs (think leaks). However, homeowners still wanted the comfortable attributes of Victorian and Classical Revival homes—particularly space—and architects designed neo-Colonial houses, which were much larger than their ancestors and included central heating, efficient kitchens, large porches, and, most important, relatively open floor plans contained within the rectangular Georgian footprint. While a few Colonial reproductions were so accurate that one could hardly distinguish them from well-preserved originals, the majority were (and are) ordinary houses given a few Colonial tokens, such as a fanlight or a swan's-neck broken pediment over the entry.

The Colonial Revival is a broad category and thus a convenient genre in which to stash many vaguely suggestive houses that don't seem to fit anywhere else. Dutch- or Flemish-style turn-of-the-century houses with gambrel roofs are often included in the Colonial Revival. Much more complex than the original Dutch farmhouses, they may sport huge cross gambrels, big dormers, bay windows, Classical porch posts, and Georgian or Federal entrances with or without Dutch doors. Some retain the typical Dutch gambrel roof profile with a "Dutch kick" at the eaves. The revivals can generally be distinguished from 17th-century Flemish houses by the lack of space between the tops of first-floor windows and the eaves. In the original houses, eaves did not appear at the second floor, as in most other styles, but a distance above due to the unique Dutch barn framing system (see pages 40–41).

The Colonial flavor of typical revival houses has become ever weaker with time. In some places, almost every house on a given street will show some Colonial trait, even if it's only an expanse of white clapboards. Largely a residential style, Colonial Revival has also been widely used for smaller municipal buildings, schools, and colleges. Today, expensive new developments are full of three-car-garage "Colonials" whose near-symmetrical façades and Palladian windows are the only signs of their origins.

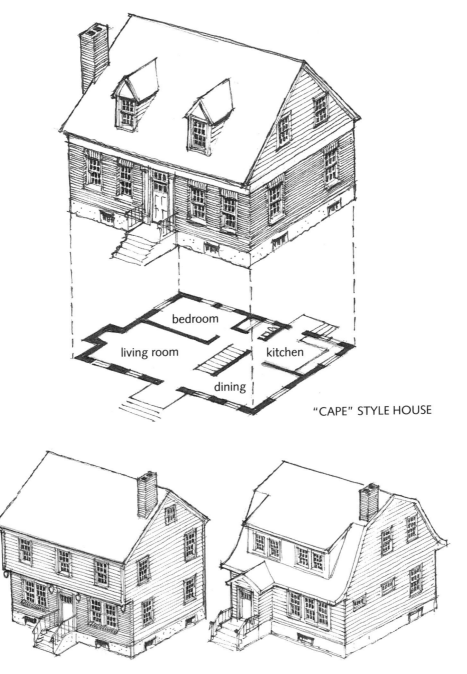

bedroom

living room

kitchen

dining

"CAPE" STYLE HOUSE

GARRISON STYLE

"DUTCH" COLONIAL

Part Three
20th-Century Revivals and Innovations

The Academic Revivals
Academic Eclecticism, The Renaissance Revival

Visitors to the 1893 World's Columbian Exposition in Chicago—a celebration of the 400th anniversary of Columbus's discovery of America—saw an array of remarkable buildings designed in a forceful yet chaste white Classicism based on the Greek and Roman orders defined during the Italian Renaissance. Designed by American architects educated at either the École des Beaux-Arts in Paris or in American schools patterned after it, these structures led to what has been called the "American Renaissance" of 1876–1917, even convincing the skeptical, Classically minded Europeans that American architecture had come of age. This new formalism was a resurgence of interest in Classical and Italian Renaissance architecture, at least in new interpretations.

These styles were applied to thousands of new buildings: government offices, museums, courthouses, hospitals, prisons, libraries, and universities. They were less successful as residential styles, for their monumental proportions and corresponding expense put them out of reach of most Americans, despite the expansion of a prosperous middle class. Only the very rich could afford such massive stone edifices.

Distinguishing these styles from one another can be difficult, for they share many features. The American Classical or Neoclassical Revival, and the Second Italian Renaissance Revival share a formal simplicity and (most of the time) an absence of the fanciful detail so prevalent in Late Victorian styles. There were a few eclectic reactions to the new symmetry, such as the Chateauesque, the Tudor Revival, and the wildly excessive Beaux-Arts. The same architects designed them all, and overlap and exchange of detail were common. Rather than advocating one particular style, society architects seemed anxious only to please their wealthy clients. The more extravagant styles, such as the Beaux-Arts and the Chateauesque, lost favor by the 1920s. The surviving styles, the Italian Renaissance Revivals and the English Tudor, could be scaled down to fit suburban building lots.

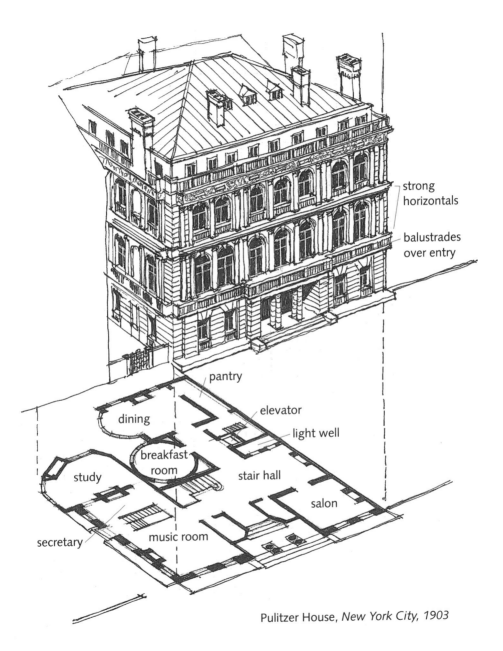

strong
horizontals

balustrades
over entry

pantry

elevator

dining

light well

breakfast
room

study

stair hall

salon

secretary

music room

Pulitzer House, *New York City, 1903*

Keith-Brown House, *Salt Lake City, Utah, 1900*

The American Classical Revival (1895–1950)
Neoclassical Revival

FORM: A 2-story rectangular block symmetrically arranged with a full-height 2-story entry porch. Side-gabled or hipped roofs are typical. Semicircular front porches common. Later versions sometimes have full-width porches.

STYLISTIC DETAIL: Classical columns, capitals, and pediments of Greek and Roman orders. Columns rarely paired. Later examples show slimmer, less detailed, round or square columns. Substantial eaves and cornices typical, as are roof balustrades. Generally smooth, clean façades with decorative entry and window treatments. Pilasters or quoins may appear at the corners. Broken pediments at the entry and windows usually occur with 2-story porch columns. Windows highly variable, though arches are uncommon. Lintels may be plain, pedimented, or keystoned. Degree of mild ornamentation varies.

CONSTRUCTION: Highly variable: stone masonry including marble and brick, and wood frame with stucco. Masonry veneer common after 1920.

The American Classical Revival style dominated the World's Columbian Exposition of 1893 in Chicago. Its New York architects had mandated a Classical design for its main buildings, even though innovative Chicago architects were already developing new concepts for offices and commercial buildings. Considering the Exposition's white plaster "temples," the Chicago architect Louis Sullivan wrote bitterly, "The damage wrought to this country by the Chicago World's Fair will last a

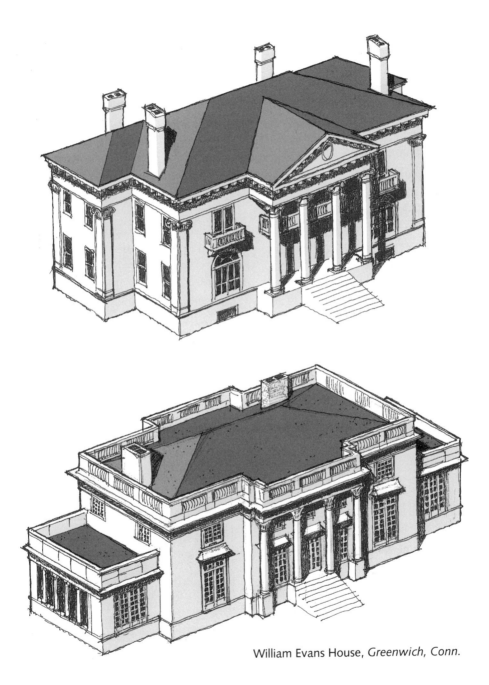

William Evans House, *Greenwich, Conn.*

half a century." The apparently stunning display of Classical architecture in a Utopian setting did renew interest in a formal, symmetrical, scaled-up architecture, and it was widely adopted for institutional and commercial buildings. Its clean, dignified lines eventually were seen on hundreds of art museums and government buildings as well as Penn Station in New York, the MIT campus, and the Lincoln Memorial.

A few of the smaller buildings at the Exposition, representing each state, suggested to some that Classical forms could again be used in residential design, at least by the affluent. The regional variations — such as full-width and semicircular porches, Georgian proportions, and ornamental traditions from the earlier Greek and Roman revivals — expressed in these state pavilions contributed elements to a national style.

Variable in form and materials, Classical Revival homes are united by their imposing columned and pedimented two-story entrances, with Greek orders outnumbering the Roman. These houses are distinguished from those of the Early Classical Revival by their larger size and scale and by the common use of broken pediments over the entry and windows. Wide porches with roofs supported by Classical columns were often added to other house styles to make them seem Neoclassical, at least to their hopeful owners. Many such examples sport pseudo-balustrades as well.

The degree of adherence to academically "correct" Classicism varied considerably; close attention to accuracy was given to earlier phases (before 1920) of the style. Later, more expedient but less skillful designs with less detail became common, though they were often clumsy and pretentious. Worn down by cost concerns and flagging interest, the American Classical Revival did not survive the Great Depression as an active residential style.

Liriodendron, *Bel Air, Md., c. 1897*

Joseph Beale House, *Washington, D.C., 1909*

The Second Italian Renaissance Revival Urban Palace (1890–1935)
Italian Renaissance, Renaissance Revival,
Northern Italian Renaissance Revival

FORM: Flat roof on a rectangular, symmetrical, 3-story box. Paired side or end porches common.

STYLISTIC DETAIL: Rusticated stone finish on first story is typical. Strong horizontal belt courses between floors may have balustrades. Ample eaves overhang a cornice and frieze. Pilasters and stone quoins common. Entry often framed by columns, standing clear or engaged. Round-arched entries flanked by Classical columns are typical. In richer examples, Classical columns may frame rows of arched windows. A balustraded balcony over the entrance and balustrades at the roofline are typical. Window treatments, likely to differ at each story, are occasionally arched. Pedimented or hooded windows at first or second floor or both. Top floor windows smaller.

CONSTRUCTION: Typically smooth ashlar stone for bearing walls or veneer. Also stucco on brick or sometimes wood frame.

The Second Italian Renaissance Revival has its roots in the northern Italian Renaissance palaces and villas of the 16th and 17th centuries. The urban palaces were grand, three-story structures (thirty feet from floor to floor!) on a rectangular plan, surrounding a colonnaded *cortile*, or courtyard. Only the nearly blank exterior walls belied their fortress heritage; eventually more windows, Classical columns, and pilasters were

The Academic Revivals

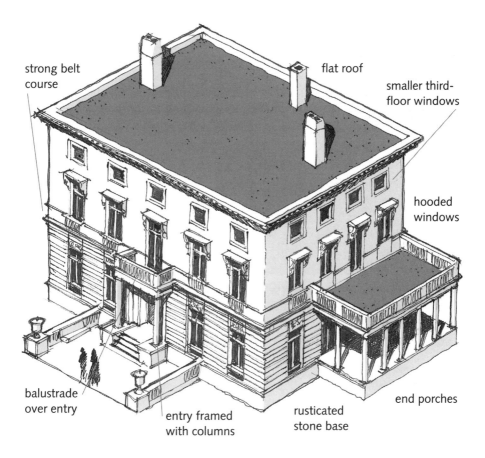

strong belt course

flat roof

smaller third-floor windows

hooded windows

balustrade over entry

entry framed with columns

rusticated stone base

end porches

Faust House, *St. Louis, Mo., c. 1900*

added, and the palaces became more open and inviting. It is these *palazzi* that inspired the flat-topped, symmetrical, American Italian Renaissance mansions shown here.

This urban expression of the Second Italian Renaissance Revival is also related to the earlier Italianate revivals in this country (see pages 246–53), although there are important differences. Second Renaissance houses are much grander in size and scale than their earlier forms, and they often include a few Classical hints of the École des Beaux-Arts by Americans who had studied there or in American architecture schools inspired by the École. It may also be worth noting that Second Italian Renaissance mansions were not based on pattern books but on close observation of the original *palazzi*, either directly or from photographs. Rich Americans adopted the façades if not the floor plans, finding the large scale suitable for their own mansions, though the new buildings rarely approached the size of the Italian originals.

Fashionable New York architects—particularly the office of McKim, Mead and White—with their access to the wealthiest clients promoted the style. The Second Italian Renaissance never became common in cities or the countryside. The Isabella Stewart Gardner Museum in Boston, once Fenway Court, Mrs. Gardner's home, is a graceful example, and, with its interior *cortile*, well represents urban Italian Renaissance architecture.

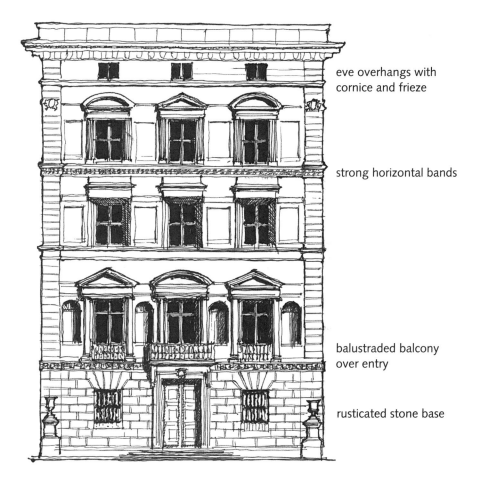

eve overhangs with
cornice and frieze

strong horizontal bands

balustraded balcony
over entry

rusticated stone base

H. C. Taylor House, *New York City, 1896*

Alonzo Roberson House, *Binghamton, N.Y., c. 1906*

The Second Italian Renaissance Revival Rural Villa (1890–1935)
Italian Renaissance, Renaissance Revival,
Northern Italian Renaissance Revival

FORM: Typically 3- or 5-bay, 2-story block under low hipped roof with substantial overhangs. May have one or two projecting full-height pavilions, usually symmetrical, but a single pavilion may be off to one side.

STYLISTIC DETAIL: Strongly horizontal with smooth, flat façades. Stucco and red tile roof. Decorative brackets on a wide cornice support generous eaves. Large round-arched openings at first floor, simpler rectangular windows above. Palladian or Serlian motif entry is likely. Quoins and a belt course common. Arched colonnades at recessed loggias. One-story entrance portico with Classical columns.

CONSTRUCTION: Smooth ashlar stone, brick, or stucco typical. A tile roof is standard.

The rural component of the Second Italian Renaissance Revival style was derived from northern Italian country villas, which were less formal and more moderate in scale than the urban *palazzi* of Rome and Florence. Predating Palladio, Classically ornamented villas of many configurations and degrees of luxury were built from the late 15th century on, as estates were consolidated following territorial conflicts.

Originally serving as spacious farmhouses, they evolved into comfortable and luxurious retreats for the prosperous, complete with fountains and extensive gardens. Though varied, the villas generally had common features, such as external loggias, stucco walls shaded by

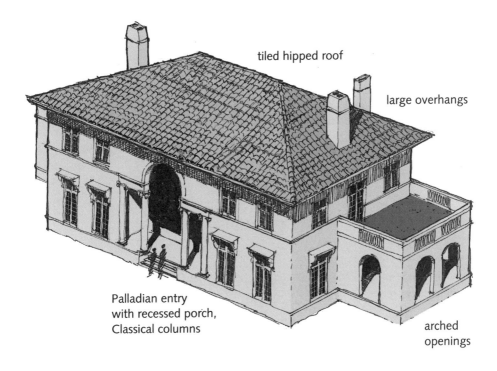

tiled hipped roof

large overhangs

Palladian entry
with recessed porch,
Classical columns

arched
openings

generous overhangs, and Classical detailing. In the 16th century, Palladio became famous for his elegant country villas, but it was the earlier rural villas of Tuscany and the Veneto that inspired American designers.

In the United States, Italian country villas are mostly suburban houses. Like their predecessors in Europe, the floor plans are quite variable but share similar characteristics, notably the sheltering hipped roof, a shaded loggia behind a row of round arches, and the relatively discreet use of ornament. An arched and columned entry, often shading a recessed porch, was first drawn by Sebastiano Serlio in 1537 and also appeared in the third of Palladio's *Four Books of Architecture* in 1570. That entrance, plus a red tile roof with broad overhangs, identifies the quintessential Italian Renaissance Revival villa. Not as strongly associated with the fashionable New York architects as the "urban palace," these villas were built as modest houses as well as mansions. Designs were available from house plan publications and local builders. Occasionally, Spanish, Mexican, and French details were mingled with the standard interpretations, resulting in a Mediterranean style. This blend became popular in the Southwest, California, and Florida.

brackets

raised terraces   recessed entry   arches

Extreme Academic Architecture

While the population of the United States nearly tripled from the Civil War to 1900, the nation's wealth increased fourfold, with almost three quarters of it concentrated in 10 percent of the population. This economic growth, gained from the spread of industry and the larger scale of agriculture, fueled a major shift westward that built new urban economic centers as well as new markets. In benefiting from this prosperity, some families, now affluent, strove to solidify their social position by building immense houses, masonry symbols of power and permanence.

Through the new convenience of mail order, the wooden Second Empire, Stick, and Queen Anne house styles were being absorbed into the American vernacular while the rich watched for more extravagant styles that could better display their wealth. Shingle Style and Colonial Revival, popular at the time, were too restrained and not sufficiently grandiose. Again, European historical traditions provided the inspiration for extravagant styles: Chateauesque, based on 16th-century French chateaux; the rambling, informal, English "cottage" revival; and the overscaled, overstated Beaux-Arts Style.

Except for the English Revival, these styles had little impact on future residential architecture — except possibly to irk the young Frank Lloyd Wright. There were too few examples, and they were too remote from most people's lives. Costly to maintain, requiring not just a maid and occasional gardener but crews of servants and full-time landscapers, these estates occupied the finest addresses and the best views in and around growing cities. The Hudson River valley, Newport, Philadelphia, St. Louis, and the north shores of Chicago and Milwaukee were typical sites of these mansions, few of which survive as homes today. Instead they are tourist attractions, religious and secular institutions, and, in Washington, D.C., embassies.

These extreme but short-lived residential styles are sometimes viewed as the peak of American domestic architecture rather than as interesting and sometimes amusing aesthetic dead ends.

Burrage House, *Boston, Mass., 1899*

The Breakers, *Newport, R.I., 1894–95*

The Beaux-Arts Style (1880–1920)
Beaux-Arts Classicism, American Renaissance Style

FORM: Monumentally scaled, symmetrical 2- or 3-story box with a flat, low-pitched, or, less frequently, mansard roof, on heavy raised masonry base. Projecting pavilions.

STYLISTIC DETAIL: Formal, large-scale elements: paired Classical columns and elaborate cornices. Windows and doors usually framed by columns or pilasters. Large windows commonly arched at main level. Stone balustrades at balconies and porch roofs, occasionally over the front cornice. Swags, medallions, and cartouches used freely, as are sculpted figures, either in relief or free-standing. Rusticated masonry is typically used at ground level. Extensive formal gardens with sculpture.

CONSTRUCTION: Massive bearing walls of smooth stone masonry with a tile roof. Some steel framing.

The American Beaux-Arts Style (among other academic styles) was created by American architects who attended the French École des Beaux-Arts or American schools modeled on it. Students were encouraged to arrive at fundamental, universal principles of design through the comprehensive study of all the earlier European architectural periods. They were discouraged from advocating a particular Classical historic legacy, although Italian Renaissance motifs were prevalent. They applied this understanding to the design of America's new buildings. Initially an architecture of monumental public buildings (Grand Central

Extreme Academic Architecture

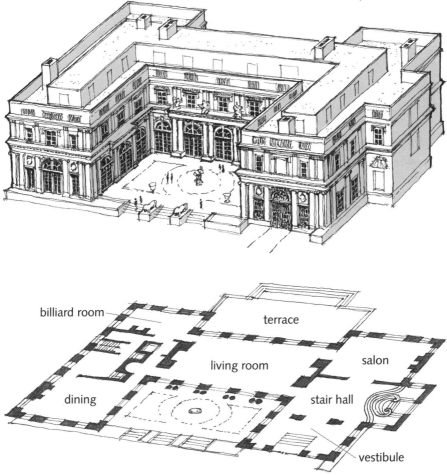

Oelrichs House, *Newport, R.I., 1902*

Terminal in New York and Memorial Hall in Philadelphia, for example), it soon became the style of choice for the grandest and most ostentatious mansions in the United States, as a drive along Ocean Avenue in Newport, Rhode Island, will demonstrate. Dominating the scene, among palatial mansions of several styles, is the Breakers, Richard Morris Hunt's monumental Beaux-Arts "cottage" designed for Cornelius Vanderbilt II. The Beaux-Arts townhouses, mansions, and country "cottages" were cut-stone monuments to the era before the income and property taxes.

Beaux-Arts was not merely the replication of Classical buildings or the imitation of Classical style that 19th-century Greek Revivalists and contemporary American Classical Revivalists advocated. Instead it focused on applying academically correct Classical elements to new building types emphasizing formality and opulence. The palatial mansion was thus not a "temple" but a Classically ornamented stone mass built on a modern floor plan intended for high-style entertaining and luxurious comfort.

Beaux-Arts mansions are an eclectic intermingling of closely copied elements of Italian Renaissance palaces and Classical orders. Outdoor sculpture and formal gardens, the paired columns and an almost flat roof, as well as their sheer mass, generally distinguish Beaux-Arts from the milder American Classical Revival of the same period (see page 294).

The interiors were at least as showy as the exteriors, with the standard magnificent grand stair gently winding its way up from the central hall, serving as a stage from which to see and be seen. The competition among the new wealthy was intense. Large rooms with high ceilings were furnished with items gathered or ordered from around the world. In some cases, entire rooms were dismantled in Europe and shipped home to be included in the new house. The enormous rooms provided plenty of space for their owners' collections of art and artifacts while advertising their refined and well-traveled, Classical taste. Murals and sculpted figures provided plenty of work for artists, perhaps the best legacy of the style.

Ironically but perhaps inevitably, Beaux-Arts, the style that burst on the scene in 1893 at the World's Columbian Exposition in Chicago, came to be seen as hopelessly decadent and irrelevant. Originally used to demonstrate America's presence among the cultured, it became the scorned symbol of all that was to be avoided by the trend-setting modernists of the Chicago School and the Bauhaus.

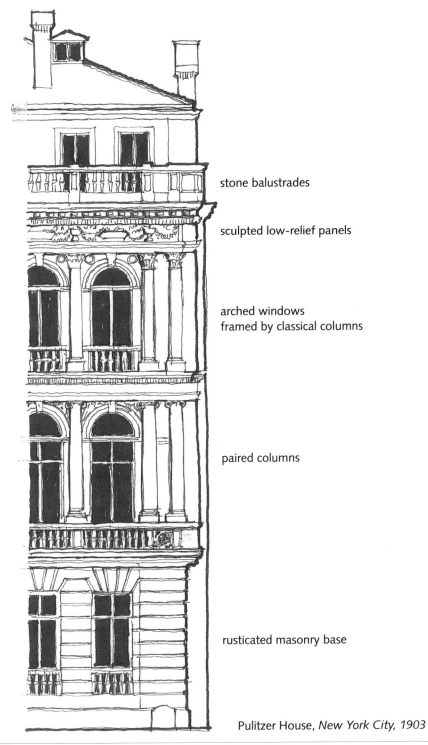

stone balustrades

sculpted low-relief panels

arched windows
framed by classical columns

paired columns

rusticated masonry base

Pulitzer House, *New York City, 1903*

Extreme Academic Architecture

Joshua Motter House, *St. Joseph, Mo., c. 1890*

The Chateauesque Style (1890–1910)
Frances I

FORM: A complex collection of flared, hipped roof forms over a 2- or 3-story heavy masonry base. Less extravagant examples may be symmetrically arranged. Roofs often truncated and flattened, suggesting Second Empire. Projecting pavilions, round towers, and turrets with conical roofs typical. Wall dormers may interrupt the cornice. Tiny attic dormers.

STYLISTIC DETAIL: Large-scale detailing approximates French 16th-century Renaissance elements, while double-curved S-shaped (ogee) moldings over entries and windows along with strong verticals suggest a Gothic character. Strong horizontal bands may include balconies. Finials, pinnacles, and cresting on the roof. Very ornate, pinnacled dormers may have paired windows. Relief carving typical. Main windows are large, hooded, and sometimes arched; round or "basket-handle" type (semi-ellipse) windows sometimes divided by carved stone mullions and transom bars. Recessed, arched entries may be canopied. Multiple tall, decorated chimneys.

CONSTRUCTION: Massive, smooth-faced stone masonry bearing walls. Slate roofs.

Chateauesque mansions, based on the magnificent 16th-century French chateaux seen by Americans on the Grand Tour and architects at the École des Beaux-Arts, were built primarily in New York, Boston, and other eastern cities, but also appear in or near St. Louis, Chicago, and Milwaukee, among other cities. Unlike the Beaux-Arts, it was primarily a

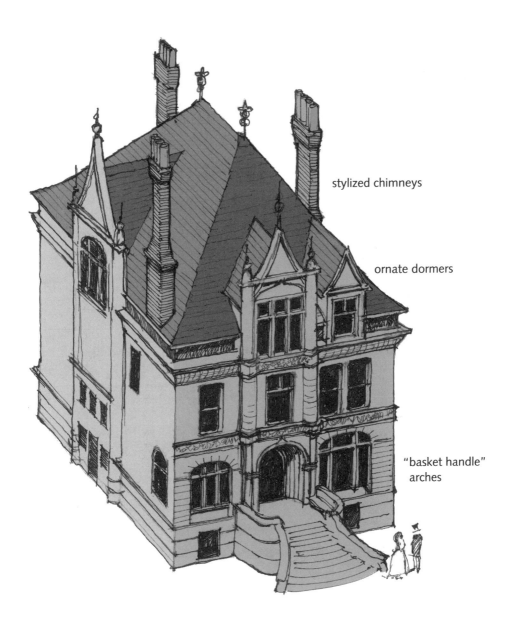

stylized chimneys

ornate dormers

"basket handle" arches

Byram House, *Chicago, Ill., c. 1880*

residential style, a true relic of the Gilded Age. While the towers, spires, turrets, sculptural chimneys, and overall mass made it difficult to translate into the vernacular, Chateauesque townhouses are some of our most recognizable urban examples of residential architecture.

Two of the best-known examples are houses designed by a master of several extravagant styles, Richard Morris Hunt, for the Vanderbilt family: W. K. Vanderbilt's imposing townhouse on Fifth Avenue in New York City (1880–84) and the spectacular Biltmore (1895), an immense chateau built for George Washington Vanderbilt in the Blue Ridge Mountains outside Asheville, North Carolina. Biltmore indeed resembles a French chateau and has come to be considered representative of American Chateauesque houses, though most of the other prominent examples are in fact urban. Other Vanderbilts built urban Chateauesque mansions with other architects, the long construction periods an indication of the effort and expense involved.

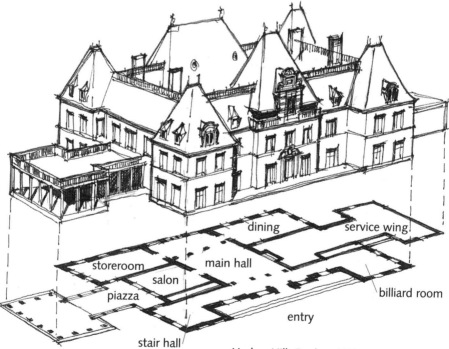

Harbor Hill, *Roslyn, N.Y., 1902*

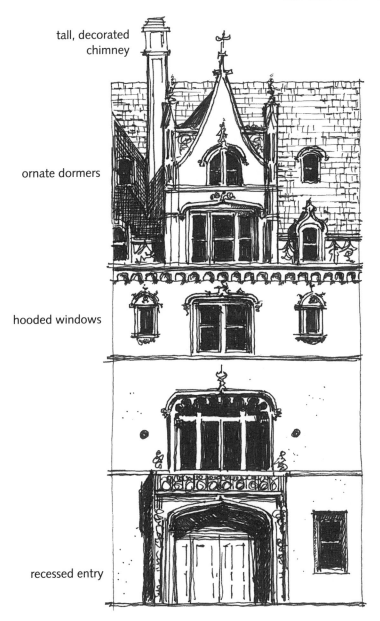

tall, decorated
chimney

ornate dormers

hooded windows

recessed entry

Fletcher House, *New York City, 1899 (partial elevation)*

Rollins House, *Des Moines, Iowa, 1925*

The English Revival (1890–1940)
Tudor Revival, Elizabethan Revival, Jacobean Revival, "Jacobethan"

FORM: Sizable, complex, 2- or 3-story house on a low base. Steep roofs, nearly always side-gabled and occasionally hipped. Dominant single cross-gable or multiple overlapping cross-gables, with an occasional jerkinhead gable. Gabled dormers and, occasionally, large shed dormers. Upper floor may project over entry. Hexagonal oriels and 1- or 2-story bay windows. Roof may extend over side porches.

STYLISTIC DETAIL: Half-timbering in gable ends. Patterned brick masonry. Tudor arches at entries. Eyebrow dormers. Small- and sometimes diamond-paned casement windows in rows of 3 or 4, with transoms. Prominent chimneys patterned at the first-floor level; decorative individual flues, both square and round, extend up well beyond chimney cap. Battlements may be seen over porches and around flat-roofed cornices. Rounded eaves with irregular shingles and eyebrow dormers sometimes used to suggest thatching. Parapet gables indicate the Jacobean variant.

CONSTRUCTION: Brick or stone masonry bearing walls full height or with half-timber and plaster nogging (very occasionally brick) from the second floor up; also stucco on wood lath. Later examples have masonry veneers and wood siding on wood frame.

Often simply called Tudor, this style is an American reinterpretation of rustic English manor houses from the 16th and early 17th centuries. Adaptations of these country homes became extremely popular after World War I, although a few prewar examples can be found on sizable

Similar to architect Bertram Goodhue's Tudor design of 1891

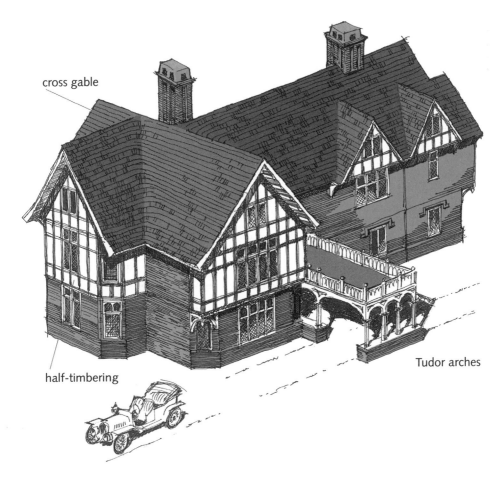

cross gable

half-timbering

Tudor arches

Extreme Academic Architecture

estates, rivaling some Chateauesque and Beaux-Arts palaces. Its main following was among successful upper- and upper-middle-class families, who found the English country house more comfortable than the Classically formal Italian and French Renaissance blocks. At first an architect's style, by the 1930s thousands of moderate imitations were becoming a part of the American vernacular.

The terms Tudor, Elizabethan, and Jacobean or Jacobethan are often used interchangeably to describe these English Revival houses. However, Tudor refers more specifically to the monolithic masonry or stucco house; Elizabethan to the "black-and-white" half-timbered house; and Jacobean to the Anglo-Dutch, parapeted-gable architecture named for James I, Elizabeth's successor. Jacobethan is the nickname for a hybrid of the latter two; many eclectic American examples include elements of two or all three varieties.

Jacobean is an interesting variant, dating from Henry VIII's importing of Flemish masons to build country homes for his court on land recently taken from the Catholic Church. The Dutch had earlier adopted elements of the Italian Baroque, simplifying it to suit their less lofty mercantile traditions. In 16th- and 17th-century England, it was a style for very large estates. Never half-timbered, its more obvious features are battlements and a parapeted gable shaped into steep triangles, steps, or compositions of curves and angles. Less common in the 20th century than Tudor or Elizabethan, its unique silhouette can occasionally be found in affluent communities.

These Flemish-English parapet gables first found their way to the American colonies in houses like Bacon's Castle in Virginia (page 101). In the United States, battlements and crenelated parapets are covered by the Jacobean banner as well, although prolonged sieges of imposing suburban houses are rare.

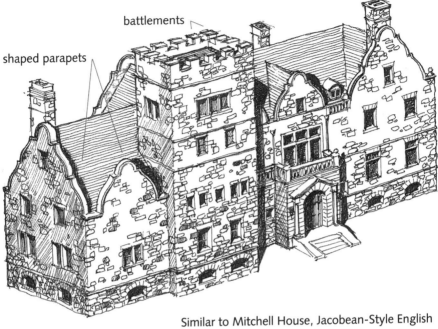

battlements

shaped parapets

Similar to Mitchell House, Jacobean-Style English
Revival mansion, *Tuxedo Park, N.Y., c. 1910*

Southwestern and California Styles

The American Southwest, from Texas across New Mexico and Arizona, then north along the Pacific coast to San Francisco, holds some of America's most interesting and beautiful architectural traditions. The blend of Spanish, Italian, Mexican, native Pueblo, and English influences has left the region with a rich collection of vernacular as well as high-fashion architectural expressions.

California's own architects barely recognized their Hispanic architectural heritage until the latter 19th century, when a few of them began to resent the eastern, English-based architecture dominating their landscape. Although the vernacular Monterey residential style had existed since the early years of the Mexican administration of California (see page 212), it was the elegant Hispanic architecture featured at important national expositions that reminded the western architects that their own region held a significant legacy waiting to be exploited.

Informal and inviting, the Mission and Mediterranean styles were well suited to the arid environment of the southwestern desert, as well as to the coasts of California and the Gulf of Mexico. Associated with patios, gardens, and cool tile floors, they promoted an easygoing way of life distinct from that of the crowded, bustling eastern seaboard. The revivals and descendants of Spanish Colonial architecture first emerged at the end of the 19th century and were built steadily until the Second World War. Now pervading the thriving American Sunbelt from Florida to California, they are some of the most elegant and comfortable homes in the United States. These styles are the most common and best suited to the Southwest and Florida, but there is hardly an eastern or midwestern suburb that doesn't feature an attempt at a Mediterranean villa or Mexican hacienda.

Interestingly, the consciously contrived, self-conscious Spanish Pueblo Revival architecture of New Mexico's Rio Grande Valley is one of the very few examples of traditional Native American architecture's influence on an American style.

Shaffer-Sherman House (has some Mission characteristics),
Rancho Santa Fe, Calif., 1920

McAneeny-Howerdd House, *Palm Beach, Fla., 1928*

Mission, *Santa Barbara, Calif., c. 1815–20*

The Mission Style (1890–1920)
Mission Revival

FORM: Variable, but usually a symmetrical 2-story square block. Low-pitched pyramidal or hipped roof typical, as are prominent, shaped parapets. One variant commonly features a bell tower or pavilion on the street-side façade. Arcaded front or wrap-around porches are common, with an occasional porte cochere.

STYLISTIC DETAIL: Curvilinear parapeted gables and wall dormers, usually over the entry. Red tile roofs extend over exposed rafter ends that may be decoratively sawn. Round or segmented unframed arched openings standard at entries and arcades. Bell towers on larger houses topped with tile pyramids or, rarely, Moorish domes. Balconies are common. Porch roofs may be supported by bulky rectangular piers. Stucco wall surfaces are undecorated white or light-colored. Usually no sculptural ornament or wrought-iron detailing. Large windows are occasionally arched and grouped.

CONSTRUCTION: Typically stucco on lath, but occasionally stone or brick walls, particularly outside California.

Spanish missions were the first colonial buildings built in what in time became Texas, New Mexico, Arizona, and California. In California, twenty-one missions were established between 1769 and 1823 along or near the Pacific coast from San Diego to San Francisco, about a day's journey from one another along El Camino Real, the coastal trail.

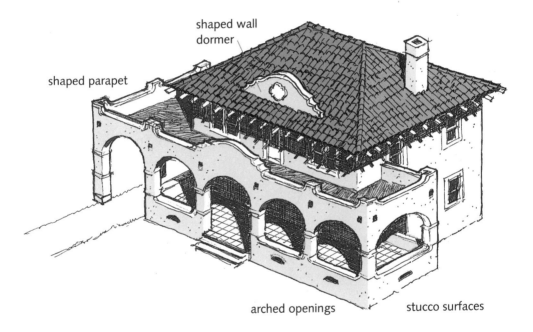

shaped wall
dormer

shaped parapet

arched openings   stucco surfaces

They were conceived by the padres and usually built by soldiers and the local Native Americans the priests had been sent to convert, a combination that led to a style that, if unsophisticated, was simple and durable. The missions usually consisted of a church, housing for the missionaries, a few troops, and any natives who chose to participate in the mission's programs. With stables and gardens, the California missions were essentially walled, self-supporting villages. The Spanish baroque architecture with its subtle Moorish elements primitively fashioned in adobe and plaster produced a building style that has been described as "consisting of a certain naive simplicity and a rugged straight-forward-ness." It was this honesty of design that appealed to later western architects in search of an ancestral architecture.

The Mission Style gained exposure after it was displayed at Chicago's Columbian Exposition in 1893, and it was further advanced when the Santa Fe and Southern Pacific railroads adopted it for train stations and hotels throughout the West. This soon led to its adoption for residential uses, and houses all over the country, large and small, borrowed its decorative parapets, bell towers, and arcaded portales. Such houses did tend to lose some of their character as they moved farther from San Diego: the standard parapeted gable was often reduced to a vestigial remnant. Some examples can be found—looking quite out of place—in sizable northeastern suburbs. In spite of its popularity, Mission remained primarily a style of the Southwest, though it did eventually reach across the Sunbelt to Florida.

In California, Mission's birthplace, the style produced some bizarre variations, in which stylistic exuberance and excessive detail overshadowed, literally, the characteristic smooth walls and clean round openings of the style. California architects themselves were appalled at many of the results of the movement they had fostered, and many eventually disowned it. Watered down by Mediterranean influences, the Mission Style was largely supplanted by the Spanish Colonial Revival (page 330).

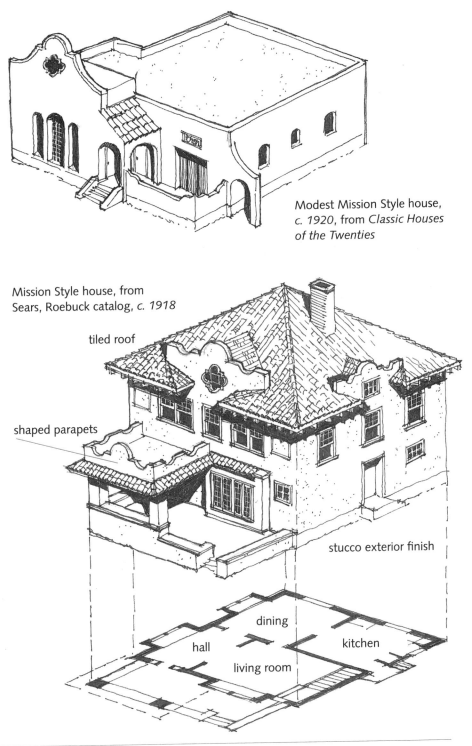

Modest Mission Style house, *c. 1920*, from *Classic Houses of the Twenties*

Mission Style house, from Sears, Roebuck catalog, *c. 1918*

tiled roof

shaped parapets

stucco exterior finish

dining

hall

kitchen

living room

John G. Kennedy House, *Palo Alto, Calif., c. 1922*

The Spanish Colonial Revival (1915–40)

FORM: Typically 1- or 2-story asymmetrical, side-gabled house with a low-pitched roof and generous overhangs. May have wings, hipped roofs, flat roofs, and arcades (*portales*). Low towers frequently seen on larger homes. Not likely to have an enclosed patio.

STYLISTIC DETAIL: Elaborate carved or cast ornament at entries and windows, though some examples may be less decorative. Red tile roofs with broad expanses of white plastered walls typical. Arches on columns or piers common, particularly at entries and arcades. Windows small and irregularly placed except for typical large, usually arched, gable-end window. Balconies typical, some only 1 window wide, with wrought-iron railings. Windows may have decorative turned wood or wrought-iron grilles. Heavy, carved wooden doors. Decorative chimney caps.

CONSTRUCTION: Plaster on brick, clay tile roof.

The interest generated by the Mission style prompted some academically oriented California architects to pursue Spanish Colonial architecture back through Mexico and eventually to Spain. However, it was the New Yorker Bertram Goodhue (1869–1924), a noted scholar of Spanish Colonial architecture in Mexico, who was named the architect for the Panama-California Exposition of 1915 in San Diego. His design for the California Building won high praise and provided an academic focus for interested designers. Although a loose Spanish Colonial Revival had existed since about 1900, after the Exposition it was refined into a

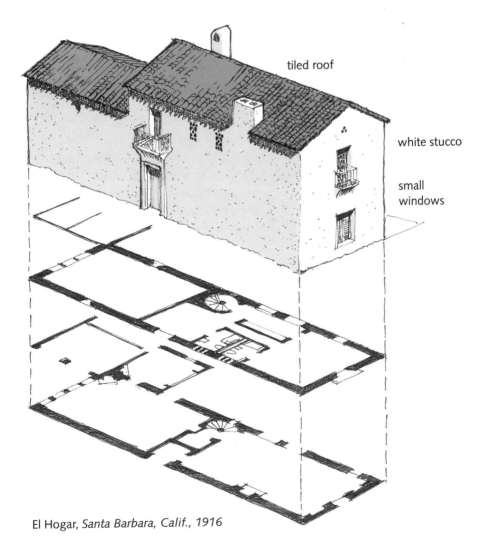

tiled roof

white stucco

small
windows

El Hogar, *Santa Barbara, Calif., 1916*

distinct style and had become popular by 1925. Adaptable for residences of all sizes, and particularly well suited to the Southern California, Texas, and Florida climates, it invaded the Midwest and other areas as well and was widely used for municipal and commercial buildings.

The distinguishing features of the Spanish Colonial Revival are the extraordinarily ornate, low-relief carvings around doors and windows. Originating in Spain in the 17th and 18th centuries, the "Churrigueresque" style was a Spanish Baroque expression of fantastic yet harmonious decoration. Originally an interior treatment, it eventually was extended to the entries and windows of churches and palaces. The Churriguera family of architects and others managed to keep the style at the forefront in Spain from 1680 to 1780. Taken to Mexico, it reached still greater heights of intricate richness, mostly on church façades. It was this exuberance that intrigued Goodhue when he toured Mexico while doing research for a book. Other influences included the architect G.W. Smith, who searched for simpler forms in the modest Andalusian farm buildings. In California his simple rooflines and a strong relationship to the patio and garden led to a more refined variant. For more luxurious homes, the villas of northern Italy provided models for California and Florida architects, as they had a century earlier in the eastern United

McAneeny-Howerdd House, *Palm Beach, Fla., 1928*

States. This derivative, without the heavy ornamentation of the Spanish Revivals, was particularly adaptable to hillside sites with terraced gardens. Classical details made their appearance again on large mansions.

These Andalusian and Italian contributions — as opposed to Mexican influences — are sometimes called the Mediterranean style of the Spanish California Revival. The term is often used as a catchall to include several turn-of-the-century styles, including the Second Italian Renaissance Revival, Mission, Spanish Colonial Revival, and others. Usually, it refers to designs with obvious Italian or Spanish features, and a house may be classified by its tendencies toward one or the other.

California Tower, Balboa Park, *San Diego, Calif., 1915,*
with Churrigueresque detailing

Applegate House, *Santa Fe, N.M., 1927*

The Spanish Pueblo Revival (1912–present)
Pueblo Style, Pueblo Revival, Santa Fe Style

FORM: A house of 1 or 2 stories, irregularly massed, with a flat roof, balconies, and recessed portales (arcades). Upper stories often set back. Walls, frequently battered, rise above the roofs to form parapets. Corner towers and bell cupolas occasionally seen on larger houses. Territorial substyle (see page 204) may be symmetrical in plan and elevation. Generally no domes or arches.

STYLISTIC DETAIL: A stucco finish with traditional punched windows (preferably casements). Corners and parapets gently rounded on more traditional houses; sharp corners may appear on less accurate examples. High-style models may have Pueblo ladders. *Vigas* (round wooden beams) may extend through the walls, appearing in a row on the outside wall. Projecting *canales* (scuppers) drain nearly flat roofs. Heavy paneled doors may be carved or paneled. Wood or iron grilles common at windows and above doors. Occasional atypical domes and arches may suggest a Mission influence. Turquoise-painted wood details common; other colors used as well.

CONSTRUCTION: Early examples may be of genuine adobe mud construction, but cement stucco finished in earth shades essentially defines the style today. The underlying structure may be of adobe brick but is more likely to be of concrete block or wood frame covered with metal lathe to receive the stucco. Exposed wood lintels appear over doors and windows.

Possibly the only style in this book that was consciously developed to attract tourists, the Spanish Pueblo Revival is derived from 18th- and

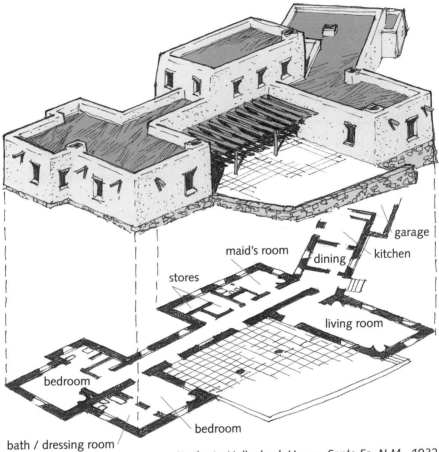

garage

kitchen

maid's room

dining

stores

living room

bedroom

bedroom

bath / dressing room

Similar to Hollenbeck House, *Santa Fe, N.M., 1932*

19th-century Spanish Colonial architecture. Combined with the native Pueblo vernacular and a pinch of Mission, the style is unique and unmistakable. It is generally confined to New Mexico's northern Rio Grande Valley, extending from Albuquerque to Taos, and is centered in Santa Fe. Because of Santa Fe's prominence as a tourist and cultural attraction, the style has more significance than its limited geography would suggest.

A Spanish Pueblo Revival variant, the New Mexican Territorial Style (see page 204), continued to be built almost without interruption through this period, leading some to call it a Territorial Revival. It attractively contrasts white-painted wood trim with adobe surfaces and so-called Territorial Greek Revival detailing.

When Santa Fe was denied a stop by the Atchison, Topeka and Santa Fe Railroad, local boosters' hopes for the town's becoming a major crossroads and New Mexico's becoming a state were deflated. Although a spur was added in 1880 that connected to the railroad stop at Lamy, Santa Fe continued to decline. However, a few influential citizens, mostly immigrant Anglos, decided to capitalize on the region's rich cultural heritage of Spanish, Mexican, Native American, and Anglo traditions by building a tourist industry. A distinct image was seen as critically important in setting Santa Fe apart from other western towns, and architecture was seen as the key.

What was adopted, however, was not the region's actual Spanish architectural heritage but an Anglo interpretation popular in the area after World War I. Over time this has congealed into what we have today: flat-roofed, multifaceted modern buildings, especially hotels and banks, but also residences, wrapped in brown stucco in imitation of adobe mud.

Despite a questionable historical rationale, the design policy has been effective in harmonizing Santa Fe's streetscapes. The insistence on a reasonably human scale, the universal stucco finish, and the consistent ratio of mass to glass have enabled Santa Fe to maintain an attractive cohesiveness.

Despite the occasional frustration of innovative architects and the inevitable gentrification that accompanies big-spending new residents and tourists, Santa Fe remains architecturally interesting, and Spanish Pueblo Revival houses encourage a comfortable, casual way of life. Other cities and towns in the Southwest, outside the Rio Grande Valley, also have Pueblo Revival houses, some looking more Pueblo than Santa Fe style. The handful outside the Southwest tend to look like alien curiosities.

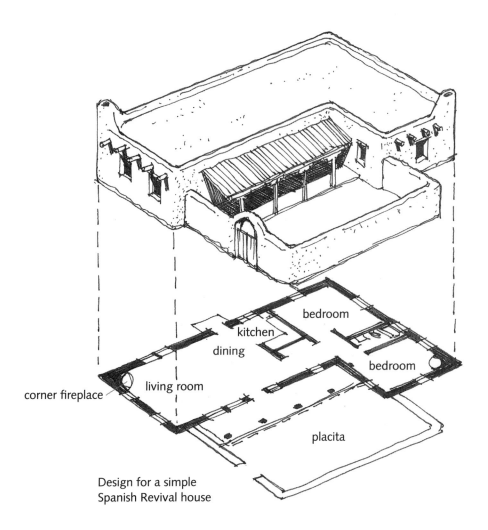

corner fireplace

bedroom

kitchen

dining

living room

bedroom

placita

Design for a simple
Spanish Revival house

Indigenous Styles and the Bungalow

Partly in reaction to the excesses of Victorian clutter and the stiff pomposities of the ubiquitous Classical revivals, several new residential designs emerged in America around the turn of the century, mainly from the Midwest. While individually distinct, they shared several characteristics: a disdain for senseless ornament, a preference for comfortable informality, and a respect for the people who would live there; most were designed by architects from the West and Midwest. In a departure from most 19th-century architecture, the new styles emphasized the horizontal, with low rooflines and deep overhangs, resulting in a uniquely American silhouette on the skyline. The houses were finished largely in natural materials and expected to relate closely to the surrounding landscape, the most ambitious examples suggesting to some a religion-free horizontal Gothic. These new approaches to house design cut through the elitist—and often confusing—Classicism that prevailed in most architects' offices. In seeing their clients as ordinary people rather than the super-rich, their advocates prepared the way for the broader modernist movement.

    Two of the new styles, Prairie and Craftsman (or Western Stick), owed a debt to the 19th-century English Arts and Crafts Movement and to H. H. Richardson's Shingle Style of the 1880s (see page 274). Inspired by the Arts and Crafts Movement, Richardson used natural building materials—stone and rough wood shingles—and created a taste among wealthy clients for rustic vacation "cottages" that were relatively free of Classical orders and ornament. Large porches, bands of windows grouped for viewing the landscape (or seascape), and the nature of shingling itself produced a unique horizontal character despite turrets, towers, and steep roofs. These conspicuous mansions, while relatively few in number, helped make this straightforward architectural expression acceptable to the public.

Additionally, some architects—among them Frank Lloyd Wright in Chicago and Bernard Maybeck and the brothers Charles and Henry Greene in California—were strongly influenced by the Japanese architecture displayed at large international expositions and featured in many illustrated books. These marvelously talented designers were aware of and generally respected one another, although it would be misleading to group them into a "school." Still, viewed a century later, their styles have appealing similarities that stand out against a background of bland neo-whatevers and severe International Style boxes.

The other major new force in residential design at the turn of the century was the arrival, in California, of the Bungalow. Although difficult to define precisely, the Bungalow's low silhouette and shady, inviting porches suggested that vacation cottages and an informal way of life were now available for one and all. The application of the Craftsman Style's naturalistic detail, inside and out, resulted in a rustic character that many still believe represents the proper Bungalow, much as the Queen Anne Style came to typify the Victorian house. "Craftsman Bungalows" are especially common in California, a few very high-styled, but thousands of simpler versions were built wherever plans or house parts could be delivered. While the simple floor plans and the porches were retained, most of these houses had little of the original Craftsman character and were absorbed into the American vernacular as affordable houses for working people.

Although the simpler Bungalows multiplied wildly, the Craftsman and Prairie traditions could not match the vigor of their architecture, and they withered after World War I, overwhelmed by people's fascination with period revivals and, of course, the Bungalow. Nevertheless, many of their features found their way into the American vernacular, particularly after World War II: open, informal floor plans, split levels, carports, attached garages, and integration with the landscape are a few.

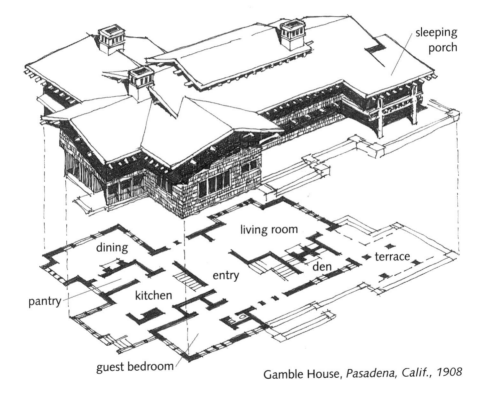

sleeping porch

living room

dining

entry

den

terrace

pantry

kitchen

guest bedroom

Gamble House, *Pasadena, Calif., 1908*

Amberg House, *Grand Rapids, Mich., 1909*

The Prairie Style (1900–1920)

FORM: Usually 2 stories, low-pitched hipped roofs (occasionally gabled), and wide, overhanging eaves. Dormers uncommon. Extended wings contain large rooms and porches. Can be symmetrical. Massing ranges from a simple "four-square" box, with a large porch or porte-cochere, to long, linear silhouettes. Massive chimneys and piers. No raised basements.

STYLISTIC DETAIL: A strong horizontal emphasis is achieved by deep, shadowed overhangs, groupings of windows in bands, thin Roman brick, and contrasting horizontal trim, among other devices. Chimneys and piers, although plain and low, are used as sturdy vertical elements anchoring the horizontal lines. Integrated with the landscape through porches, terraces, planters, and window boxes. Inside are large fireplaces, built-in amenities, and rich wood finishes on trim and paneling. Ornament usually limited to abstract leaded glass patterns.

CONSTRUCTION: Brick masonry or stucco over wood frame. Occasional steel members for long spans.

Perhaps the only well-defined American school of architecture, the Chicago School's residential Prairie Style totally departed from the vertical towers and turrets of the Victorian era as well as the strained academic interpretations of Beaux-Arts Classicism. Prairie's origins have been traced back to H. H. Richardson's Romanesque and Shingle styles, which must have impressed young Wright as it did his California contemporaries, Bernard Maybeck and the Greene brothers, Charles and

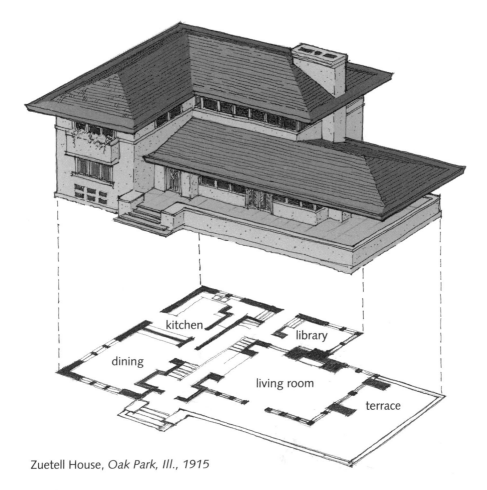

kitchen

library

dining

living room

terrace

Zuetell House, *Oak Park, Ill., 1915*

Henry. There is also a connection with Japanese architecture, which had been so well received by American architects at international expositions, including, significantly, the Chicago World's Fair of 1893.

A small group of Chicago architects led by Louis Sullivan and Frank Lloyd Wright launched an entirely new residential aesthetic between 1900 and World War I. They were part of an Arts and Crafts Movement that originally arose in England, but there were some important differences in outlook between advocates of the English style and those of the Chicago School. The English reformers rejected the machine, but Wright and his group welcomed mechanization and saw the positive attributes of machine-made materials; Wright was particularly emphatic on this point. The English also preferred to look to the past for design inspiration, while the Chicagoans tried to ignore the European influences in order to discover their own new aesthetic.

With the Prairie Style, they succeeded. Prairie architecture's strong horizontality, limited building materials, and emphasis on free and open spaces are seemingly inspired by the prairies themselves. The style's most striking characteristic is a flowing plan of interpenetrating, overlapping spaces. Free of columns, posts, and punched-out windows, the Prairie home spreads from a solid masonry core—a massive fireplace at the crossed axis of the floor plan—into the landscape through extended living spaces and porches. Panels of windows define spaces and connect with the outdoors to effectively "destroy the box," a stated aim of the Prairie School.

Short-lived and never as popular with the American public as period revival styles were, Prairie failed to attract the interest of a public more concerned with traditional symbols of affluence than spatial concepts and design philosophies. Still, it produced many remarkably beautiful homes, primarily in the northern Midwest. The style was well received in Europe, where modern trends like Art Nouveau and the Bauhaus school were well under way.

Of the original group, only Wright seems to have survived the failure of the Prairie School. With his typical vigor, he went on to design Usonian houses, the Johnson's Wax complex, Fallingwater, Taliesin West, and New York's Guggenheim Museum. Because of his later great success, Prairie is often seen as Frank Lloyd Wright's style, but his fellow revolutionaries also deserve to be recognized: Walter Burley Griffin, George Grant Elmslie, William Grey Purcell, Barry Byrne, and Robert C. Spenser are a few of the names that should be better known today.

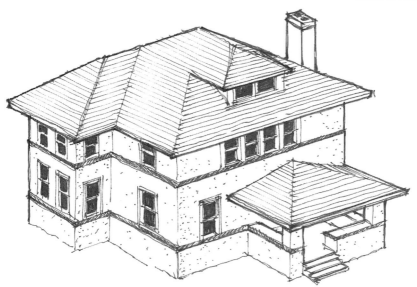

SIMPLE PRAIRIE STYLE TWO-STORY HOUSE

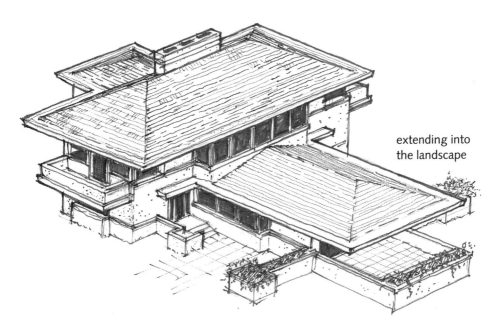

extending into
the landscape

J. Kibben Engalls House, *River Forest, Ill., 1909*

Hanchett Residence, *San Jose, Calif., c. 1911*

The Craftsman Style (1905–30)
Western Stick Style

FORM: Typically a rectangular, 1- or 1½-story bungalow. Occasionally 2 stories. Front-gabled, side-gabled, or less frequently, with a hipped roof, all gently sloped with wide overhangs. Cross gables uncommon. Full-width porches are typical. More elaborate massings appear in California.

STYLISTIC DETAIL: Displays a wooden structure, with exposed rafter ends at unboxed eaves and exposed beam ends at gables (often knee-braced). Tapered lower portion of walls common, along with massive, tapered porch columns or short square columns on heavy tapered supports. Deep shadows under extended eaves emphasize the horizontal. Windows may be grouped in rows. Ideally, a strong relationship to gardens and the outdoors is made from porches and pergolas.

CONSTRUCTION: Wood frame with natural, rustic materials, often on a stone foundation or stone foundation and first floor with patterned shingles above. Horizontal wood siding, vertical board-and-batten siding, though siding may be any material in marginal examples.

The American Craftsman Style, like the Prairie Style, was influenced by England's Arts and Crafts Movement of the late 19th century. Gustav Stickley, a New York furniture maker, published *Craftsman* magazine, originally to advocate the value of handicrafts but also to discus furniture and home and interior design, as well as philosophies of country living. The "Craftsman Idea," Stickley wrote, sought to replace the increasingly

Similar to "House Design for Outdoor Life in a Warm Climate," *Craftsman*, Jan. 1909

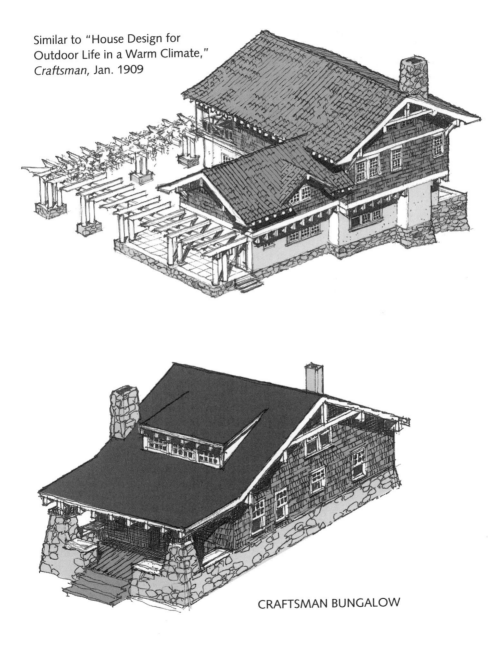

CRAFTSMAN BUNGALOW

commercial values of American society with a simpler way of life: one based on a "wholesome country life" rather than "restless and feverish ambition." Unlike the English Arts and Crafts Movement, however, Craftsman valued efficiency and modern conveniences. It was Stickley who proposed the modest Bungalow as a practical expression of the Craftsman philosophy. Many styles and types of homes were featured in Craftsman, but all had simple, informal floor plans, interiors of wood detailing with built-in seating, sideboards, and bookcases, large fireplaces, and a direct relationship to the natural surroundings. (Many of the Craftsman principles can be found in Frank Lloyd Wright's work and writings.)

The Craftsman Style was developed and carried to new heights in California, most notably by the Greene brothers in Pasadena and Bernard Maybeck in San Francisco. The Greenes became acquainted with H.H. Richardson's work while studying architecture at MIT. Moving to California in 1888, they were exposed to Japanese forms and craftsmanship, and with these influences they eventually produced some of the most original and elegant residential architecture in the country, strongly influencing other architects and going far beyond the fundamental Craftsman concepts, both in scale and refinement of detail. Their luxurious superbungalows are sometimes called Western Stick Style, which implies a connection to the earlier Stick Style that doesn't really exist.

The rustic architecture of the Craftsman Style outlasted its philosophy. Along with a hint of Mission Style, it was applied to modest housing in California, resulting in a fresh, new approach after the scorned excesses of high Victorian fashion. Along with the bungalow craze, rustic Craftsman details, however sparse, eventually appeared in thousands of homes across the country. The Craftsman Style is not synonymous with the Bungalow, although the terms are closely allied in history, and "Craftsman Bungalow" or "California Bungalow" describes a lot of houses, especially in California. However, regardless of the house form, it is the rustic detailing, even the barest vestigial remnant, that determines a Craftsman home.

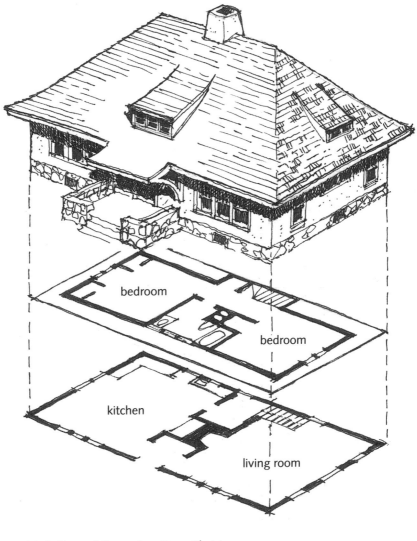

bedroom

bedroom

kitchen

living room

"A Cottage of Cement or Stone That Is
Conveniently Arranged for a Small Family,"
Craftsman, Apr. 1905

Miller House, *Altoona, Pa., c. 1921*

The Bungalow (1900–1930)
The Craftsman Bungalow

FORM: Typically a 1½-story, rectangular-plan house of moderate size on a raised foundation. A gently sloped roof with wide overhangs may be front-gabled or side-gabled with dormers at the front or both front and rear. The front-gabled model is approximately twice as deep as its width, built perpendicular to the street; the side-gabled plan is squarer. Wide, deep front porches typical, as are bay windows along one side. Prominent brick chimney. Large, high-styled bungalows are rare.

STYLISTIC DETAIL: May have Craftsman exposed beam and rafter ends, deep overhanging eaves, and massive porch roof supports. Rustic building materials may include stone and rough shingling.

CONSTRUCTION: Generally wood frame, but stone commonly used for exposed foundations and porches.

In British India, the Bungalow was an open wayside structure surrounded by a veranda. In California, diverse architectural styles—ranging from Japanese and Craftsman to English Arts and Crafts and Shingle—came together to make the Bungalow a distinctively American concept. As the style spread from California, however, it lost many of its special characteristics, becoming a popular mail-order house, with "bungalow" becoming a general term for smaller houses.

Bungalows featured sheltering rooflines, inviting porches, and rustic detail. They were also more efficient in terms of space and less expensive

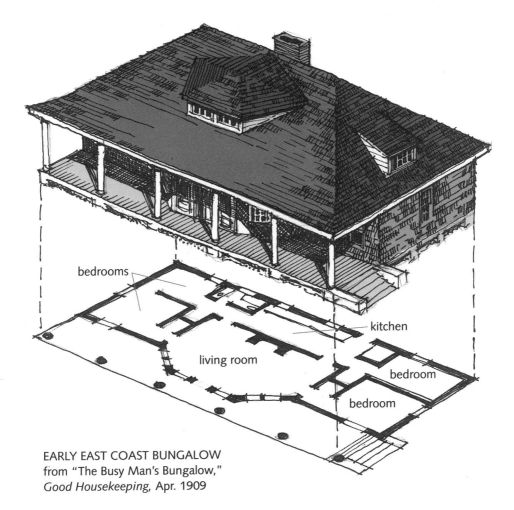

bedrooms

kitchen

living room

bedroom

bedroom

EARLY EAST COAST BUNGALOW
from "The Busy Man's Bungalow,"
Good Housekeeping, Apr. 1909

to build than the complex massing of Victorian houses. The cost of labor and materials had risen appreciably during the last decades of the 19th century, and fewer ordinary citizens could afford Queen Anne or Second Empire houses. The term "Bungaloid" has been coined to deal with the many varieties of bungalow and the application of bungalow features that are commonly seen across the country.

However, two floor plans with different roof configurations have emerged that are generally recognized as constituting a "true" Bungalow. Both are one-and-a-half-story buildings, and both are intended for building lots in small towns. The first type, sometimes called a Box Bungalow, is front-gabled and much deeper than wide, built perpendicular to the street, typically allowing space for a driveway and a garage in the rear. The sizable front porch is under a second gable. The front door is to one side and opens directly into the living room. Behind is the dining room and kitchen with a back door. Next to the living room is a front bedroom with a bath and another bedroom to the rear served by a minimal corridor. There is little space upstairs. The second version is side-gabled and may have a similar plan to the Box Bungalow, but often it is more square. The side-gabled roof dramatically sweeps from front to rear, covering a full-width porch, and, with dormers, it provides space upstairs for another bedroom or even two.

Garden Valley Bungalow, *Boise, Idaho*

In its broadest sense, Bungalow is a conceptual term, referring not to a specific type or style of house but to an early-20th-century architectural notion that suggested simple, informal living. Bungalows evoked thoughts of exotic India, the Far East, and Old (Spanish) California and at the same time appealed to the latest trends with their Craftsman details.

REPRESENTATIVE STYLED BUNGALOWS, c. 1920

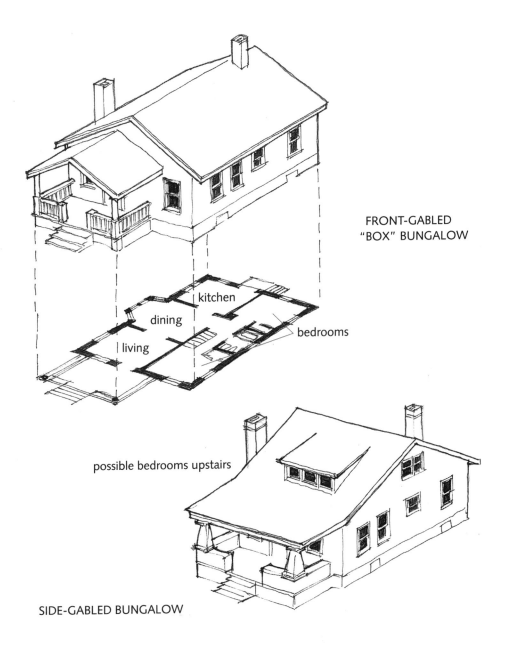

FRONT-GABLED
"BOX" BUNGALOW

kitchen

dining

bedrooms

living

possible bedrooms upstairs

SIDE-GABLED BUNGALOW

Modern Trends

While American home buyers were absorbed by bungalows and "period" houses during the 1920s, a few architects—and their clients—considered more forward-looking concepts that, to them, expressed the technological vitality of American society. The collapse of the Prairie School after World War I and the waning influence of a few innovative California architects left open an opportunity for others dissatisfied with the prevailing Victorian, Neoclassical, and other revival fantasies. The Modern aesthetic originated in Europe and the United States as the architectural expression of the Western world's industrial expansion and business development in the latter 19th century. The new architecture was needed for new types of buildings: factories, office buildings, mercantile centers, and economical urban housing for the multitude of workers required by the rapid expansion of business and industry.

Thus Modern architecture arrived more by demand than by aesthetic choice. There was no way that the traditional styles could accommodate the sudden requirements of industry, commerce, and a restive, growing population. The heavy masonry construction of Neoclassical or late Gothic styles was impractical and expensive; Victorian and Georgian motifs were obviously limited in scale and structural capacity. New designs in new materials—concrete, steel frame, and glass—provided rational, well-lighted, flexible, and efficient space. Buildings needed to be relatively quick to erect, enclosing large, clear-span and high-rise spaces. As we now see, the new architecture more than fulfilled its promise, and the world is now overrun with its products.

The first attempts at Modern design were interesting if not widely accepted. Early rumblings in 19th-century Europe produced Art Nouveau's plant-form designs and the geometric patterns of Art Deco. Both were decorative styles that addressed the desire for modernity. Art Deco eventually traveled to the United States, where, with Art (or "Streamline") Moderne, it expressed Americans' fascination with airplanes, trains, and speed. More energetic thrusts of modern design came from the Chicago School's high-rise buildings, Frank Lloyd Wright's interpenetrating floor plans, and European attempts to merge industry, engineering, and architecture. Germany's Bauhaus School had an enormous impact on design, eventually leading to the renowned International Style. These approaches all shared a common goal: to entirely eliminate historical architectural influences by dispensing with all ornament and style, thereby distilling architectural design to its essence.

In the United States there were two main Modernist thrusts: Frank Lloyd Wright's teachings on organic architecture and what came to be called the International Style, advocated by former Bauhaus faculty fleeing Europe before World War II. These émigrés spread the word effectively, writing and teaching at leading architectural schools and turning out young Internationalists. Wright, on the other hand, started his own small school and advocated very personal philosophies of design. His ideas so relied on his considerable talents, not only as an architect but as teacher and promoter, that his work seems to constitute a one-man style. Although he was much more prolific than any of his International Style peers, the latter won the larger nonresidential commissions and, reaching a much broader audience, swept away any remaining romantic or neoclassical tendencies. Both made major contributions, however: Wright distinctively settling his low-slung buildings harmoniously in the landscape; the others building pristine geometrical shapes that might fit anywhere, often in striking contrast to the natural surroundings.

Modernism in U.S. residential architecture was slow to gain acceptance, and it acted more as an influence on American house design rather than succeeding as a specific style. To most Americans, International Style houses and even Frank Lloyd Wright's designs were (and are) considered extreme, and although certain aspects of them have been adopted into our everyday architecture, most single-family homes built in the later 20th century are based on conservative designs intended to resemble farmhouses or Georgian colonials, with the occasional faux chateau or suburban antebellum plantation thrown in. Still, examples of Modern houses can be found in many communities.

For many, Modernism had rationalized the art out of architecture, reducing it to mere problem-solving exercises in efficiency: efficiency in the use of space, construction time, and building costs. These concerns led to a reaction against the "glass box" sameness of so much of modern design. Postmodernism is more intellectual and philosophical than visual; it defines itself by what it is not rather than by any positive theory of design. No clear new direction has yet emerged in residential design, although the Postmodern era has produced some strange and very self-conscious efforts. Interestingly, it has also built some rather conventional-looking houses, even using a few Classical details. Although Postmodernism is much discussed in academic circles, the architecture of the 20th century, and so far the 21st, remains effectively "Modern" to most of us, whatever our intellectual discipline.

Witten House, *Morrisville, Vt.*

Butler House, *Des Moines, Iowa, c. 1937*

Art Moderne (1920–50)
Moderne, Streamline Moderne

FORM: Variable, asymmetrically massed, 1- and 2-story, flat-roofed houses. Rounded, protruding rooms and balconies.

STYLISTIC DETAIL: Strong horizontal emphasis with flat roofs, trim lines, and bands of windows. Also, corner windows, large panels of glass block, steel pipe handrails and balustrades. Rounded corners. Generally free of decorative ornament, although some Art Deco detail may be found at doorways.

CONSTRUCTION: Standard wood frame with smooth stucco surfaces. Steel casement windows.

After World War I, the new aircraft industry presented Americans with sleek forms and streamlined shapes. Graphic arts and industrial design, two relatively new professions, exploited this fascination, producing streamlined motorboats, railroad locomotives, and even household appliances. In the automobile industry, fenders, hoods, and trunks began melting into a single fluid shape. However immobile, a few streamlined buildings also appeared, giving the impression that they too were rushing toward the future.

Though never common, Art Moderne was a far more popular residential design than the geometric Art Deco: it was truly a style of architecture, whereas Art Deco was paint and decoration, angular, stylized floral forms, zigzags and chevrons, with a vertical emphasis.

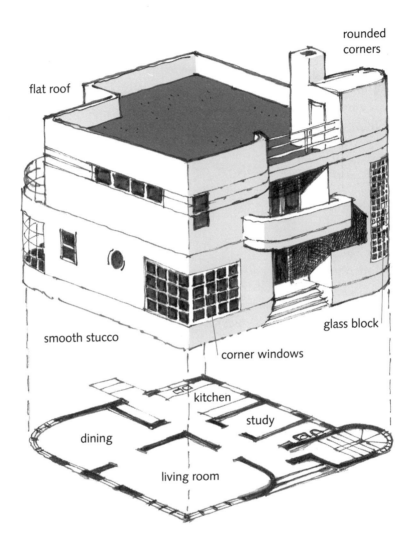

rounded corners

flat roof

smooth stucco

glass block

corner windows

kitchen

study

dining

living room

Both were popular for commercial buildings: Moderne for transportation buildings, airport terminals, and railroad depots, Art Deco for hotels, apartments, and office buildings (notably New York's Chrysler Building), and the two were often combined on the same structure. Both styles were fleeting notions and contributed nothing new in floor plan or construction; though some later Moderne houses resemble the emerging International Style, they were for the most part streamlined shells over conventional floor plans. Art Deco faded by 1930, but Moderne struggled on into the 1950s.

MODEST MODERNE COTTAGE

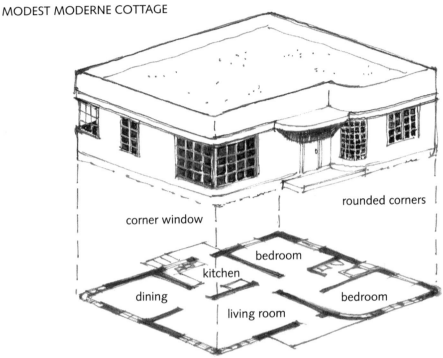

rounded corners

corner window

bedroom

kitchen

dining

bedroom

living room

Farnsworth House, *Plano, Ill., 1951*

The International Style (1930–present)

FORM: Asymmetrical, rectangular, 1- or 2-story block or assembly of blocks with a flat or shed roof. Typically no roof overhangs, but cantilevered roof extensions as sun shading or applied screening devices are common.

STYLISTIC DETAIL: Emphasis is on the horizontal. A determined avoidance of any applied ornament or decoration. Smooth, plain surfaces, typically painted white. Windows may be in large panels, horizontal bands, or punched openings installed nearly flush with outside wall surface. Metal industrial casement windows are common. Floor-to-ceiling glass is juxtaposed with panels of plain wall material. Corner windows. Glass block is occasionally used, possibly in large panels. Featureless entry. In rural settings, contrasts sharply with natural surroundings.

CONSTRUCTION: Originally intended as modular, steel frame and stucco, curtain-wall structure (exterior panels mount outside the columns) but more often built of conventional wood frame and siding. Exposed tubular steel "Lally" columns common.

Emerging from Europe, particularly Germany, after World War I, what was to become the International Style eventually conquered the commercial architectural world, not necessarily for its aesthetic appeal, but for its modular efficiency in sizable projects. Named in 1923 after a book describing an exhibition of European and American avant-garde architecture in New York, the style was a purposeful renunciation of historic architectural tradition; its stated goal was to strip away all

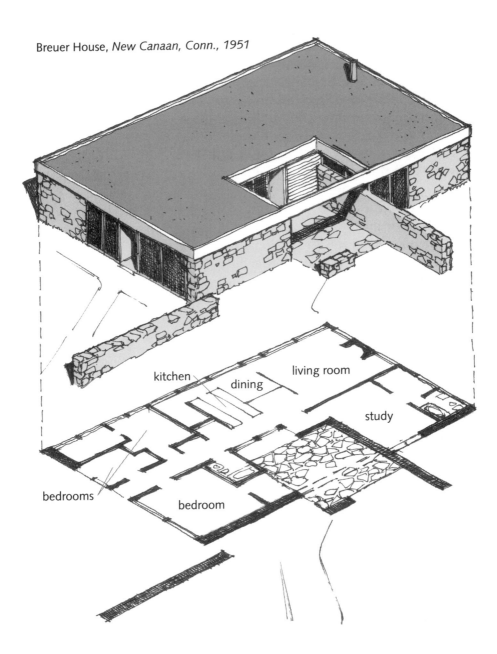

Breuer House, *New Canaan, Conn., 1951*

kitchen

dining

living room

study

bedrooms

bedroom

previously established design elements in order to arrive at the essential core of architectural design. Strongly associated with the German Bauhaus design school, the International Style's leading proponents came to the United States in the late 1930s, leaving Hitler's harassment behind. These men found quick acceptance in American academia. Most notable among them were Walter Gropius and Marcel Breuer at Harvard and Ludwig Mies van der Rohe at the Illinois Institute of Technology in Chicago.

The International Style did not have a serious impact on American house design, though every sizable city has an example or two, usually hidden away in exclusive suburbs, homes of affluent architecture buffs or the architects themselves. The style's austerity and open plans did not appeal to typical households and it was relatively expensive to build. When interpreted in more affordable materials, like plywood, the look tended toward cheap-ness, which gave so-called modern architecture a bad name to many.

The International Style was somewhat adjusted to American tastes by architects who used more practical floor plans and visually softer, warmer elements—wood siding and rough stone, for instance.

Le Corbusier's Villa Savoye (1930), in Poissy, France, is perhaps the best-known International Style house and was an early rallying point for the style's crusaders. The austere but elegant Farnsworth House (1951) by Mies van der Rohe, in Plano, Illinois, and Philip Johnson's own little steel and glass hideaway in New Canaan, Connecticut, carried the style's concept to its inevitable extreme: the glass box.

These houses remain, even to those interested, handsome but unlivable design exercises. More homelike examples are the Gropius House (1938) in Lincoln, Massachusetts; any of Marcel Breuer's designs; and Richard Neutra's Tremaine House near Santa Barbara, California (1948). With the incomparable Fallingwater (1935) in Bear Run, Pennsylvania, Frank Lloyd Wright, an outspoken foe of the International Style, claimed to have outdone the Europeans at their own game.

Interest in the style faded in the 1960s, when architects were reduced to decorating their boxes. However, in the 1970s a renewed interest in International Style residential design was shown by a group of eastern architects known as the New York Five. Of that group, Richard Meier has been particularly successful in further refining and developing the American International Style home. This "revival" produced highly sophisticated designs of complex, pristine structures, typically pure white, perched in and contrasting sharply with the natural environment. Summer houses and vacation cottages were favorite projects.

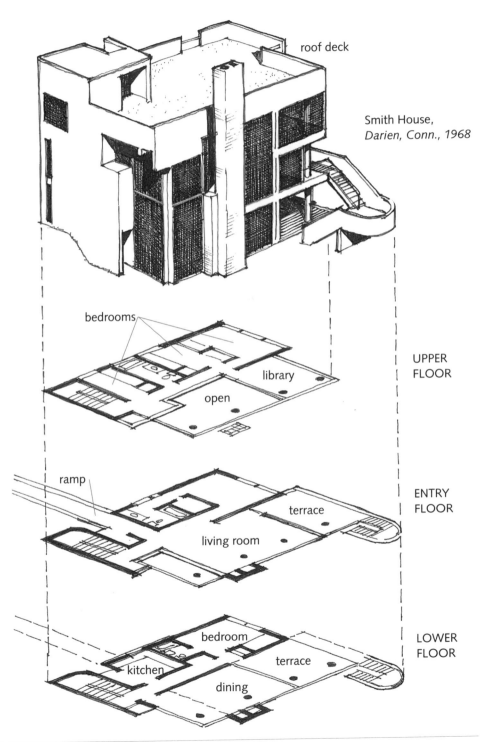

roof deck

Smith House,
Darien, Conn., 1968

bedrooms

library

open

UPPER
FLOOR

ramp

terrace

living room

ENTRY
FLOOR

bedroom

kitchen

terrace

dining

LOWER
FLOOR

Glossary

acanthus · A Mediterranean plant whose foliage inspired the carved and cast capitals on Corinthian and Composite columns.

Adam Style (Adamesque) · A refined architectural style named for the English architects Robert Adam (1728–92) and his three brothers. It is noted for its delicate Neoclassical ornament, particularly for interiors. A major influence on the American Federal style.

adobe · A Spanish-Arabic word for the clay or mud mixture used in making sun-dried (not oven-baked) bricks of mud and straw. Also a structure of adobe mud or brick, plastered with a mud finish.

aggregate · A hard, stable material, such as crushed stone, gravel, or sand, mixed with cement to make concrete or mortar.

airhole · A ventilation opening in a masonry foundation wall.

American Style · Italianate.

anchor plate · A visible plate connected to a tie rod in masonry construction, often decoratively shaped.

antebellum · Before the Civil War.

arcade · A covered exterior corridor with a series of arches along one or both sides.

arch · A masonry construction that spans an opening or the shape of an arch in other materials.

architrave · In Classical architecture, the lowest band of the entablature, which rests directly on the supporting columns.

Art Deco (Zigzag Style) · A decorative style of the early 20th century characterized by angular geometric forms and applied to a range of products, including furniture and jewelry. As architectural motifs, usually applied to commercial buildings. Frequently included with Art Moderne. See page 358.

Art Moderne (Moderne, Streamline Moderne) · A horizontal and sometimes rounded antihistorical style of the 1920s and '30s that attempts to look streamlined. Frequently includes Art Deco elements.

Art Nouveau · A turn-of-the-century European design motif of fluid, organic forms, decorative rather than architectural.

Arts and Crafts Movement · A philosophy of design stressing handicrafts and a return to preindustrial design. Popular in England in the late 19th century, it had some influence on the American Prairie and Craftsman styles.

ashlar · Smoothly finished, squared stone blocks. May be regularly or randomly coursed.

ballflower · A spherical Gothic decoration consisting of a ball held by three stylized petals.

balloon framing · A system of light timber framing with studs and corner posts that reach from sill to roof plate. Joists are nailed to the studs or supported on girts. Balloon framing, which was faster and less expensive than timber frame construction, revolutionized home building in the United States from the 1830s on.

baluster · Each of the small vertical members supporting a railing.

balustrade · A railing or parapet made of balusters, pedestals, and rails.

band (band molding) · A horizontal, flat wall molding.

banister · A baluster, or a stair railing consisting of balusters, posts, and rails.

bargeboard (vergeboard) · A trim board attached to extended eaves at a gable end, often ornately sawn or carved on Gothic Revival houses.

barn framing · Timber frame construction without studs between posts.

Baroque · A European Renaissance architecture characterized by the free use and distortions of Classical elements, including curved surfaces, color, and the use of sculpture.

basket-handle arch · An elliptical arch suggesting the shape of a basket handle.

bas-relief · A low carving protruding somewhat from the background plane.

batten · A narrow board. See **board-and-batten**.

battered wall · A wall with a slanted outer surface narrowing toward the top.

battlements (castellations, crenelations) · In residential design, a decorative, notched stone parapet suggesting castle fortifications. Can also be exterior wall moldings shaped like battlements, as on Bacon's Castle (page 101).

Bauhaus · An influential German design school established by Walter Gropius in 1919 that sought to combine art, industrial technology, and crafts into a theory of functional design, particularly in architecture.

bay · Originally, in timber framed houses, the wall space between two vertical framing members where a door or window could be installed. After the advent of light framing (balloon, western), a bay refers to the regular spacing of windows and doors; a "five-bay Georgian" façade, for instance, will have a central doorway and two windows on either side.

bay window · A window or assembly of windows projecting from the outside wall.

beam · A horizontal, structural (load-bearing) member going from post to post.

bearing wall · A continuous load-bearing, structural wall with minimal penetrations.

Beaux-Arts · 1. A general term describing the application of various Classical elements to architectural designs according to the principles set forth at the École des Beaux-Arts in Paris, especially in the latter 19th century. 2. A particularly ostentatious American architectural style used for monumental buildings and a few flamboyant mansions around the turn of the 20th century.

belt course · A projecting horizontal molding used to divide a wall and emphasizing floor levels, usually in masonry construction. May be of brick or molded cement plaster.

belvedere · (cupola) A small, open-sided rooftop structure, usually centered, typical of Italianate and Octagon houses.

bent · A rigid transverse frame assembly used in series such as the anchor-bent Dutch barn framing system.

black-and-white · Exposed timber framing with white infill, as seen on Elizabethan and Tudor houses.

blind arch · A masonry arch with the opening filled in, usually recessed from the arch face.

board-and-batten · An exterior wall finish of vertical planks where the joints are covered with a narrow board, the batten.

bond · The pattern of brick or stone, including the joints, in a masonry wall.

bond course · A row of brick headers in a masonry wall.

bousillage (Fr.) · A "nogging" wall infill made of mud and lime with straw, animal hair, or Spanish moss as a binder and applied on a horizontal lattice between posts or studs. Typical of French Mississippi Colonial construction.

bracket · A projecting structural or decorative member supporting or appearing to support extended eaves, cornices, porch roofs, or upper floors. Commonly found on Italianate, Italian Renaissance Revival, and some later Victorian houses.

Bracketed Style · Another term for Italianate.

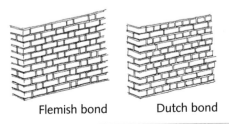 

| Flemish bond | Dutch bond | running bond | English bond |

breast · 1. A part of the chimney exposed to the interior, usually above the fireplace, and often plastered. 2. The interior wall space between floor and window.

brick veneer · A single layer of brick applied to the face of a wood framed wall.

broken pediment (open pediment) · A pediment with its cornices interrupted at the midpoint or peak, usually to frame a decorative detail such as a cartouche or urn. Commonly seen over Federal doorways and windows.

bull's-eye window · A round or oval window often occurring in pediments and gable ends.

bungalow · A general term for a small, one-and-one-half-story rectangular house, usually sited perpendicular to the street, typically with some Crafts-man detailing and a wide front porch.

buttery (17th- and 18th-century English Colonial) · A room for storing provisions and cooking equipment, usually off the kitchen.

buttress · An external masonry pier supporting a masonry wall, designed to resist lateral forces.

cabin · A small rustic dwelling, crudely built, often only one room with a fireplace.

camelback · A one-story house with a two-story section at the rear. Associated with 19th-century New Orleans.

canales (Sp.) · Spouts or roof-draining scuppers projecting through an adobe wall.

cantilever · An unsupported building element extending out past the bearing wall or supporting post.

Cape Cod house · 1. A one-and-a-half-story New England house, end-gabled with central chimney floor plan and steep roof, originally built in Massachusetts from 1700 on. 2. Today, a small end-gabled house common in lower-cost housing developments, barely resembling the original.

capital · The topmost part of a column.

Carpenter Gothic · A highly ornate, mid-19th-century variant of Gothic Revival with richly applied wood scrollwork at porch railings, bargeboards, and brackets. An expression of the new availability of power woodworking tools such as the lathe and scroll saw.

cartouche · A cast or carved raised relief decorative element in the shape of a scroll or an oval frame surrounded by scrollwork. Commonly associated with Beaux-Arts architecture.

casa (Sp.) · House.

casement window · A window hinged at the side (jamb) that can swing either in or out.

castellate · Suggesting the appearance of a castle with ornamental battlements or crenelations.

Catslide · An English term for a small southern house, end-gabled, with a shed added at the rear, similar in silhouette to the New England Saltbox.

center-passage plan · A two-room floor plan with an entry and central corridor dividing the house. A refinement of the hall-and-parlor house, particularly in Virginia and Maryland from the latter 18th century on.

chamber (English colonies, 17th, 18th century) · 1. The smaller of two rooms in a hall-and-chamber house, typically a bedroom. 2. A second-floor room, also usually for sleeping.

chamber chamber · An upstairs room over the chamber in a hall-and-chamber house.

chamfer · A bevel cut into the edges of beams and columns or posts. A decorative detail but functional as well in reducing damage to sharp corners while saving heads from nasty bumps. Common during Colonial times, when wood structural members were exposed inside.

Chateauesque · A late-19th- and early-20th-century, elegant American style supposedly derived from 16th-century French châteaux.

chinking (nogging) · The material used for filling gaps in exterior walls, particularly in log construction. Clay was generally used, often with an aggregate of twigs, stones, hair, or Spanish moss.

Churrigueresque · A Spanish baroque style developed by the Churriguera family of architects in the 17th century and noted for its extravagant yet harmonious decorative detail. Brought to Mexico, it became even more intricately fantastic when applied to church doorways. It came to the United States as much more modest ornamentation on Spanish Colonial Revival houses.

clapboard · A piece of wood siding mounted horizontally and overlapping another. The top edge of the board is thinner than the bottom. Before the advent of sawmills, clapboards were riven (split) by hand from large timbers.

Classical architecture (Classicism) · The architecture of Greece and Rome that inspired Italian Renaissance architecture as well as the classical revivals that followed.

Classical orders · See **orders**. The arrangement of columns and entablature used in Classical architecture, including the Greek and Roman orders: Doric, Ionian, Corinthian, Tuscan, and Composite.

Classical revivals · Early-19th-century American styles that used Classical

Greek and Roman elements. In the late 19th and early 20th centuries, a more academic Classical Revival produced imposing stone mansions.

clerestory · A raised section of exterior wall fitted with high windows for light and ventilation.

collar tie (collar beam) · A horizontal structural member connecting two opposite roof rafters and forming the letter A.

Colonial Revival · A very popular late-19th- and 20th-century style further embellishing Georgian and Dutch Colonial themes. Elements of the style are still with us in high-styled subdivisions as well as on more modest suburban homes.

colonette · A small decorative column.

colonnade · A series of equally spaced columns supporting an entablature or porch roof.

column (post, pillar) · The slim vertical structural member supporting a roof or upper story. May be round, square, or geometric in a sectional view.

Composite order · See **orders**.

corbeling · Decorative masonry details where a projecting course of masonry is topped by another projecting course and yet another, creating a stepped brick or stone cantilever. Commonly seen on chimney caps, brick parapets, and cornices.

Corinthian order · See **orders**.

cornice · The exterior trim at the top of a wall where it meets the roof. In classical architecture, the uppermost projection of the entablature above the frieze and architrave.

cornice return · The point at the eave where the cornice line turns the corner to reach the gable end and stops.

cortile · An Italian courtyard.

course · A single horizontal run of masonry.

coursed masonry · A masonry wall with all the elements of a course of the same height, although the courses themselves may vary in height.

Craftsman · A popular American style in the early 20th century exemplified by wide eaves, exposed rafter and beam ends, large porches, and the use of rustic materials.

crenel (crenelle) · One of the open spaces in a battlement parapet.

crenelated (crenellated) · Having a battlement-shaped parapet.

Creole · Originally a person of European ancestry born in the West Indies or Louisiana during the French Colonial period. Soon expanded to include the descendants of French soldiers and African–West Indian women. Finally, it came to distinguish one likely to be of mixed racial and cultural background who, unlike strangers and foreigners, spoke the Creole language and was well acclimated to the complex culture and difficult environment of the New Orleans area.

cresting (roof crest) · A decorative ornament, usually of sawn wood or cast metal, installed along the ridge of a roof or wall, typical of the Second Empire and Queen Anne styles.

cross gable · A gable intersecting the main roof at right angles, typically over the front entry.

Cross House · A house with a cross-shaped plan where a building element intersects with the rectangular main structure, usually at the center entrance, and extends through the house to the rear, particularly in the 17th-century Chesapeake Bay region.

crow step · The stepped parapet gables commonly used in Dutch urban architecture from at least the 16th century, once a familiar sight on New York City streets.

cupola (belvedere, lantern) · A small rooftop structure, often decorative but able to provide ventilation and light to the center of the house. Typical of Octagon and Italianate houses.

curtains · See **hyphens**.

curtain wall · A nonloadbearing wall of any material, entirely hung from and outside the structural frame of a building.

cushion capital · A cushion-shaped column capital appearing to be "pushed out" by the weight of the load above.

dentil · One of a continuous row of regularly spaced small blocks installed along and under the projecting cornice of Classically detailed buildings.

dependencies (flankers) · Smaller outbuildings symmetrically placed on either side of a main house, often connected by a colonnade or enclosed "hyphen." Inspired by drawings of Palladio's country villas outside Venice, a typical arrangement of large plantations in Maryland, Virginia, and North Carolina in the latter 1700s. Used as kitchens, living quarters for servants, and offices.

diapering · In Colonial Maryland and Virginia, a decorative masonry effect achieved by creating patterns of glazed brick in monolithic brick walls.

Dog-Trot house · A two-room log cabin with an open, outdoor passage between the rooms, all under a single end-gabled roof.

doorjamb · One of the two vertical sides of a door frame.

Doric order · See **orders**.

dormer · A small gable or shed projecting from a sloped roof containing a window to bring light and ventilation into an attic or upper floor.

Double-Cell house · A Double-Pen house.

Double House · In Charleston, South Carolina, a formal, two- or three-story townhouse, generally symmetrical with a center entry and large central hall. Not two Charleston Single Houses combined.

double-hung window or sash · A window consisting of two vertically sliding sashes, one mounted above and just outside the other. In a single-hung sash, only the bottom sash moved. A triple-hung sash was uncommon.

Double-Pen · A two-room log cabin with a dividing log wall.

double-pile · A house two rooms deep.

dovecote (*pigeonnier*) · A structure housing tame doves or pigeons for roosting and nesting.

Dutch bond (English cross bond) · See **bond**.

Dutch Colonial · 1. The houses built by Dutch settlers and others in New Netherlands, particularly along the Hudson River, in northern New Jersey, and in eastern Long Island during the Colonial era. 2. Today, a vague house style usually having a gambrel roof, possibly with extended eaves in imitation of an actual Colonial house popular in New Jersey and Long Island after 1750.

Eastlake · A style of architectural decoration characterized by extravagantly turned spindle work, porch posts, brackets, and railings. Named for an English furniture designer and architect, Charles Lock Eastlake, the style is really a result of American power tools embellishing his peculiar angled and notched furniture designs. Eastlake was

not pleased that his name was attached to such excesses.

eave · The lower edge of a pitched roof that extends past the supporting wall, particularly the underside.

eclecticism · In the latter 19th century, the free use and mixing of architectural elements from earlier European styles.

École des Beaux-Arts · The influential French art school founded in 1648. It had a considerable effect on American architects in the late 19th century, advocating the use of Classical and Renaissance elements in grand designs.

Egyptian Revival · A minor 19th-century style with battered walls and massive "papyrus" columns. Rarely seen in housing, it was occasionally used for dark public buildings and cemeteries. There was a brief Neo-Egyptian revival in the 1930s.

elevation · A scale drawing of a building façade.

Elizabethan · In the United States, the term often refers to late-19th- and early-20th-century English Revival architecture that used "black-and-white" half-timbering. Based vaguely on late medieval, rambling English cottages, it is often used interchangeably with Tudor.

ell · An extension of a house at right angles to the main structure.

engaged column · A column attached to and part of the wall behind it, similar to a pilaster.

English bond · See **bond**.

entablature · In Classical architecture, the entire horizontal span supported by columns comprising the architrave, the frieze, and the cornice.

entresol · A mezzanine floor, as seen in some New Orleans townhouses.

eyebrow · A low, rounded dormer with a window, appearing as a wave in the roof but not interrupting its shingles or slates.

eyebrow window (frieze-band window) · A small window, which can be opened, built into the frieze of some Greek Revival houses.

façade · The main exterior wall of a building, usually at the front or entry wall.

fanlight (fan) · An arched window over the main entrance, often with radial muntins suggesting a fan or sunburst. Common on Georgian houses.

Federal Style (Adamesque, Adam) · Successor to the pre-Revolutionary Georgian style and the initial Classical Revival style. Strongly influenced by the work of the British architect Robert Adam and his brothers.

fenestration · The arrangement of windows on a building's façade.

festoon (swag) · A decorative representation of a garland or ribbon suspended in a curve between two points. Seen on Classical Revival architecture.

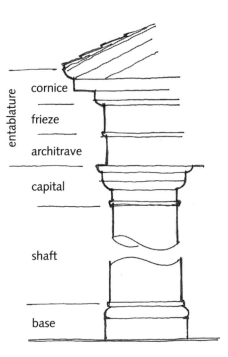

fieldstone · Rough, natural stone used in the uncoursed construction of walls and foundations.

finial · An ornamental spire often used at the top of the roof peak on Gothic Revival houses.

Flemish bond (Flemish cross bond, Flemish diagonal bond) · See **bond**.

fluting · The vertical grooves cut into Classical columns (except Tuscan).

foliated · Adorned with leafy decoration.

frieze · That part of the Classical entablature between the cornice above and the architrave below.

front-gabled · Having the house entry and a gable end facing the street, with the eaves on the sides.

gable · The triangular wall at the end of a gable roof.

gable end · That end of a house under the peak of a gabled roof.

gable front · Having the main entry at the gable end.

gable front-and-wing · A front-gabled house with an ell at the rear.

gable roof · A roof of two equal slopes joined to create a gable at each end.

galérie (Fr.) (veranda) · In the French Mississippi Colonial era, the outside passageway or porch.

gambrel roof · A roof shape using two slopes per side, a gentle pitch from the ridge, then steeper to the eaves. Common from English and Dutch Colonial hearths to the present, the Dutch gambrel having shorter, flatter pitches at the top and long sweeping slopes to extended eaves.

garçonnière (Fr.) · In French and Cajun Louisiana, a sleeping loft or separate dormitory for young men.

gargoyle · A decorative stone spout, often grotesquely carved, that drains water from a roof.

Garrison · Originally a New England Colonial house with a second-story overhang, or "jetty," at the front façade, a feature said to resemble fortress design, allowing defenders to shoot down at their attackers. Today, any builder's house with such a feature is called a Garrison Colonial.

gauged brick · Brick cut and rubbed into special shapes for the arches and heads of windows, particularly in the Colonial Chesapeake Bay region.

Georgian · A pre–Revolutionary War style common in the English colonies, noted for its rigid symmetry of rectangular floor plans, central axial entry and hall passage, evenly sized and spaced windows, and dual, symmetrical chimneys. Georgian followed the medieval and transitional Colonial styles, representing a new sophistication and a connection to the English class society. It became very desirable in the increasingly prosperous and status-conscious colonies.

Georgian Revival · A rediscovery of Georgian Colonial architecture in the late 19th and early 20th centuries as part of the broader Colonial Revival, which Georgian Revival is some-times called.

Gothic Revival (Perpendicular) · A style of the mid-19th century in the United States that attempted to reinterpret the romantic images of the earlier Gothic architecture of France and England.

great house · The main house on a plantation.

Greek Revival · A 19th-century American style based on the Classical forms of Greek antiquity.

hacienda · In the Southwest, a large, self-sufficient estate or ranch, or the main house on a large ranch.

half-timbered · A type of construction using a timber frame filled in with nogging. The frame is exposed, creating a visible pattern on the exterior wall.

hall · In residential architecture: 1. The larger room with the entry of a hall-and-parlor or hall-and-chamber house. 2. The passage connecting several rooms in a house.

Hall-and-Parlor, Hall-and-Chamber House · A two-room plan common in the English colonies. The hall served as a general reception, entertaining, and work space while the parlor was usually for sleeping, although there were many variations.

hall chamber · The upstairs room over a hall.

hand-hewn · Hewn or shaped by hand using tools such as axes and adzes.

head · The horizontal top member of a door or window frame.

header · A brick laid flat with the end exposed in order to bond two wythes (thicknesses) of brick together in a wall.

header course · A masonry course consisting only of headers.

hearth · Aside from the fireplace, the term is used here to describe the core area of a distinct established culture, from which elements diffused to new areas. Examples of cultural hearths are the Delaware Valley and the New England hearths.

hewn (hewed) · Roughly shaped with hand tools such as axes and adzes.

hipped roof · A gabled roof "beveled," or hipped, at both ends so that it slopes toward the peak from all four sides.

hoodmold (dripstone) · In Gothic architecture, a stone molding projecting over a window or door to divert rainwater; also a common detail of the Gothic Revival style executed in wood.

hyphens · Connecting corridors or colonnades from the main house to two symmetrically flanking outbuildings. Typical of plantation layouts in the 18th-century Tidewater region.

"I" house · A symmetrical two-story, gable-ended house with a rectangular, one-room-deep floor plan, center entry, and three or five bays.

International · A starkly functional style developed in Europe after World War I that tried to avoid any historical reference. Successfully used for commercial projects; with notable exceptions, it was seldom used for homes in the United States.

Ionic order · See **orders**.

Italianate (Tuscan) · A style inspired by the villas and manors of Renaissance northern Italy. Squarish in plan and somewhat formal, Italianate houses were well suited for suburban building lots and were extremely popular in the mid-19th century. "Italianate" is often used for Italian Villa homes as well.

Italian Renaissance Revival · Arriving in the late 19th century, this style was a much grander interpretation of northern Italian Renaissance villas and palaces than the earlier Italianate and Italian Villa styles, resulting in more luxurious mansions.

Italian Villa · Concurrent with the Italianate Style, the Italian Villa was also drawn from northern Renaissance Italy but had a more rural, asymmetrical character.

jacal · A type of simple construction once common in the American Southwest that uses vertical poles or logs embedded in trenches, then chinked with mud.

Jacobean · A style named for James I (1603–25), one of the English Revival styles popular with the gentry at the turn of the 20th century. Characterized by stone construction, steep roofs, and shaped parapet gables. The occasional result of combining its features with an Elizabethan motif has been slyly called Jacobethan.

jamb · Either of the two vertical side pieces of a door frame.

Jeffersonian Classicism (Roman Revival, Early Classical Revival) · A Neoclassical style based on Roman public buildings and strongly advocated by Thomas Jefferson.

jerkinhead · A gable end "beveled" at the peak to form a partial hip; used also at dormers.

jetty · The overhang of the upper floor of a house, usually at the front over the entry, as seen on a Garrison Colonial house.

joist · In wood construction, one of a series of closely spaced parallel beams supporting an upper floor.

keystone · The center block of a masonry arch, often larger than the other stones and ornamental.

lantern · A small structure with a window on the top of a roof or dome, similar to a cupola or belvedere.

latillas (Sp.) · Saplings laid across *vigas* (roof beams) as the base for a flat mud or earthen roof on adobe houses.

leaded glass · Glazing held in place with lead "cames," or thin mullions.

lime · A material made from limestone or seashells by crushing or heating into a powdery form; used in making mortar, plaster, and whitewash.

living hall · The large first-floor circulation space in a Queen Anne house, with fireplace and stairs accessed from the main entry and opening to living areas through large doorways.

Lombard · Italianate.

loophole · For defensive purposes in Colonial times, a narrow vertical opening in the exterior wall from which to observe the enemy and return fire. In masonry construction, the sides of the opening are splayed, making it much wider on the inside.

Mansard (Mansard roof) · A roof of two pitches on all four (or more) sides of the house, the outer slope quite steep and the inner gently sloped. Named for the French architect François Mansart, it is typical of the American Second Empire style and mansions showing a Beaux-Arts influence. It is sometimes confusingly (and wrongly) referred to as a gambrel roof, which has gable ends.

masonry · Stone, brick, concrete block, and adobe construction, typically of bearing walls.

massing · The exterior sculptural composition of the volumes of a building.

medallion · An ornamental panel of flowers or other decoration in bas-relief, typically set into a wall, ceiling surface, or frieze.

mezzanine (*entresol*) · A partial second level typically overlooking the floor below as a balcony.

midden · A communal dump associated with pre-European contact, Native American settlements that, along the Atlantic coast, provided European settlers with mounds of oyster shells, a valuable source of lime for making mortar.

Miesian · Architecture in the manner of Ludwig Mies van der Rohe (1886–1969), a German architect noted for rational, austere designs devoid of any ornament.

Mission · An early-20th-century style looking to the historic Spanish California missions for architectural inspiration.

Moderne · See **Art Moderne**.

molding · Any linear decorative trim shaped in countless geometric profiles;

used on wall surfaces, cornices, columns, door and window frames, and the like, often to hide uneven construction joints.

Monterey · A style (c. 1830) originating before the Anglo-American cultural assault on California. Characterized by a pitched roof, adobe construction, and second-level balconies.

mortar · The cementitious material used for bonding masonry units, stone, brick, and concrete block.

mortar joint · The mortar-filled space between masonry units. The joints may be tooled to be flush, concave, or raked, among other treatments.

mullion (muntin) · A vertical member separating multiple windows or panels of glass in a window.

muntin (muntin bar) · Similar to a mullion but typically smaller, separating individual panes of glass in windows and doors vertically and horizontally.

Neoantique · Neoclassical.

Neoclassical, Neoclassicism · Art and architecture in the 18th and 19th centuries based on the Classical design principles taken from Greek and Roman antiquity.

nogging · In timber frame construction, the material used to fill the space between the structural members in the exterior wall.

Octagon house · An eight-sided house, much publicized in the mid-19th century.

ogee · The decorative, double-curved S shape used in ogee arches, in the cross section of ogee moldings, and in the profile of an ogee roof.

one-over-one · A double-hung window with one pane of glass in each sash. Also six-over-six, twelve-over-twelve, etc.

onion dome · Reminiscent of Byzantine architecture, a bulbous dome, shaped like an onion, that terminates in a point at the top. Rare, but seen on a few flamboyant, eclectic mansions in the United States.

open cornice · A cornice in which overhanging eaves are not boxed in and the rafters and the undersides of the roof sheathing are exposed but trimmed with a fascia board.

open pediment · Broken pediment.

orders · Classical design principles that determine the proportions, size, and shape of columns and entablature. The Greek orders were the Doric, Ionian, and Corinthian; the Romans added the Tuscan and Composite.

organic architecture · A philosophy of design espoused by Louis Sullivan and Frank Lloyd Wright that was based on using natural forms in harmony with the natural environment and resulting in a unified, integrated "organism" of a building.

oriel · An aboveground projection from the wall of a house in the form of a bay window.

overdoor · A window above the doorway that has been incorporated into the door frame assembly like a fanlight.

oxeye · A round or oval window typically in a gable end or dormer.

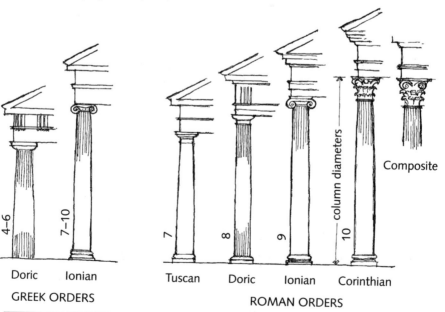

GREEK ORDERS — Doric   Ionian

ROMAN ORDERS — Tuscan   Doric   Ionian   Corinthian   Composite

palisade · A stockade fence built by setting logs with pointed tops into the ground in long rows.

Palladian · Architecture influenced by the Renaissance Italian architect Andrea Palladio (1508–80), largely through his widely published drawings of country villas. Characterized by symmetrical massing under a hipped roof and pro-jecting, pedimented central porticos, all with Classical Roman elements and proportions.

Palladian motif (Serlian motif, Venetian motif) · A three-part opening of vertically proportioned shapes, with the center, taller opening arched, the spring line or full diameter of its arch resting on the flat lintels of the other two openings.

Palladian window (Venetian window) · A triple window shaped in accordance with the Palladian motif (see above).

panel door · A door of wood panels held by a framework of horizontal wood rails and vertical wood stiles.

paneled, paneling · Faced with wood panels held in a frame.

parapet · That part of an exterior wall extending above the roof.

parapet gable · That part of a gable-end wall extending above a sloping roof.

parlor · Originally a room used for sleeping as well as entertaining guests and eating, particularly in a hall-and-parlor house. It was more private than the hall, with the main entry.

Palladian window

passage · An interior corridor. In the center-passage house, a narrow space running from front to rear, the main entry at one end and a secondary entrance at the other.

patio · An open courtyard.

pattern book · Imported beginning in the 18th century, a book of drawings intended as a guide for American housewrights and carpenters to the popular English styles of the time. In the 19th century, pattern and plan books were published in the United States by American designers and were very influential in promoting specific styles and philosophies for living.

pavilion · In residential architecture, a prominent, projecting section of the main façade of a large house, identified by its full height, roof shape, and other architectural elements.

pavilion roof · A steeply pitched rectangular-plan hipped roof, likely to be steeper on the ends. Typical of French Colonial architecture in Canada and the Mississippi Valley.

pebbledash, pebble dash · The technique of applying pebbles or gravel to a wet layer of exterior stucco wall. The term has also been used to describe the first 19th-century attempts in the United States to build cast-in-place concrete walls for houses, using pebbles as aggregate.

pedestal · In Classical architecture, the structural element at floor level on which a column rests.

pediment · The form of the triangular, gently sloped gable over the entablature on a Classical building, made up of the tympanum, or center panel, enclosed by two raking cornices above and a horizontal cornice at its base. As a style element, it may be found over doors and windows and above porches and pavilions, as well as at the gable ends of a building. Over windows, it may be rounded, like an arch.

pendant · A suspended ornament or carved corner post, particularly at the overhanging corners and at either side of the front entry on Colonial Garrison houses in New England.

pent · 1. A secondary, shed-roofed structure added against the main house. 2. A small roof or hood over an entry or window.

pent eave · An additional narrow shed roof running the length of the eaves

at the level of the second floor on the front only. Less commonly, it was built also on the rear, the gable ends, or on all four façades. Typical of Pennsylvania farmhouses from the 18th century on.

penthouse · The first definition of "pent" above. Also a modern rooftop or top-floor residence.

pergola · An open grid of wood beams supported by posts, usually attached to a house, to hold shade or climbing plants. A common accessory of Craftsman homes.

piazza · In residential architecture, particularly in the southeastern United States, a covered open space or veranda attached to the side or sides of a house. The distinguishing feature of the Charleston Single House, used for receiving visitors and entertaining.

Picturesque Movement · A romantic reaction to the prevailing Classical Revival style during the first half of the 19th century. Originating in England, it was expressed in the United States by Victorian styles: Gothic Revival, Italianate, and Second Empire.

pier · A square or rectangular column of wood or masonry, free standing or projecting from a wall, that typically carries the structural loads from above the first story to the foundation.

pilaster · An "engaged" (part of a wall) column or pier, typically of Classical design with base and capital. Although originally structural, it is now usually a decorative addition.

pile · 1. An uncommon reference to the depth (front to back) of a house; a double-pile house is two rooms deep. 2. A wood or metal shaft driven into the ground as part of a foundation.

pineapple · Actually a pinecone, an 18th-century and earlier symbol of fertility and hospitality when carved or cast into moldings, decorative pendants, or finials on hipped roofs.

pinnacle · A vertical rooftop ornament usually tapering to a point or ending in a ball. Similar to a finial.

pipe rail · A handrail made from lengths of stock steel pipe.

pitch · The slope of a roof.

pit sawn · Lumber sawn lengthwise from large timbers by two workers using a large two-handed saw (a pit saw). One person stands on the horizontal timber, the other is below in a pit. Boards for house construction were cut this way until the early colonists could build sawmills powered by waterwheels.

placita (Sp.) · A small courtyard or plaza enclosed on three or four sides by the wings of a house.

plantation · In the 19th century, a large, often immense, agricultural operation owned by a single person or family. It concentrated on a particular cash crop, such as cotton or tobacco, typically relying on slave labor. In the Colonial period, plantation was synonymous with farm.

plate · The horizontal framing member at the top of a wood frame wall.

plaza · A public square. Also see ***placita***.

porch · Typically an open-sided structure attached to a house to protect the entry and provide covered receiving and living space, similar to a piazza or veranda. In 17th-century Tidewater Cross Houses, the porch may be fully or partially enclosed as a room.

porch chamber · In a Cross House, the room above the porch or entry.

portales (Sp.) · Long, covered porches facing a *placita* or plaza.

porte-cochere (carriage porch) · A structure over an entry or porch extending over part of the driveway.

portico · A formal entry porch covered by a roof supported by columns, particularly a pedimented, projecting Classical Greek or Roman pavilion.

post · A simple column; a vertical structural member.

post-and-beam · A simple framing system that used vertical posts and columns to support horizontal beams and rafters.

post-in-the-ground · A construction method using vertical posts set directly in the ground in rows to form walls. In French Colonial regions, called poteaux-en-terre.

postmedieval · The continuing use of medieval English architectural elements by the 17th-century English colonists, particularly in the Tidewater region and New England. Included steeply pitched gable roofs (often thatched), small, diamond-paned windows, and massive, decorative masonry chimneys.

poteaux-en-terre (Fr.) · Vertical post-in-the-ground log construction in the French Colonial regions.

poteaux-sur-sole (Fr.) · Vertical log construction with the posts resting on a timber sill that could be supported by a stone foundation.

Prairie School, Prairie Style · An early-20th-century design that rejected historical and Classical styles in favor of open, flowing floor plans and a strongly horizontal character, suggesting, some say, the midwestern prairie. Centered in Chicago, it is strongly associated with its boldest practitioner, Frank Lloyd Wright, although he worked beside several capable peers.

puddled adobe · The Native American construction technique using separate layers of wet, hand-laid mud to build walls, in contrast with the Spanish method of building up walls with sun-baked adobe bricks.

pueblo · 1. A settlement. 2. A Native American settlement or village in the Southwest, typically consisting of attached and terraced multistoried adobe or stone dwellings. 3. An individual house in the village.

Pueblo Revival · See **Spanish Colonial Revival**.

puncheons · Slablike planks split or sawn from a log.

pyramid roof · A hipped roof of four roughly equal sides meeting at the top in a pyramid.

Queen Anne · In the United States, a flamboyant interpretation in wood of the earlier English Queen Anne style; popular with the general public from about 1880 through 1910.

quoin · Dressed stone used as a decorative corner on Renaissance houses, suggesting stacked and rusticated finished stonework. Also, its imitation in wood or brick.

rafter · One of a row of similar, sloping beams supporting a pitched roof.

raised panel · The beveled-edged wood panel held by vertical styles and horizontal rails in a raised panel door or wall paneling.

rake · Slope or pitch.

raking or raked cornice · The sloping cornice of a triangular pediment or gable.

ramada (Sp.) · An arbor or open porch.

relief · Sculpture engaged with its background, as seen on Classical friezes and pediments.

Renaissance Revival · Design recalling the Italian Renaissance architecture of the 15th century. In the United

States, note the relatively minor Italian Renaissance Revival of 1840–60 and the academic Second Italian Renaissance Revivals of 1880–1935.

ribbon window · An uninterrupted horizontal band of windows typically seen on Moderne, Prairie, and International houses.

Richardson Romanesque, Richardsonian · A heavy masonry style advanced by H. H. Richardson (1838–86); inspired by the Romanesque architecture of southeastern France, sometimes called Romanesque Revival.

ridge beam, ridge pole · The longitudinal beam at a roof's ridge that receives the rafters.

riven, rived · Hand-split from a log, like the early clapboards and shingles (shakes).

Roman arch · Round arch.

round arch · A semicircular arch.

rubbed bricks · Bricks that have been smoothed or shaped by rubbing against each other or an abrasive surface, producing a consistent, lighter color. Typical of Chesapeake Bay Tidewater Georgian architecture, where they were used as subtle trim around doors and windows and at corners.

running bond · See **bond**.

rustication · The emphasis on masonry joints by beveling, champhering, or rounding the exposed edges of stones, often at the foundation walls and quoins.

Saddle Bag · A log structure of two rooms (pens) backed up to a central chimney.

saddle notch · A system used at the corners of log structures.

Saltbox · A two-story New England Colonial house extended by a shed at the rear, creating the profile of a Colonial table salt box.

sash · The frame of a window holding the glass. It may be fixed or movable, swinging (casement), or vertical sliding (single-, double-, or triple-hung).

scrollwork · Decorative curved shapes formed with lathes, scroll saws, and band saws. Commonly seen on high-styled Victorian houses.

scupper · An opening in a parapet wall with a spout, allowing water to drain through from a roof or balcony.

Second Empire (Mansard) · Eclectic Victorian style derived from the French architecture associated with Napoleon's Second Empire (1852–70). Often elaborate and ornate, it is most noted for the Mansard roof.

section · An architectural scale drawing that shows a structure as though cut by a vertical plane; typically used for construction detail.

segmental arch · An arch constituting less than a half-circle, common over windows in Chesapeake Bay Tidewater area.

semicircular arch (round arch) · A half-circle arch.

Serlian motif · Palladian motif. Named for Sebastiano Serlio (1475–1555), an early interpreter of Classical design principles and a precursor of Andrea Palladio.

shake · A wood shingle split from a short log by hand.

shed dormer · A dormer with a shed roof.

shed roof (pent roof) · A sloping roof with a single pitch.

Shingle Style · A style popular in the late 19th century, featuring a monolithic exterior finish of wood shingles, the large massing of many elements, and minimal ornament.

shiplap · Horizontal wood siding that, unlike clapboards, has rabbeted edges forming a flush, horizontal, overlapping joint.

Shotgun House · A simple dwelling of three or four rooms lined up one behind the other, with the connecting doors aligned, theoretically allowing a shotgun to be fired through the house without hitting anything.

side-gabled (end-gabled) · Having the house entry and an eave side facing the street, with gables at the ends.

sill · A horizontal wood member on the foundation that serves as the base of a wood-framed structure. Also, the horizontal base of a door or window of any material.

Single House · In Charleston, South Carolina, a long, two- or three-story, one-room-deep house with a central stair, sited perpendicular to the street. It is entered at midpoint, usually along a full-length porch or piazza.

soffit · The exposed underside of an overhanging surface, such as an extended eave.

soldier · A brick installed vertically with the narrow face exposed.

soldier course · A horizontal run of soldier bricks.

Spanish Colonial · The Spanish Baroque architecture adapted to the American Southwest, associated with the building of missions in Mexico, Texas, New Mexico, and California from the 16th through the 18th centuries.

Spanish Colonial Revival · Early-20th-century style using elements of Spanish Colonial architecture.

Spanish Pueblo Revival (Santa Fe, Pueblo Revival) · A style consciously developed by Santa Fe businessmen in the early 20th century to appeal to tourists. Loosely derived from Spanish Colonial architecture and Pueblo villages, it appears mainly along the Rio Grande in northern New Mexico. It features adobe-like construction, with flat roofs, portales, vigas, canales, and carefully managed ratios of mass to glass.

spindlework · The use of multiple decorative spindles as architectural ornaments, along porch and stair railings, for example. Wood spindles are made from doweling turned on a lathe, shaped somewhat like the spindles used in spinning yarn. Associated with Queen Anne and other Victorian styles.

Steamboat Gothic · Similar to Carpenter Gothic, a decorative elaboration of Gothic detail found along major midwestern rivers after 1850 and thought to resemble the ornamentation on steamboats.

stick chimney · Typical of log construction techniques, a chimney framed with sticks and packed with mud inside.

Stick Style · A style of wood construction that appeared after the Civil War, designed to suggested the wood framework beneath. Vertical, horizontal, and diagonal flat boards organize the exterior elevations by outlining panels of various siding textures. "Sticks" were also used to decorate gables, porch supports, and brackets.

Stone-Ender · A gable-ended, timber-framed Colonial house strongly associated with early Rhode Island and known for the massive fireplace that constituted nearly the entire end of the house, as seen from the outside.

stoop (stoup) · From the Dutch *stoep*, a small front porch, possibly with benches on either side, perpendicular to the front door.

story-and-a-half · A one-story building having an attic with windows.

Streamline Moderne · See **Art Moderne**.

stretcher · A brick laid horizontally.

stretcher course (stretching course) · A course of brick made up of only stretchers.

string course (belt course) · In masonry construction, a horizontally projecting molding intended to visually break up a plain wall surface, most often at second-floor levels.

stucco · A lime and sand plaster finish on an exterior wall.

stud · A vertical wood structural member spaced between posts, common to wood frame construction. Metal studs are used as well on modern buildings.

superstructure · The part of a building above the foundation.

swag · See **festoon**.

swan neck · The curved shape of the pair of cornices of a broken pediment.

Swiss Chalet · A minor style vaguely recalling a Swiss chalet, promoted in pattern books in the mid-19th century. Generally with a gable in front, it was identified by gable-end balconies with decorative railings and extended roof overhangs.

tabby · A concrete-like material of oyster shells, sand, water, and lime (from oyster shells) used for making walls in roughly 1-foot-high courses. Used by the 16th-century Spanish in Florida and adopted in 17th-century South Carolina.

temple form · A late-18th-century Virginia three-part house, consisting of a two-story central block with a lower form on either side, smaller than the grand plantation houses of the period.

temple front · A central formal entrance of Classical columns, entablature, and pediment, usually a full two stories high.

Territorial · An adobe style created by adding Greek Revival and other wood detailing to adobe homes in the Southwest, particularly in the Rio Grande Valley, in the late 19th century.

Territorial Revival · A revival of the Territorial Style after 1920.

thatched roof · A roof of reeds, straw, or other plant material, tied in bundles and attached to horizontal roof members; used primarily by early English settlers. Also, a name for an amusing imitation of thatched roofing, made with shingles, on a very few English Revival houses at the turn of the 20th century or later.

timber frame · A heavy wood structural system of posts, beams, and studs, used before the advent of balloon and platform framing.

top plate · The continuous, horizontal wood member, attached to the tops of the studs, that receives the foot of the rafters.

tracery · A decorative pattern of mullions or muntins applied to a window, particularly typical of Adamesque designs during the Federal period.

transom · 1. In Colonial times, a horizontal bar between the top of a door and the window above it, or a fixed horizontal bar dividing a tall window. A transom bar is a slimmer transom. 2. Contemporary use refers to a window directly over a door.

transom light (transom window) · The rectangular or fan-shaped glazing over a door.

trefoil · A decorative three-part cloverleaf design element used often in the upper part of Gothic windows and arches.

Tudor arch · A low, pointed arch commonly used in English Tudor architecture.

Tudor Revival · A masonry or stucco style that recalls the English architecture of the Tudor period (1485–1588), featuring steep roofs, cross gables, and massive chimneys.

Turkish dome · See **onion dome**.

turret · A round or octagonal tower-like projection at the corner of a large house, usually with a conical roof.

Tuscan · Italianate.

Tuscan order · See **orders**.

tympanum · The triangular wall enclosed by the raking and horizontal cornices forming a pediment.

valley · The angle where two sloping roof surfaces meet.

veneer · In cabinetwork, a thin wood finish. Also, a wythe of brick or stone constituting the exterior finish of a wall over a backing material and a thin coat of plaster known as veneer plaster.

Venetian motif · Palladian motif.

Venetian window · Palladian window.

veranda · *Galérie*, piazza.

verge · The extension of the roof past the gable end.

vergeboard · A bargeboard.

vernacular · Architecture based on traditional regional or ethnic forms, not involving an architect or trained designer.

vertical plank frame (box frame) · Heavy planks attached to the sills and plates of a structure, creating a structural box.

Victorian · Any of the styles built roughly during the reign of Queen Victoria (1837–1901).

Victorian Gothic · High Victorian Gothic.

viga (Sp.) · In adobe construction, an exposed horizontal roof beam, often projecting beyond the outside wall.

villa · From Roman times and the Renaissance, a large country home with outbuildings and extensive gardens.

wainscoting · The wood covering of the lower part of an interior wall.

wall dormer · A dormer with its front wall flush to and integral with the building's wall,

water table · The point at which the thicker foundation wall projects slightly from the main wall surface above. It usually occurs at the first floor on brick masonry buildings and is marked by specially molded brick.

wattle-and-daub · A wall construction technique using thin, flexible sticks or vines intertwined with vertical poles (wattling) and covered on both sides with a clay mud and straw mixture (daub).

weatherboard · A horizontal board used as the exterior wall or roof covering on 17th- and 18th-century Colonial houses. Clapboards are one example.

Welsh chimney · A stick chimney.

Western frame · A platform frame.

wigwam · A Native American structure of wood poles covered with bark or hides.

wing · A sizable extension on the side of a house.

wrought-iron work · Gates, fences, grilles, balconies, and other hardware made by hammering or forging wrought iron (iron that has been formed by shaping ingots).

wrought nail · A hand-forged iron or mild steel nail, usually square in cross section with a large head, used until the late 18th century.

wythe · A single thickness of brick or other masonry material.

zaguan (Sp.) · In Spanish Colonial architecture, a covered passage connecting the patio to the street.

zapata (Sp.) · In Spanish Colonial architecture, a corbeled wooden capital over a wooden column, often decoratively carved or sawn.

Recommended Reading

General

Brunskill, R. W. 1970. *Illustrated Handbook of Vernacular Architecture*. New York: Universe Books.

Bucher, Ward. 1996. *Dictionary of Building Preservation*. New York: John Wiley.

Bushman, Richard L. 1992. *The Refinement of America*. New York: Vintage Books.

Candee, Richard M. 1992. *Building Portsmouth*. Portsmouth, N.H.: Portsmouth Advocates.

Conzen, Michael P. 1990. *The Making of an American Landscape*. New York: Routledge.

Easton, Robert, and Peter Nabokov. 1989. *Native American Architecture*. New York: Oxford University Press.

Glassie, Henry. 1968. *Pattern in the Material Folk Culture of the Eastern United States*. Philadelphia: University of Pennsylvania Press.

———. 2000. *Vernacular Architecture*. Bloomington: Indiana University Press.

Gowans, Alan. 1992. *Styles and Types of North American Architecture*. New York: HarperCollins.

Kaye, Myrna. 1998. *There's a Bed in the Piano: The Inside Story of the American Home*. Boston: Bulfinch Press.

Kennedy, Roger G. 1985. *Architecture, Men, Women, and Money in America, 1600–1860*. New York: Random House.

Kornwolf, Georgiana W., and James D. Kornwolf. 2002. *Architecture and Town Planning in Colonial North America*. Baltimore: Johns Hopkins University Press.

Lounsbury, Carl R. 1994. *An Illustrated Glossary of Early Southern Architecture and Landscape*. New York: Oxford University Press.

Massey, James C., and Shirley Maxwell. 1996. *House Styles in America*. New York: Dovetale.

Noble, Allen G. 1992. *To Build in a New Land*. Baltimore: Johns Hopkins University Press.

————, ed. 1984. *Wood, Brick & Stone*. Amherst: University of Massachusetts Press.

Palladio, Andrea. 1965. *The Four Books of Architecture*. New York: Dover.

Pierson, William H., Jr., and William H. Jordy. 1970. *American Buildings and Their Architects*, Vols. 1–4. New York: Oxford University Press.

Rybczynski, Witold. 1986. *Home: A Short History of an Idea*. New York: Viking Penguin.

————. 1989. *The Most Beautiful House in the World*. New York: Penguin Books.

Upton, Dell. 1998. *Architecture in the United States*. New York: Oxford University Press.

Upton, Dell, and John Michael Vlach, eds. 1986. *Common Places: Readings in American Vernacular Architecture*. Athens: University of Georgia Press.

Ware, William R. 1994. *The American Vignola: A Guide to the Making of Classical Architecture*. New York: Dover.

Whiffen, Marcus. 1996. *American Architecture Since 1780*. Cambridge, Mass.: MIT Press.

Whiffen, Marcus, and Frederik Koeper. 1981. *American Architecture*, Vols. 1–2. Cambridge, Mass.: MIT Press.

Northern Colonial Hearths

Benjamin, Asher. 1969. *The American Builder's Companion*. New York: Dover.

Cohen, David Steven. 1992. *The Dutch American Farm*. New York: New York University Press.

Cummings, Abbott Lowell. 1979. *The Framed Houses of Massachusetts Bay, 1625–1725*. Cambridge, Mass.: Harvard University Press.

Eberlein, Harold Donaldson, and Cortlandt Van Dyke Hubbard. 1990. *Historic Houses of the Hudson Valley*. New York: Dover.

Fischer, David Hackett. 1989. *Albion's Seed*. New York: Oxford University Press.

Garvin, James L. 2001. *A Building History of Northern New England*. Hanover, N.H.: University Press of New England.

Kelly, J. Frederick. 1963. *Early Domestic Architecture of Connecticut*. New York: Dover.

Kimball, Fiske. 1966. *Domestic Architecture of the American Colonies and of the Early Republic*. New York: Dover.

Stachiw, Myron O. 2001. *The Early Architecture and Landscapes of the Narragansett Basin*. Newport, R.I.: Vernacular Architecture Forum.

Southern Colonial Hearths

Ekberg, Carl J. 1996. *Colonial Ste. Genevieve*. Tucson: Patrice Press.

Glassie, Henry. 1975. *Folk Housing in Middle Virginia*. Knoxville: University of Tennessee Press.

Lane, Mills. 1993. *Architecture of the Old South*. New York: Abbeville Press.

Lapham, Samuel, Jr., and Albert Simons. 1970. *The Early Architecture of Charleston*. Columbia: University of South Carolina Press.

Smith, J. Frazer. 1993. *Plantation Houses and Mansions of the Old South*. New York: Dover.

Stoney, Samuel Gaillard. 1989. *Plantations of the Carolina Low Country*. New York: Dover.

Vlach, John Michael. 1993. *Back of the Big House: The Architecture of Plantation Slavery*. Chapel Hill: University of North Carolina Press.

Ware, Donna M. 1990. *Anne Arundel's Legacy*. Annapolis: Anne Arundel County.

Waterman, Thomas Tilestone. 1946. *The Mansions of Virginia, 1706–1776*. Chapel Hill: University of North Carolina Press.

Southwest and California

Longstreth, Richard. 1983. *On the Edge of the World*. Berkeley: University of California Press.

Reeve, Agnes Lufkin.1988. *From Hacienda to Bungalow: Northern New Mexico Houses, 1850–1912*. Albuquerque: University of New Mexico Press.

Wilson, Chris. 1997. *The Myth of Santa Fe: Creating a Modern Regional Tradition*. Albuquerque: University of New Mexico Press.

Woodbridge, Sally B. 1988. *California Architecture*. San Francisco: Chronicle Books.

American Styles

Lancaster, Clay. 1985. *The American Bungalow, 1880–1930*. New York: Dover.

Pearson, Clifford A., ed. 1996. *Modern American Houses*. New York: Harry N. Abrams.

Scully, Vincent J., Jr. 1971. *The Shingle Style and the Stick Style*. New Haven: Yale University Press.

Stickley, Gustav. 1979. *Craftsman Homes: Architecture and Furnishings of the American Arts and Crafts Movement*. New York: Dover.

Photo Credits

The photos on pages xii, 85, 88, 90, 96, 110, 120, 170, 172, 218, 228, 278, and 357 are by the author. The photo on page 152 is by Mark Foster. All other photos are courtesy of the Historic American Buildings Survey (HABS), Library of Congress.

Uncaptioned Photos at Chapter Openings

page

xii · Captain William Smith House, Lincoln, Mass., late 18th century

2 · Parson Capen House, Topsfield, Mass., c. 1683

36 · Dutch gable, Albany, N.Y. (demolished)

54 · John Chad House, Chadds Ford, Pa., early 18th century

80 · John Rideout House, Annapolis, Md., c. 1765

130 · Middleburg, Dufer, S.C., c. 1699 or 18th century

162 · Magnolia Mound, Baton Rouge, La., c. 1795

196 · Acoma Pueblo, N.M., c. 1000

218 · Monticello, Charlottesville, Va., c. 1772–1809

236 · Bowen House, Woodstock, Conn., c. 1846

258 · Thorpe House, Cambridge, Mass., c. 1887

290 · Liriodendron, Bel Air, Md., c. 1897

306 · Joshua Notter House, St. Joseph, Mo., c. 1890

322 · Mission San Diego de Alcala, San Diego, Calif., c. 1808–1813

338 · Frank Lloyd Wright's Robie House, Chicago, Ill., 1906

354 · Walter Gropius House, Lincoln, Mass., 1938

Index

Index   **397**